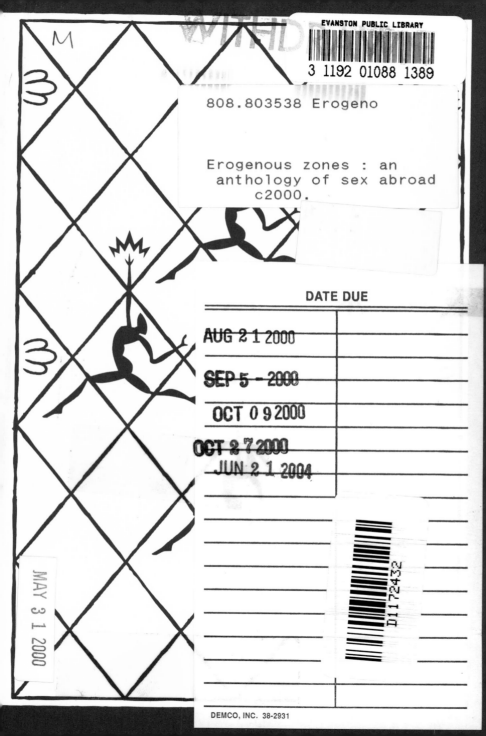

# EROGENOUS

# ZONES

# EROGENOUS ZONES

## ZONES

*An Anthology of Sex Abroad*

EDITED, AND WITH AN INTRODUCTION,
BY LUCRETIA STEWART

MODERN LIBRARY

NEW YORK

2000 Modern Library Original

Copyright © 2000 by Lucretia Stewart

All rights reserved under International and Pan-American Copyright
Conventions. Published in the United States by
Random House, Inc., New York, and simultaneously in Canada
by Random House of Canada Limited, Toronto.

MODERN LIBRARY and colophon are registered trademarks
of Random House, Inc.

Owing to limitations of space, permissions acknowledgments
can be found beginning on page 327.

Library of Congress Cataloging-in-Publication Data is available
0-679-60323-9

Modern Library website address: www.modernlibrary.com

Printed in the United States of America on acid-free paper

2   4   6   8   9   7   5   3   1

To Vicki Woods
who hates to travel


In memory of Robert Powell Jones
1954 – 1998

Think of the long trip home.
Should we have stayed at home and thought of here?
Where should we be today?
... Oh, must we dream our dreams
and have them, too?

—ELIZABETH BISHOP, *Questions of Travel*

# ACKNOWLEDGMENTS

This anthology was Ben Sonnenberg's idea. Without him, it wouldn't exist. Ian Jackman, as commissioning editor, also deserves a special mention.

I am grateful to the following for their suggestions: Martin Amis, Michael Carroll, Patrick Cockburn, Marie-Claude de Brunhoff, Holly Eley, John Fleming, Jonathan Fryer, Antonia Gaunt, Charles Glass, Francis Graham-Harrison, John Hatt, Christopher Hitchens, Hugh Honour, Richard Howard, Ian Jack, Tess Jaray, Francis King, Peter Parker, Patrick O'Connor, Duncan Fallowell, David Jenkins, Jonathan Keates, Rhoda Koenig, James Lord, Patrick Marnham, J. D. McClatchy, Janet Montefiore, Andrew Motion, John Ryle, Marilyn Schaefer, Jon Swain, Colin Thubron, Gore Vidal, and Edmund White. My thanks also to Sarah Anderson for advice; to Sean Swallow for research; to Mhairi Brennan for uncomplaining photocopying, word counting, and general help; and to Matthew Thornton for his efforts in getting all the necessary permissions.

# CONTENTS

## AUSTRALASIA

## THE AMERICAS

# INTRODUCTION

I seem to have spent my life traveling. My father was a diplomat and my childhood was spent abroad, first in Asia, then America and finally in Europe. Even when I was young, travel and foreign parts always seemed romantic and rather daring; the passage of time has not caused me to change my mind. I began to travel as an adult in 1985, when I returned to China, where I had lived as a small child, and I have continued to do so for the last fifteen years. During this time I have visited Laos, Vietnam, Cambodia, Thailand, Burma, Indonesia, Korea, Hong Kong, Macao, China, Singapore, Malaysia, France, Germany, Switzerland, Italy, Spain, Portugal, Greece, Poland, Russia, America, the Caribbean, and Australia—and most of my traveling has been done alone. Like the writer Colin Thubron I believe that, if you travel with another person, you travel in "a little bubble of Englishness" (or Americanness, Frenchness, etc.). Some years ago a friend described me as "addicted to travel." I wouldn't go that far, but it is true that travel has always seemed some kind of solution. In addition, I believe that it really does broaden the mind.

So, when this anthology was proposed, I was enthusiastic. I have, for exactly fifteen years—since 1985, in fact—been aware of the relationship, you might almost say kinship, between sex and travel; and before I was formally conscious of it, I am certain that I suspected its existence.

Travel is, above all, the search for the unknown, for the other; so, in its purest form, is sex (the pre–skin cancer obsession with the sun is a less forthright form of this; even today people associate the two, traveling to the Caribbean in search of sun and sex—the sea coming a poor third in the desire stakes). Travel and sex both involve exploration and experimentation; linking the two is almost irresistible. As Pico Iyer writes in *The Lady and the Monk,* "Besides the pairing of Western men and Eastern women was as natural as the partnership of sun and moon. Everyone falls in love with what he cannot begin to understand. And the other man's heart is always greener."

From the outset, I decided to restrict the collection to nonfiction: to mix fiction and nonfiction would only obscure the purpose of the anthology. But my criteria for inclusion has been that the *foreignness* of either the setting, or of the object of desire, should quite demonstrably have had a transforming effect on the traveler, and therefore on the quality of the experience itself. (Ideally these factors should coincide with literary merit, as in the case of Gustave Flaubert, whose travels in Egypt reveal him to be the very model of an erotic traveler; but, in some cases, where the writing is less strong, the experience itself has been sufficiently unusual, sufficiently *sexy,* to merit inclusion here.)

So, Duncan Fallowell, a gay writer, finds himself engaging in heterosexual sex in St. Petersburg when he is caught off guard by a masseuse/prostitute. Geoff Dyer finds himself on the verge of public masturbation on a beach in Mexico; after making love to a girl in Los Angeles, Richard Rayner dons her Bunny costume and transforms himself into Bunny Richard; Aimée Crocker, an American woman traveler who explored the Far East in the thirties, found Shanghai a most liberating place. And so on.

For the travelers/writers who are featured in this anthology, the whole business has assumed a sort of tripartite quality—rather like the Holy Trinity, one and three at the same time: traveling, fucking/making love/falling in love/yearning, then writing about it. The last, I imagine, gives the experience, or the memory of the experience, an extra frisson.

A romantic and unusual, preferably exotic, setting compounds the thrill. The more exotic the setting the greater the kick. It doesn't need to be about danger, though some of the writers whose work I have included in this collection clearly find an element of risk a turn-on (for example, the extract from *Cleopatra's Wedding Present* by Robert Tewdwr Moss, a handsome young homosexual, who, in reality, survived his Syrian adventures, only to be murdered in London on the day that he finished writing the book).

In 1980, the Anglophile American scholar Paul Fussell published a book called *Abroad* and subtitled it "British Literary Traveling Between the Wars." The wars in question were the two world wars of this century, and the period between them saw the Golden Age of travel writing, particularly in Britain, where undertaking a difficult and arduous journey, then writing a book about it, became a rite of passage for young men.

This was for two reasons: first, because traveling had suddenly become easier (communications were better, people were more prosperous, etc.) and, second, because the world then hadn't changed (or shrunk) as much as it has now. It was still possible to find remote places where few people had been; as a travel writer, you could still address your subject almost as if you were an anthropologist, something impossible to get away with today, that is, unless you actually are an anthropologist.

The book contained a chapter entitled *"L'Amour du Voyage,"* in which Fussell claimed that "Making love in a novel environment, free from the censorship and inhibitions of the familiar, is one of the headiest experiences travel promises."

The operative word here is "promises." The traveler, like the sexual adventurer (of whom homosexuals seem to be the most daring—although some people might think "reckless" a better word), embarks on his quest in the hope of encountering the unknown. Erotic travelers are the original strangers in the night; for these lovers at first sight, love (and sexual adventure) is simultaneously just a glance away and many miles from home. The promise of a foreign affair, that enticing combination of the erotic and the exotic, can prove unbearably alluring.

The trailer which advertises the video of the film version of Han Suyin's novel *Love Is a Many-Splendored Thing* promises that "Passion loses control in exotic Hong Kong." Implicit is the suggestion that uncontrollable passion and sexual adventure (even, with luck, depravity) beyond wildest imaginings are possible only in such places as "exotic Hong Kong." But, in E. M. Forster's story "The Obelisk," written in 1939, the travel undertaken by a schoolmaster and his wife is merely to an out-of-season seaside resort. Nonetheless it leads to a chance encounter with two sailors, which in turn leads to sex, which leads to unprecedented perception, none of which would have been possible if the couple had not "traveled."

In Alison Lurie's novel *Foreign Affairs,* two Americans, a middle-aged spinster and a young married man, find themselves in London for several months. Both form relationships about which, at home in America, they might have hesitated: the woman, an academic specializing in children's literature on a foundation grant, with a Texan tourist; the man with an unstable English actress eight years his senior. Both characters feel free to act, as it were, out of character, because they are far from home. The journey has taken the travelers from a world of middle-class values and expectations to at least the possibility of a new order of experience.

Anyone who has ever enjoyed a brief encounter with someone unknown or barely known recognizes that it carries with it a particular thrill. In *Delta of Venus*, Anaïs Nin fantasizes about being brought to orgasm in the subway at rush hour by a total stranger, a man who, as soon as the train stops, gets out and disappears. His anonymity—she does not know his name, she cannot see his face—adds to her arousal. This is not an uncommon fantasy, but, while Nin's experience may have been invented (at the time, in 1941, she, Henry Miller, the English poet George Barker, and several others were all writing erotica for a dollar a page to make money and to feed the fantasies of a rich book collector) the extract included here from *The Empty Mirror* by Janwillem van de Wetering describes the almost identical situation actually occurring on a train to Kobe.

For some writers, the presence of a beloved friend is the catalyst, or, at the very least, the icing on the cake. After a trip to Sicily in the spring of 1927, Cyril Connolly wrote to Nöel Blakiston as follows: "Thank you for coming to Sicily and for contributing to the most sustained ecstasy of my life. . . . I shall never be able to travel with anyone else . . . for I on honey dew have fed and drunk the milk of paradise . . . O Nöel!" O Nöel indeed.

Norman Douglas's preferred traveling companions were young boys (his taste was for boys between ten and twelve), which may account for the fact that he rarely mentioned his companions in his writing (and which is why Douglas does not feature in this anthology). In *Alone*, far from being alone, he was accompanied for most of the walking tours described in the book by René Mari, a boy of fourteen. In *Old Calabria*, his companion was twelve-year-old Eric, a Cockney he had picked up in Crystal Palace. Eric kept his own diary of the trip (in which he wrote, "Salami is a kind of sousage it is very beastly"). In *Fountains in the Sand*, Douglas's companion was a "tall, young and attractive" German schoolmaster. Douglas told Harold Acton that "each of his books had ripened under the warm rays of some temporary attachment: unless he was in love he had little or no impulse to write." He was convinced that the Mediterranean was the natural locale for the seduction of very young persons and, in fact, ended his days in a handsome villa in Capri, attended by a ten-year-old Neapolitan boy, Ettore, much beloved by Douglas, but written off as "a little tart" by others.

Not all the extracts I have included come from the work of *real* writers. In twentieth-century travel writing, the tradition has been for a young man to set off on a sort of Grand Tour—usually to the Middle East, North Africa, Sub-Saharan Africa, or Asia—and then to write about it, as if to justify the enterprise. The Arabist explorer Freya Stark once summarized the difference between herself and Peter Fleming (*News from Tartary, One's Company*, etc.) as follows: "Peter travels and then writes about it; I travel in order to write about it."

I think that that's a valid distinction: Fleming, as it happens, was a gifted writer—lively and informative (his unhappy companion on the journey that produced *News from Tartary*, Ella Maillart, herself wrote a not very good book, *Forbidden Journey*, about the same trip). Most of these travelers were men, with some notable—and notorious, such as Lady Hester Stanhope and her late twentieth-century counterpart Fiona Pitt-Kethley—exceptions. In the extracts included in this collection, some are quite obviously by writers. Others are the work of gifted—or, in some cases, less gifted—amateurs.

One of my favorite extracts comes from *Italian Journeys* by the British writer and critic Jonathan Keates. While staying at a *pensione* in Venice, Keates overheard an exchange between "a bald, bespectacled Frenchman of a certain age" and a couple of sailors—"country boys from a village somewhere down south, doing their military service on the lagoon"— whom the Frenchman had brought back to the *pensione* late one night. It's a sad, rather shoddy little encounter, but, before recounting its humiliating *denouement*, Keates remarks that "in garrulous Italy the talk which follows sex is worth everything else for pleasure. . . ."

Some travelers—of whom Giacomo Casanova, the great eighteenth-century lover whose name is now synonymous with sexual promiscuity (as in "he's a real Casanova"), is perhaps the best example—have journeyed, it would appear, almost solely for the purpose of erotic titillation and gratification. Casanova's travels were really just one long, erotic pursuit, perhaps the best example of the fusion (or confusion) of sex and travel.

Casanova's fictional counterpart is Don Juan. In Mozart's opera *Don Giovanni,* Leporello, Don Giovanni's manservant, sings the famous "catalogue" song in which he enumerates his master's conquests. It is clear from the outset that Don Giovanni was as much as a traveler as he was a lover, visiting Italy, Germany, France, Turkey, and Spain (where he had slept with 1,003 women—the music rushes to a crescendo of excitement with the repetition of the phrase *mille e tre*), in relentless pursuit of country girls, domestic servants, and city beauties, as well as countesses, baronesses, marchionesses, and princesses—women of every rank, every size, and every age: blondes, brunettes, fat ones (in winter), thin ones (in summer).

With comparable energy and enthusiasm (or was it simply a lack of discrimination?), Flaubert, according to letters and diaries he wrote during his travels in Egypt, flung himself wholeheartedly into the gratification of his libido and effectively set out to embrace and explore the country through its women. A century later, his sexual abandon is evoked in *No Particular Place to Go,* an account by the British poet Hugo Williams of a three-month poetry-reading tour in the United States in the mid-1970s, three indefatigable months during which he cut a considerable swathe through the numerous women he encountered.

A comparison of the two writers illustrates some of the most salient characteristics of the sexual traveler. Williams's adventures were enjoyed at the height of the sexual revolution and Flaubert's escapades predated, or so one would imagine, sexual liberation and feminism (in any case, the women he slept with were usually professionals; if not actual prostitutes, then courtesans or dancers). But, though Flaubert indicates a degree of sensitivity and tenderness towards some of his sexual partners, in particular Kuchik Hanem (of whom he wrote, "I stared at her for a long while, so as to be able to keep a picture of her in my mind"), the general impression is, as with Williams, one of careless, indiscriminate lust.

When Edmund White (an extract from whose cool, almost anthropological *States of Desire* is included) published his autobiographical novel *The Farewell Symphony,* he encountered a fair amount of criticism of his promiscuity—some critics couldn't resist indulging in a Leporello-style exercise, counting the number of the unnamed narrator's sexual partners (the narrator was, of course, assumed to be White himself), and attributing his promiscuity to the fact that he was homosexual. In truth, as the accounts of Flaubert and Williams, among other heterosexuals, testify, sexual orientation has nothing to do with it. Straight men abroad felt just as free as gays to indulge in an orgy of intercourse. At home, it was the constraints of family or society, rather than their sexual preferences, that restricted their behavior.

For Joe Orton, abroad—specifically North Africa—became virtually indistinguishable from sexual pleasure. As Orton's diaries clearly reveal, for him and for his companion, Kenneth Halliwell, the whole point of taking their holidays in Tangier was to have as much sex as was humanly possible with young Arab boys. In the case of writers such as J. R. Ackerly and John Haylock, both acknowledged homosexuals, abroad was not so much about sexual gratification but about liberation from the constraints and pretenses of "home." And it was only when André Gide—at home in France a respectable married man—was abroad (and in the Third World) that he could reveal—and give full expression to—his true nature, his homosexuality. In the extract from *Si le Grain Ne Meurt (If It Die)* which I have included here, Gide describes his first and second homosexual encounters, the latter in particularly explicit terms.

This passage appeared, of course, in the original French and then in Dorothy Bussy's translation, of which a special limited edition of 1,500 copies was published in 1950. It was, however, omitted from the 1951 edition of the work (in every other respect, the same translation), presumably because it was deemed too shocking. The British writer Francis King had recommended this passage to me, but I could find only the censored edition in the London Library. King put me in touch with Jonathan Fryer, the author of a book about Wilde and Gide (*André & Oscar*); I was able to borrow a copy from him of the original translation and find the relevant passage—far more daring than any other Gide that I had come across.

Robin Maugham describes his first homosexual experience, which took place in Nice, on a yacht belonging to Gerald Haxton, a friend of his Uncle Willie (Somerset Maugham). In a paragraph preceding the extract I have included, he writes, "I was still pleased with myself because I had so thoroughly enjoyed making love to the girl in Nice the previous night," yet when Gerald offers him Laurent, "a blond boy of about seventeen," he doesn't hesitate.

The practice of homosexuality was, for most men in the "civilized" world, a risky business. It still is—legally. Since 1885, both "gross indecency" and buggery have been illegal in Britain; in America, the law varies from state to state. However, thankfully, things have become somewhat easier since the sixties (the 1967 Wolfenden Report went some way towards de-criminalizing gay sex in England and Wales). Before then, however, it was easier and safer to go abroad. More fun too, probably.

Fussell says of Christopher Isherwood: "Because of the risks of enjoying them in London, boys became for Isherwood an emblem of abroad. One such was Bubi, who he became infatuated with during his first stay in Berlin. 'By embracing Bubi,' he [Isherwood] writes, 'Christopher could hold in arms the whole mystery-magic foreignness. . . . Berlin meant boys.' " And boys meant Berlin, just as for some travelers, Africa meant not simply the dark continent but also an entire continent of dark and infinitely alluring flesh.

Now, of course, the risks have changed. AIDS has put something of a dampener on erotic travel, for homosexuals and heterosexuals alike. The extract from Ed Hooper's *Slim* is a timely reminder of the risks of sex with a stranger. Hooper, a journalist reporting from AIDS-ravaged Uganda, fell passionately in love with a woman whom he met casually in a bar, and the specter of AIDS dogged their relationship. AIDS, in a way that nothing else has done before (syphilis seems usually—except presumably in its terminal and grotesquely deforming stages—to have been regarded with remarkable insouciance), has cast a shadow over hitherto lighthearted promiscuity. Would Paul Theroux have been as carelessly eager in Africa today as he was before the discovery of AIDS?

The Victorian writer Frank Harris, who was resolutely heterosexual and fairly sleazy with it, demonstrated a robust crudity about his encounters that is refreshing, if a little repetitive and boastful. Other writers doubtless had exactly the same motives (to go forth and conquer), but they were less open about them. I suspect that Mark Hudson (*Our Grandmothers' Drums*) attributed purer motives to his pursuit of the African girl he desired, though he rather gives the game away when he writes, "I decided when all was said and done it was an intelligent face." Does he expect us to believe that he wouldn't have slept with her if she had been merely beautiful?

Another and higher order of traveler and writer was the great Victorian explorer Richard Burton. Burton was, everyone agrees, extremely interested in sex and sexual behavior, both from a personal and anthropological point of view. However, after his death, his wife, Isabel, anxious that there should be no stain on his reputation, destroyed almost all of his journals and diaries and ceremoniously burnt his translation of *The Scented Garden.* The writings that remain are, therefore, as it were, at one remove; we can only speculate as to what he actually got up to and, accordingly, I haven't included anything from Burton.

For some travelers, Africa could always come to them in the person of an exotic stranger. Some travelers have fallen so much in love with a particular place that they feel impelled to express their love, to consummate, as it were, their love affair with a human being. Pico Iyer now lives with the Japanese woman he wrote about in *The Lady and the Monk.* Both Isabelle Eberhardt (*Prisoner of the Dunes*) and Jane Digby El Mezrab (who, with Eberhardt, Isabel Burton, and Aimée Dubucq de Rivery, is discussed in Lesley Blanch's *The Wilder Shores of Love*) were driven to express both their restlessness and their love of a particular country and people by forming a series of romantic attachments, then finally marrying into the country.

In a variation on this theme, the Guadeloupean writer Franz Fanon commented: "Talking recently with several Antilleans, I found that the dominant concern among those arriving in France was to go to bed with a white woman. As soon as their ships docked in Le Havre, they were off to the houses. Once this ritual of initiation in to 'authentic manhood' had been fulfilled, they took the train for Paris." The men were proclaiming not just their manhood but also their Frenchness.

Others, such as Laurie Lee (*A Moment of War*) and Dom Moraes (*My Son's Father*) found themselves caught up in a particular situation which led to an encounter which combined the romantic and the erotic. In Lee's case, the excitement of war was mirrored by the excitement of a chance and highly charged encounter. Moraes's experience is more tender.

———

I've enjoyed my share of lovemaking in exotic spots and understand all too well the relationship between the place, the moment, the situation, and the person, which all combine mysteriously to create an atmosphere ripe for adventure. There's something magical about tropical countries: the strangeness, the dreamy warmth, the scent, the fact that no one in the real world knows where you are or what you are doing. It was, on the whole, adventure, rather than "relief," that these writers were after. In the right circumstances, that most depressing of encounters, the one-night stand, can seem positively thrilling. As the old poem has it, "Wouldn't you like to sin / On a tiger skin / With Elinor Glyn?" The tiger skin is the real attraction.

I first understood the erotic potential of the East in Canton, China, in a Ferris wheel that revolved slowly, high above the city. Later that evening, back at a hotel on the banks of the Pearl River (the name alone evokes a kind of magic) with the sounds of the boatmen in their sampans on the water, all scruples were forgotten, all cares banished, London, other obligations, other people, everything ceased to exist. Only the moment remained. You can recognize such moments, not just afterwards when they linger in your memory with a crystalline clarity, but at the time, almost as if you have taken a drug that intensifies your senses—of smell, of sight, of hearing.

My experience in China was followed by others—to the extent that I came to associate the Far East with a particular kind of erotic experience—and, when I was back in England with its monochrome colors and its gloomy climate, I would take out and examine my store of such memories rather as a miser might gloat over a secret hoard. The second time was on the Star Ferry pier in Hong Kong; the third in Raffles Hotel in Singapore. Raffles, that is, in its last, great, seedy days before it was refurbished and lost all its character.

I had just arrived from London. When I got to my hotel, a gleaming, modern skyscraper, I found a message telling me that an old boyfriend also happened to be in Singapore. He was staying at Raffles. I caught a cab and went over. We had one drink, then another, and then dinner. Just as I was almost fainting with exhaustion, saying, "I really must get some sleep," he said, "Come and have a look at the Tiffin Room."

The Tiffin Room, as far as I can remember, was a monument to colonial glory, festooned with stuffed tigers' heads and glass showcases containing reports of sporting triumphs. So, when he kissed me and said, "Come upstairs for a bit," I thought "Well, why not? How often does opportunity knock in Raffles?" There were other times too—in Luang Prabang, in Angkor—until my travels ceased to take me to the Far East and I discovered that it was possible to enjoy myself in Martinique, Guadeloupe, St. Vincent, Grenada, New York, Paris, Venice, Seville, on the night train to St. Petersburg. . . . Anywhere but here, in fact.

# EUROPE

# Laurie Lee

## A Moment of War: A Memoir of the Spanish Civil War

The girl wore the tight black dress of the villages, and had long Spanish-Indian eyes. She pushed the old man up the stairs and told him to go to bed. Doug, Ulli and Danny followed behind him, singing brokenly and urging him on.

A winter sunset glow shone through a high grille in the wall, and I was aware, behind the sharp smell of coñac, of something softer and muskier. The young girl, crouching low in the shadows, had loosened her dress and was pouring brandy over her bare bruised shoulder.

She rubbed the liquor into her flesh with long brown fingers and watched me warily as she did so. Her eyes were like slivers of painted glass, glinting in the setting sun. I heard the boys upstairs stamping and singing to the breathy music of an old accordion. But I couldn't join them. I was trapped down here, in this place, this cellar, to the smell of coñac and this sleek animal girl.

She was stroking, almost licking, her upper arms, like a cat, her neck arched, her dark head bowed. She raised her eyes again, and we just stared at each other before I sat down beside her. Without a word, she handed me the flask of coñac, turned her bare shoulder towards me, and waited. Her skin was mottled by small purple bruises that ran backwards under her dress. I poured some drops of coñac into the palm of my hand and began to rub it awkwardly over her damp hot flesh. The girl sighed and stiffened, then swayed against me, leading me into a rhythm of her own.

The frayed black dress was now loose at the edges and gave way jerkily to my clumsy fingers. The girl's eyes were fixed on mine with a kind of rapt impatience. With a slight swerve of her shoulders she offered more flesh for healing. I rubbed more coñac into the palms of my hands. Slowly, as my touch followed her, she lay back on the sacking. The boys upstairs were singing "Home on the Range."

Apart from the quick stopping and starting of her breath, the girl was silent. The red blanket of sunset moved over her. Her thin dancer's body was now almost bare to the waist and revealed all the wispy fineness of a Persian print. It seemed that in some perverse way she wished to show both her beauty and its blemishes. Or perhaps she didn't care. She held my hands still for a moment.

"Frenchman," she said thickly.

"English," I said woodenly.

She shrugged, and whispered a light bubbling profanity—not Catalan but pure Andaluz. Her finger and thumb closed on my wrist like a manacle. Her body met mine with the quick twist of a snake.

When the square of sunset had at last moved away and died, we lay panting gently, and desert dry. I took a swig from the goatskin and offered it to her. She shook her head, but lay close as though to keep me warm. A short while ago she had been a thing of panicky gasps and whimpers. Now she looked into my eyes like a mother.

"My little blond man," she said tenderly. "Young, so young."

"How old are you, then?" I asked.

"Fifteen . . . sixteen—who knows?" She sat up suddenly, still only half-dressed, her delicate bruised shoulders arched proudly.

"I kill him."

"Who?"

"The old one. The grandfather. He maltreats . . . Thank God for the war."

The chicken, huddled fluffily against the wall in the corner, seemed now to be asleep. The girl turned and tidied me briskly, then tidied herself, settling her clothes around her sweet small limbs. Then she lifted her long loose hair and fastened it into a shining bun. The stamping and singing upstairs had stopped.

I was astonished that this hour had been so simple yet secret, the opening and closing of velvet doors. Eulalia was not the sort of Spanish girl I'd known in the past—the noisy steel-edged virgins flirting from the safety of upstairs windows, or loud arm-in-arm with other girls in the paseo, sensual, cheeky, confident of their powers, but scared to be alone with a man.

Eulalia, with her beautiful neck and shoulders, also had a quiet dignity and grace. A wantonness, too, so sudden and unexpected, I felt it was a wantonness given against her will. Or at least, if not given willingly, it was now part of her nature, the result of imposed habit and tutoring.

As she pulled on her tattered slippers, she told me she would not stay long in Figueras. She'd come from the south, she said—she didn't know where—and had been working here as a house-drudge since she was ten. Once she would have stayed on till body and mind were used up; the sexually abused slattern of some aged employer, sleeping under the stairs between calls to his room. Not any more, she was now free to do as she wished. Spain had changed, and the new country had braver uses for girls such as she. She need stay no longer with this brutal pig of an innkeeper. She would go to Madrid and be a soldier.

It had grown dark and cold in the cellar. Suddenly she turned and embraced me, wrapping me urgently in her hot thin arms.

"Frenchman!" she whispered. "At last I have found my brother."

"Englishman," I said, as she slipped away.

# PATRICK LEIGH FERMOR

## *Between the Woods and the Water: On Foot to Constantinople from the Hook of Holland*

One day when we were invited to luncheon by some neighbours, István said, "Let's take the horses" and we followed a roundabout, uphill track to look at a remaining piece of forest. "Plenty of common oak, thank God," he said, turning back in the saddle as we climbed a path through the slanting sunbeams, "you can use it for everything." The next most plentiful was Turkey oak, very good firewood when dry, also for stablefloors and barrelstaves. Beech came next, "It leaves scarcely any embers"; then yoke elm and common elm, "useful for furniture and coffins." There was plenty of ash, too—handy for tools, axe-helves, hammers, sickles, scythes, spades and hay-rakes. Except for a few by the brooks, there were no poplars up there but plenty by the Maros: useless, though, except for troughs and wooden spoons and the like. Gypsies made these. They settled in the garden and courtyard of the kastély with their wives and their children and whittled away until they had finished. "There is no money involved," István said. "We're supposed to go halves, but, if it's an honest tribe, we're lucky to get a third. We do better with some Rumanians from out-of-the-way villages in the mountains, very poor and primitive chaps, but very honest."*

In a clearing we exchanged greetings with a white-haired shepherd

---

*I think they must have belonged to the interesting ancient community of the Motsi, who inhabit peaks and valleys deep in the western Transylvanian massif.

leaning on a staff with a steel hook. The heavily embroidered homespun cloak flung across his shoulders and reaching to the ground was a brilliant green. His flock tore at the grass among the tree-stumps all round him. Then a path led steeply downhill through hazel-woods with old shells and acorns crunching and slipping under the horses' hoofs.

It was a boiling hot day. On the way back from a cheerful feast, we went down to the river to look at some wheat. Overcome by the sight of the cool and limpid flood, we unsaddled in a shady field about the size of a paddock, took off all our clothes, climbed down through the reeds and watercress and dived in. Swimming downstream with lazy breast-stroke or merely drifting in the shade of the poplars and the willows, we talked and laughed about our recent fellow guests. The water was dappled with leafy shade near the bank and scattered with thistle-down, and a heron made off down a vista of shadows. Fleets of moorhens doubled their speed and burst noisily out of the river, and wheat, maize and tiers of vineyard were gliding past us when all at once we heard some singing. Two girls were reaping the end of a narrow strip of barley; going by the colours of their skirts and their embroidered tops, braid sashes and kerchiefs, they had come for the harvest from a valley some way off. They stopped as we swam into their ken, and, when we drew level, burst out laughing. Apparently the river was less of a covering than we had thought. They were about nineteen or twenty, with sunburnt and rosy cheeks and thick dark plaits, and not at all shy. One of them shouted something, and we stopped and trod water in mid-Maros. István interpreted, "They say we ought to be ashamed of ourselves," he said, "and they threaten to find our clothes and run off with them."

Then he shouted back, "You mustn't be unkind to strangers! You look out, or we'll come and catch you."

"You wouldn't dare," came the answer. "Not like that, naked as frogs."

"What are these for?" István pointed to the branches by the shore. "We could be as smartly dressed as Adam."

"You'd never catch us! What about your tender white feet in the stubble? Anyway, you're too respectable. Look at your hair, going bald in front."

"*It's not!*" István shouted back.

"And that young one," cried the second girl, "he wouldn't dare."

István's blue eye was alight as he translated the last bit. Then without exchanging another word we struck out for the shore as fast as crocodiles and, tearing at poplar twigs and clumps of willow-herb, bounded up the bank. Gathering armfuls of sheaves, the girls ran into the next field, then halted at the illusory bastion of a hay-rick and waved their sickles in mock defiance. The leafy disguise and our mincing gait as we danced across the stubble unloosed more hilarity. They dropped their sickles when we were almost on them and showered us with the sheaves; then ran to the back of the rick. But, one-armed though we were, we caught them there and all four collapsed in a turmoil of hay and barley and laughter.

# GIACOMO CASANOVA

## *History of My Life*

### (VOLUME II)

### CHAPTER I

*My short and too lively stay in Ancona. Cecilia, Marina, Bellino.*
*The Greek slave girl from the Lazaretto. Bellino unmasks.*

I reached Ancona at nightfall on the 25th of February in the year 1744
and put up at the best inn in the town. Satisfied with my room, I tell the
host that I wish to eat meat. He replies that in Lent Christians eat fish. I
say that the Pope has given me permission to eat meat; he tells me to show
him the permission; I say that he gave it to me by word of mouth; he will
not believe me; I call him a fool; he tells me to go and lodge elsewhere;
and this last proposition of his, which I do not expect, astonishes me. I
swear, I curse; whereupon a solemn-looking individual comes out of a
room and proceeds to tell me that I *was wrong* to want to eat meat, since
fish was better in Ancona; that I *was wrong* to expect the innkeeper to take
my word for it that I had permission; that, if I had permission, I *was wrong*
to have asked for it at my age; that I *was wrong* to have called the
innkeeper a fool, since he was free to refuse to lodge me; and, finally, that
I *was wrong* to raise such a row.

This man who was sticking his nose into my business unasked, and
who had come out of his room only to tell me how unimaginably *wrong* I
was, had very nearly set me laughing.

"Sir," I said, "I subscribe to all your accusations. But it is raining, I am extremely hungry, and I have no wish to go out looking for another lodging at this hour. So I ask you if, since our host refuses, you will provide me with supper."

"No, for I am a Catholic and hence am keeping the fast; but I will undertake to calm our ruffled host, who will give you a good supper, though of fish."

So saying, he started downstairs; and I, comparing his cool common sense with my hasty petulance, acknowledge that he is worthy of teaching me a thing or two. He comes back upstairs, enters my room, says that all is well again, that I shall have a good supper, and that he will keep me company at it. I reply that I shall consider it an honor and, to oblige him to tell me his name, I tell him mine, adding that I am Cardinal Acquaviva's secretary.

"My name," he says, "is Sancho Pico, I am a Castilian and Proveditor of the army of His Catholic Majesty, which is commanded by the Count de Gages under orders from the Generalissimo, the Duke of Modena."

After exclaiming over the appetite with which I ate all that was set before me, he asked me if I had dined; and he seemed relieved when I answered that I had not.

"Will the supper you have eaten," he asked, "make you ill?"

"I have reason to hope that, on the contrary, it will do me good."

"Then you have deceived the Pope. Follow me to the next room. You will have the pleasure of hearing some good music. The first actress is lodging there."

The word "actress" arouses my curiosity, and I follow him. I see a woman rather well on in years eating supper at a table with two girls and two handsome youths. I look in vain for the actress. Don Sancho introduces her to me in the person of one of the youths, who was ravishingly handsome and could not have been more than sixteen or seventeen years old. I think at once that he is the castrato who had played the part of first actress at the theater in Ancona, which was subject to the same regulations as the theaters in Rome. The mother introduces her other son, a good-looking boy too, but not a castrato, whose name was Petronio and who appeared as prima ballerina, and her two daughters, the elder of whom, named Cecilia, was studying music and was twelve years old; the other, who was a dancer, was eleven and named Marina; they were both pretty. The family came from Bologna and made a living by its talents. Affability and lightheartedness made up for their poverty.

When Bellino (for such was the name of the castrato who was first actress) rose from table he yielded to Don Sancho's urging and sat down at the harpsichord and accompanied himself in an air which he sang with the voice of an angel and enchanting *fioriture*. The Spaniard listened with his eyes closed and seemed to be in ecstasy. For my part, far from keeping my eyes closed, I was admiring Bellino's which, black as carbuncles, sparkled with a fire which burned my soul. This anomalous being had some of Donna Lucrezia's features and certain gestures reminiscent of the Marchesa G. The face seemed to me feminine. And the masculine attire did not prevent my seeing a certain fullness of bosom, which put it into my head that despite the billing, this must be a girl. In this conviction, I made no resistance to the desires which he aroused in me.

After two pleasant hours Don Sancho saw me to my room and told me that he was leaving early in the morning for Sinigaglia with the Abate Vilmarcati, and would return the following day in time for supper. Wishing him a good journey, I said that I should meet him on the road, since I wished to sup at Sinigaglia that day. I was stopping in Ancona only for a day, to present my bill of exchange to the banker and get another for Bologna.

I went to bed full of the impression which Bellino had made on me and sorry to leave without having given him proof of the justice I did him in not being hoodwinked by his disguise. But the next morning I had no more than opened my door when he appears before me and offers me his brother to serve me instead of a hired manservant. I agree, he comes at once, and I send him to bring coffee for the whole family. I make Bellino sit down on my bed, intending to treat him as a girl; but his two sisters come running to me and thwart my plan. I could not but delight in the charming picture I had before my eyes: gaiety, of three different kinds, unadorned beauty, familiarity without presumption, the verve of the theater, a pretty playfulness, little Bolognese grimaces with which I was not yet familiar and which I found most charming. The two little girls were perfect living rosebuds, and more than worthy of being preferred to Bellino if I had not taken it into my head that Bellino was a girl too. Despite their extreme youth the sign of their precocious puberty was visible on their white bosoms. . . .

I gave [the mother] a doblon de a ocho, at which she wept for joy. I promise her another if she will tell me a secret.

"Admit," I say, "that Bellino is a girl."

"You may be sure he is not; but he does look it. So much so, indeed, that he had to submit to being examined."

"By whom?"

"By the very reverend confessor of Monsignor the Bishop."

"I will not believe a word of it until I have examined him myself."

"Very well; but in conscience I can have nothing to do with it for, God forgive me, I do not know what your intentions are."

I go to my room, I send Petronio out to buy a bottle of Cyprus wine, he gives me seven zecchini in change from a doblon I had given him, and I divide it among Bellino, Cecilia, and Marina; then I ask the two girls to leave me alone with their brother.

"My dear Bellino," I say, "I am sure that you are not of my sex."

"I am of your sex, but a castrato; I have been examined."

"Let me examine you too, and here is a doblon for you."

"No, for it is clear that you are in love with me, and religion forbids me to let you."

"You were not so scrupulous with the Bishop's confessor."

"He was old, and all he did was take a hasty look at my unfortunate condition."

I put out my hand, he pushes it away and rises. This obstinacy angers me, for I had already spent fifteen or sixteen zecchini to satisfy my curiosity. I sit down to dinner in the sulks, but the appetite of the three pretty creatures restores my good humor and I make up my mind to obtain a return for the money I had spent from the two younger sisters.

With the three of us sitting before the fire eating chestnuts, I begin distributing kisses; and Bellino, on his side, shows no want of compliance. I touch and then kiss the budding breasts of Cecilia and Marina; and Bellino, with a smile, does nothing to stop my hand from slipping behind his shirt ruffle and laying hold of a breast which leaves me in no possible doubt.

"This breast," I said, "proclaims you a girl, and you cannot deny it."

"All we castrati have the same deformity."

"So I am aware. But I know enough about it to tell the one kind from the other. This alabaster breast, my dear Bellino, is the charming breast of a girl of seventeen."

Completely on fire, and seeing that he offered no resistance to my hand, which was delighting in possessing such a breast, I make to approach it with my panting lips, which were pale from the intensity of my ardor; but the impostor, as if he had only that moment become aware of the forbidden pleasure I was enjoying, rises and walks off. I am left raging, yet unable to blame him. . . .

Just as I was going to shut my door, I see Cecilia, wearing little more than a shift, coming to tell me that Bellino would consider it a favor if I would take him with me as far as Rimini, where he was engaged to sing in an opera which was to be produced after Easter.

"Go and tell him, my little angel, that I am ready to do him the favor if he will first do me that of showing me, in your presence, whether he is a girl or a boy."

She goes, and comes back to tell me he is already in bed, but that if I would put off my departure for only one day he promised to satisfy my curiosity.

"Tell me the truth and I will give you six zecchini."

"I cannot earn them, for I have never seen him naked and so cannot be sure of my own knowledge; but he is certainly a boy, otherwise he would not have been allowed to sing in this city.". . .

When I sent for Bellino and demanded that he keep his promise, he replied with a smile that the day was not over yet and that he was sure he would travel to Rimini with me. I asked him if he would like to take a walk with me, and he went to dress. . . .

I went out to get money from Bucchetti, since I did not know what might happen to me on my journey before I reached Bologna. I had enjoyed myself, but I had spent too much. I still had to consider Bellino, who, if he was a girl, must not find me less generous than his sisters had done. Whether he was must inevitably come out during the course of the day; and I thought I was certain of it. . . .

At suppertime I waited on Don Sancho, whom I found alone and in a very decent room. His table was laid with silver dishes and his servants were in livery. Bellino, whether from whim or as a ruse, enters dressed as a girl, followed by his two very pretty sisters but whom he totally eclipsed, and at that moment I became so sure of his sex that I would have staked my life against a paolo. It was impossible to imagine a prettier girl.

"Are you convinced," I asked Don Sancho, "that Bellino is not a girl?"

"Girl or boy, what does it matter? I think he is a very handsome castrato; and I have seen others as good-looking as he."

"But are you sure of it?"

"*Valgame Dios!* I am not interested in making sure."

Respecting the Spaniard for possessing a wisdom which I lacked, I made no answer; but at table I could not take my eyes from this being whom my depraved nature impelled me to love and to believe a member of the sex to which it was necessary to my purposes that he should belong.

Don Sancho's supper was exquisite and, as was to be expected, better than mine, for otherwise he would have considered himself dishonored. He gave us white truffles, several kinds of shellfish, the best fish from the Adriatic, still champagne, Peralta, sherry, and Pedro Ximenes. After supper, Bellino sang in a fashion to make us lose the little reason the excellent wines had left us. His gestures, the way he moved his eyes, his gait, his bearing, his manner, his face, his voice, and above all my instinct, which I concluded could not make me feel its power for a castrato, all combined to confirm me in my idea. Yet I still needed to make certain from the testimony of my own eyes.

After duly thanking the noble Castilian, we wished him a good sleep and went to my room, where Bellino must either keep his promise to me or earn my contempt and resign himself to seeing me set off alone at dawn.

I take his hand and I make him sit down beside me before the fire, and I ask his two young sisters to leave us alone. They go at once.

"This business," I said, "will not take long if you are of my sex, and if you are of the other you will have only to spend the night with me. I will give you a hundred zecchini in the morning and we will leave together."

"You will leave alone, and you will be generous enough to forgive my weakness if I cannot keep my promise to you. I am a castrato, and I cannot bring myself either to let you see my shame or to expose myself to the loathsome consequences which convincing you of it may have."

"It will have none, for as soon as I have seen, or touched, I will myself beg you to go to bed in your own room; we will leave tomorrow the best of friends and there will be no more of this matter between us."

"No, my mind is made up: I cannot satisfy your curiosity."

At these words I am out of all patience, but I control myself and try gently to advance my hand to the place where I should find if I was right or wrong; but he uses his to stop mine from pursuing the investigation I was set on making.

"Take your hand away, my dear Bellino."

"No, absolutely not! For I see you are in a state which horrifies me. I knew it, and I shall never consent to such infamies. I will go and send my sisters to you."

I hold him back, and pretend to regain my calm; but suddenly, thinking I could take him unawares, I stretch out my arm to the bottom of his back, and my quick hand would have learned the truth from that direction if he had not parried the thrust by rising and blocking my hand, by which I was still holding on, with his, which he had been keeping over what he called his shame. It was at this moment that I saw he was a man, and believed that I saw it against his will. Astonished, angered, mortified, disgusted, I let him leave. I saw that Bellino was in truth a man; but a man to be scorned both for his degradation and for the shameful calm I observed in him at a moment when I ought not to have seen the most patent evidence of his insensibility. . . .

So now I was traveling with Bellino, who, believing that he had disillusioned me, might well hope that I would no longer be curious about him. But a quarter of an hour had not passed before he found that he was mistaken. I could not look into his eyes and not burn with love. I told him that since his eyes were a woman's and not a man's, I needed to convince myself by touch that what I had seen when he had run away was not a monstrous clitoris.

"It may be that," I said, "and I feel that I shall have no difficulty in forgiving you for such a defect, which in any case is merely a trifle; but if it is not a clitoris, I need to convince myself of it, which is a very easy matter. I no longer want to see; all I ask is to touch, and you may be sure that as soon as I am certain I will become as gentle as a dove, for once I discover that you are a man, I cannot possibly continue to love you. That is an abomination for which—God be praised!—I feel no inclination in myself. Your magnetism and, what is more, your breasts, which you abandoned to my eyes and my hands expecting that they would convince me I was mistaken, instead of doing so gave me an invincible impression which makes me still believe that you are a girl. Your build, your legs, your knees, your thighs, your hips, your buttocks are a perfect replica of the Anadyomene, which I have seen a hundred times. If after all that it is true that you are simply a castrato, permit me to believe that, knowing you look exactly like a girl, you hatched the cruel scheme of making me fall in love and then driving me mad by refusing me the proof which alone can restore me to sanity. An excellent physician, you have learned in the most diabolical of schools that the one way to make it impossible for a young man to be cured of an amorous passion to which he has succumbed is to aggravate it; but, my dear Bellino, you must admit that you cannot practice this tyranny unless you hate the person upon whom it is to produce such an effect; and, that being the case, I should use what reason I have left to hate you in the same measure, whether you are a girl or a boy. You must also be aware that your obstinate refusal to give me the certainty which I ask of you forces me to despise you as a castrato. The importance you attribute to the matter is childish and malicious. If you have human feelings, you cannot persist in your refusal, which, as the logical consequence of my reasoning, reduces me to the painful necessity of doubt. Such being my state of mind, you must finally realize that I cannot but resolve to use force, for if you are my enemy I must treat you as such without further scruples."

At the end of this too threatening harangue, to which he listened without once interrupting me, he answered only in the following few words:

"Consider that you are not my master, that I am in your hands on the strength of the promise which you sent me by Cecilia, and that you will be guilty of murder if you use force on me. Tell the postilion to stop; I will get out, and I will complain of your conduct to no one."

After this short answer, he melted into tears which reduced my poor soul to utter desolation. I almost believed that I was wrong—I say "almost," for if I had been sure of it I would have begged him to forgive me. I was unwilling to set myself up as the judge of my own cause. I withdrew into the bleakest possible silence, and found the strength of mind not to speak another word until halfway through the third post, which ended at Sinigaglia, where I intended to sup and spend the night. Before we reached there, things had to be settled. I thought there was still hope that I could make him see reason.

"We could," I said, "have parted at Rimini good friends, and that would have been the case if you had felt any friendship for me. At the price of a compliance which would have led to nothing, you could have cured me of my passion."

"It would not have cured you," answered Bellino, firmly, but with a sweetness which surprised me, "for you are in love with me whether I am a girl or a boy, and when you found that I am a boy, you would have continued to love me, and my refusals would have made you even more furious. Finding me still inexorably determined, you would have run into excesses which would later have made you shed useless tears."

"So you say, and think you are proving that your obstinacy is reasonable; but I have every right to contradict you. Convince me, and you will find me a good and loyal friend."

"You will be furious, I tell you."

"What has infuriated me is the way you deliberately displayed your charms, when, you must admit, you knew the effect they would have on me. You did not fear my amorous fury then; and do you expect me to believe that you fear it now, when all that I ask of you is to let me touch an object which cannot but fill me with disgust?"

"Ah! disgust! I am certain of the contrary. Here is my reasoning, and let it be the end of the matter. If I were a girl, I could not help loving you, and I know it. But since I am a boy, my duty is not to comply in the least with what you demand, for your passion, which is now only natural, would at once become monstrous. Your ardent nature would become the enemy of your reason, and your reason itself would soon surrender, to the point of becoming the accomplice of your frenzy, thus seconding your nature. This inflammatory revelation which you desire, which you do not fear, which you demand of me, would leave you with no control over yourself. Your sight and your touch, seeking what they cannot find, would want to avenge themselves on what they found, and the most loathsome thing that can happen between men would happen between you and me. How can you, with your intelligence, cozen yourself into thinking that when you found me a man you would cease to love me? Do you believe that after your discovery what you call my charms, which you say have made you fall in love, would vanish? No, they might even grow more powerful, and then your ardor, become merely animal, would employ every means your amorous mind could conjure up to calm itself. You would manage to persuade yourself that you could change me into a woman, or, imagining that you could become a woman yourself, you would want me to treat you as such. Led astray by your passion, your reason would invent sophism after sophism. You would say that your love for me, a man, is more reasonable than it would be if I were a girl, for you would find the source of it in the purest friendship, and you would not fail to cite me examples of such anomalies. Led astray yourself by the specious brilliance of your arguments, you would become a torrent which no dam could hold back, and I should be at a loss for words to demolish your specious reasoning, and lack the strength to repulse your furious efforts. You would finally threaten me with death, if I denied you entrance to an inviolable temple, whose gate wise nature made to open only outward. It would be a loathsome profanation, which could not be accomplished without my consent, and you would find me ready to die before I would give it."

"Nothing of the sort would happen," I answered, rather shaken by his cogent reasoning, "and you exaggerate. Yet I feel obliged to tell you, if only as a matter of form, that even if all you say should happen, it seems to me there would be less harm in allowing nature an aberration of this kind, which philosophy may well consider a mere folly without consequences, than to follow a course which will make an incurable disease of a sickness of the mind which reason would render only momentary." . . .

Having reached Sinigaglia in comparative calm, and the night being dark, we stopped at the posthouse inn. After having our trunks untied and brought to a good room I ordered supper. As there was only one bed I asked Bellino in a perfectly calm voice if he wished to have a fire lighted for him in another room. He surprised me by gently answering that he had no objection to sleeping in my bed. . . .

## CHAPTER II

*Bellino unmasks; his story. I am arrested. My involuntary flight.*
*My return to Rimini and my arrival in Bologna.*

I had scarcely got into the bed before I was overcome to see him moving toward me. I clasp him to me, I see that he is fired by the same transport. The exordium of our dialogue was a deluge of mingling kisses. His arms were first to slip down from my back to my loins. I stretch mine still lower, it is revelation enough that I am happy, I sense it, I feel it, I am convinced of it. I am right, I am vindicated, I cannot doubt it, I do not want to know how, I fear that if I speak I shall no longer be happy, or be happy as I would not wish to be, and I give myself, body and soul, to the joy which flooded my entire being and which I saw was shared. The excess of my bliss seizes all my senses with such force that it reaches the degree at which nature, drowning in the highest of all pleasures, is exhausted. For the space of a minute I remain motionless in the act of mentally contemplating and worshiping my own apotheosis.

Sight and touch, which I had thought would be the leading actors in this drama, play only secondary roles. My eyes ask no greater bliss than to remain fixed on the face of the being who held them spellbound, and my sense of touch, concentrated in my fingertips, fears to move elsewhere since it cannot imagine that it could find anything more. I should have accused nature of the most despicable cowardice if, without my permission, it had dared to leave the place of which I could feel I was in possession.

Scarcely two minutes had passed before, without breaking our eloquent silence, we set to work together to give each other fresh assurances of the reality of our mutual happiness—Bellino by assuring me of it every quarter of an hour by the sweetest moans; I by refusing to reach the end of my course again. I have all my life been dominated by the fear that my steed would flinch from beginning another race; and I never found this restraint painful, for the visible pleasure which I gave always made up four fifths of mine. For this reason nature must abhor old age, which can itself attain to pleasure, but can never give it. Youth shuns its presence, for youth's deadly enemy is age, sad, weak, deformed, hideous age, which drives it into lonely seclusion at last, and always too soon.

We finally broke off. We needed an interval. We were not exhausted; but our senses demanded that our minds be calm so that they could return to their proper seats.

Bellino, the first to break the silence, asked me if I had found him a good mistress.

"Mistress? Then you admit you are a woman? Tell me, tigress, if it is true that you loved me, how could you put off your happiness, and mine, for so long? But is it really true that you belong to the bewitching sex of which I believe I have found you to be?"

"You are the master now. Make certain."

"Yes. I need to convince myself. Good God! what has become of the monstrous clitoris I saw yesterday?"

After a complete conviction, which was followed by a long outpouring of gratitude, the fascinating creature told me her story as follows:

"My name is Teresa. The poor daughter of an employee at the Institute at Bologna, I made the acquaintance of the celebrated castrato singer Salimbeni, who lodged in our house. I was twelve years old and had a good voice. Salimbeni was handsome; I was delighted to find that I pleased him, and to have him praise me, and eager to learn music from him and to play the harpsichord. Within a year I had acquired a fairly good grounding and was able to accompany myself in an air, imitating the *fioriture* of the great master, whom the Elector of Saxony, the King of Poland, had summoned to serve him. His reward was such as his affection made him demand of me; I did not feel ashamed to grant it to him, for I worshiped him. Men like yourself are certainly to be preferred to men like my first lover; but Salimbeni was an exception. His good looks, his intelligence, his manners, his talent, and the rare qualities of his heart and soul made him preferable to all the whole men I had known until that time. Modesty and discretion were his favorite virtues, and he was rich and generous. He could never have found a woman to resist him; but I never heard him boast of conquering any woman. In short, his mutilation made him a monster, as it could not but do, but a monster of adorable qualities. I know that when I gave myself to him he made me happy; but he did so much that I can only believe I made him happy too.

"Salimbeni had a protégé whom he was boarding in the house of a music teacher in Rimini, a boy of my own age whom his dying father had had castrated to preserve his voice, so that he could turn it to profit for the benefit of the numerous family he was leaving behind, by appearing on the stage. The boy was named Bellino and was the son of the good woman whose acquaintance you just made at Ancona and whom everyone believes to be my mother.

"A year after I first came to know this being so favored by Heaven, it was he himself who told me the unhappy news that he must leave me to go to Rome. I was in despair, even though he assured me that I would soon see him again. He left my father the charge and the means to continue the cultivation of my talent; but within a few days a malignant fever carried him off; and I was left an orphan. After that Salimbeni could no longer resist my tears. He decided to take me with him as far as Rimini and leave me to board with the same music teacher in whose house he was keeping the young castrato, the brother of Cecilia and Marina. We left Bologna at midnight. No one knew that he was taking me with him—which was easy enough, for I knew no one, and no one took any interest in me, except my dear Salimbeni.

"As soon as we reached Rimini he left me at the inn and himself went to see the music teacher and make all the necessary arrangements with him for me. But half an hour later he is back at the inn, lost in thought. Bellino had died the day before our arrival. Thinking of the grief his mother would feel when he wrote her the news, it occurs to him to take me back to Bologna under the name of the Bellino who had just died and put me to board with his mother, who, being poor, would find it to her advantage to keep the secret. 'I would give her,' he said, 'sufficient means to have you complete your musical studies, and four years from now I will bring you to Dresden, not as a girl but as a castrato. We will live there together, and no one can say anything against it. You will make me happy until I die. All that is necessary is to make everyone believe you are Bellino, which you will find easy enough, since no one knows you. Only Bellino's mother will know the truth. Her children will not suspect that you are not their brother, for they were infants when I sent him to Rimini. If you love me, you must renounce your sex and even forget it completely. You must now take the name of Bellino and leave with me at once for Bologna. Within two hours you will be dressed as a boy; all you need do is to keep anyone from knowing that you are a girl. You will sleep alone; you will keep out of sight when you dress; and when in a year or two your breasts begin to develop it will be of no consequence, for having too much bosom is a defect in which all we castrati share. In addition, before I leave you I will give you a little apparatus and teach you how to adjust it so well to the place which shows the difference of sex that the deceit will pass unnoticed if it ever happens that you have to undergo an examination. If you like my plan, you will enable me to live in Dresden with you without giving the Queen, who is very devout, any occasion to object. Tell me if you consent.'

"He could be sure that I would. I could have no greater pleasure than to do whatever he wished. He had me dressed as a boy, he made me leave all my girls' clothes behind, and after ordering his servant to wait for him in Rimini, he took me to Bologna. We arrive there at nightfall, he leaves me at the inn, and goes at once to see Bellino's mother. He explains his plan to her, she assents to it, and it consoles her for the death of her son. He brings her back to the inn with him, she calls me her son, I address her as 'Mother'; Salimbeni goes off, telling us to wait. He comes back an hour later and takes from his pocket the apparatus which in case of necessity would make me pass as a man. You have seen it. It is a sort of long, soft gut, as thick as one's thumb, white and with a very smooth surface. I had to laugh to myself this morning when you called it a clitoris. It was attached to the center of an oval piece of very fine transparent hide, which was five or six inches long and two inches wide. When this is fixed with gum tragacanth to the place where sex can be distinguished, it obliterates the female organ. He dissolves the gum, tries the apparatus on me in the presence of my new mother, and I find that I have become like my dear lover. I should really have laughed if the imminent departure of the person I adored had not pierced my heart. I was left more dead than alive, with a presentiment that I should never see him again. People laugh at presentiments, and with good reason, for not everyone can hear the voice of his heart; but mine did not deceive me. Salimbeni died still a young man in the Tyrol last year, with the resignation of a philosopher. I was left under the necessity of turning my talent to account. My mother thought it a good plan to continue passing me off as a man, for she hoped she could send me to Rome to sing. In the meanwhile she accepted an offer from the theater in Ancona, where she also put Petronio to dance as a girl.

"After Salimbeni, you are the only man in whose arms Teresa has truly sacrificed to perfect love; and you have but to ask and I will from this day on abandon the name of Bellino, which I loathe since Salimbeni's death and which is beginning to cause me difficulties for which I have no patience. I have appeared in only two theaters, and to be admitted to both of them I had to submit to the same degrading examination, for wherever I go people think I look so much like a girl that they will not believe I am a man until they have been convinced. Until now I have had to deal only with old priests, who were innocently satisfied with having seen, and then certified me to the bishop; but I have continually to defend myself against two kinds of people, who assail me to obtain illicit and loathsome favors. Those who, like you, fall in love with me and so cannot believe that I am a man, insist upon my showing them the truth; and that I cannot bring myself to do for fear they will want to convince themselves by touch as well; in such a case I am afraid not only that they will strip off my mask but that, becoming curious, they will want to use the apparatus to satisfy monstrous desires which may come to them. But the wretches who persecute me beyond endurance are those who declare their monstrous love to me as the castrato I pretend to be. I fear, my dear one, that I will stab one of them. Alas, my angel! Rescue me from my shame. Take me with you. I do not ask to become your wife, I will only be your loving mistress, as I would have been to Salimbeni; my heart is pure, I know that my nature is such that I can live faithfully with my lover. Do not forsake me. The affection you have inspired in me is true love; what Salimbeni inspired in me was the fondness of innocence. I believe I did not become truly a woman until I tasted the perfect pleasure of love in your arms." . . .

"Please let me see you once again with the strange device which Salimbeni gave you."

"At once."

She gets out of bed, pours water into a glass, opens her trunk, takes out her apparatus and her gums, dissolves them, and fits on the mask. I see something unbelievable. A charming girl, who looked it in every part of her body, and who, with this extraordinary attachment, seemed to me even more interesting, for the white pendant offered no obstruction to the well of her sex. I told her that she had been wise not to let me touch it, for it would have intoxicated me and made me become what I was not, unless she had instantly calmed me by revealing the truth. I wanted to convince her that I was not lying, and our skirmish was comical. We fell asleep afterwards and did not wake until very late. . . .

# DORIS LESSING

## *Walking in the Shade:*
## *Volume Two of My Autobiography, 1949–1962*

And yet . . . We slept wrapped in blankets out in a field, in the open because of the stars. One morning, already hot, though the sun was just rising, we sat up in our blankets to see two tall dark men on tall black horses,
each wearing a red blanket like a serape, riding past us and away across
the fields, the hot blue sky behind them. They lifted their hands in greeting, unsmiling.

We ate our bread and olives and drank dark-red wine under olive trees
or waited out the extreme heat of midday in some little church, where I
had to be sure my arms were covered, and my head too.

We went to a bullfight, where Jack wept because of the six sacrificed
bulls. He was muttering, Kill him, kill him, to the bulls.

In Madrid beggar women sat on the pavements with their feet in the
gutters, and we gave them our cakes and ordered more for them.

We felt in the Alhambra that this was our place—the Alhambra affects
people strongly: they hate it or adore it.

We quarrelled violently, and often. It is my belief and my experience
that energetic and frequent sex breeds sudden storms of antagonism. Tol-
stoy wrote about this. So did D. H. Lawrence. Why should this be? We
made love when we stopped the car in open and empty country, in dry
ditches, in forests, in vineyards, in olive groves. And quarrelled. He was
jealous. This was absurd, because I loved him. In a town in Murcia, where

it was so hot we simply stopped for a whole day to sit in a café, in the shade if not the cool, he was convinced I was making eyes at a handsome Spaniard. This quarrel was so terrible that we went to a hotel for the night, because Jack, the doctor, said that our diet and lack of sleep was getting to us.

# NED ROREM

## *Knowing When to Stop*

Between the two appointments with Poulenc came an occurrence that changed my life. (Well, yes, any occurrence, even daily ones of buying the *Times* or brushing the teeth, changes our life, but not necessarily geographically.) Did I mention that the Reine Blanche is a quite small establishment—a narrow twenty-five-foot-long bar with a dozen stools on the right as you enter, and on the left a four-foot-wide walkway—made to look bigger with mirrors? There at midnight on 6 July, while chatting with Alvin Ross as we swigged Pernod, I leaned toward the reflecting wall and kissed my image on the mouth. From behind me a voice in accented English said: "I could do it better than that." I turned around to a *coup de foudre.*

Guy Ferrand, twenty-nine, stocky with a salt-and-pepper crew-cut and a hint of five-o'clock shadow, bad teeth (like everyone in France), and keen oriental eyes, immediately struck me as very sexy. A Bordelais by birth, he now lived in Fez, Morocco, where, as a professional doctor he headed a plan at the Hôpital Cocard to inoculate indigenous tribes and rid the land of malaria. For the moment he was on vacation, so why shouldn't he come home with me? I hesitated to bring him upstairs. Instead, in the dark before dawn, we made love on the mildewing hallway stairs, and next day motored to Chartres in his Citroën 4-chevaux. The cathedral seemed then, as on every subsequent visit, dingy and cheerless. But the apricot sherbet in the medieval café *en face*, accompanied by Guy's descriptions of North Africa's lunar landscape, remains indelible, as does his singing of raunchy French folk songs as we drove back to Paris at dusk through the flat and prosperous be-poplared countryside.

# JAMES BOSWELL

## *Boswell on the Grand Tour:*
## *Italy, Corsica and France, 1765–1766*

MONDAY 7 JANUARY. I arrived in the evening at Turin, which made me think of Lord Eglinton, who passed some time here and advised me to do the same. I put up at the Bonne Femme, a most magnificent *auberge*. I went dirty to the opera. The superb theatre struck me much, and the boxes full of ladies and gallants talking to each other, quite Italy. So fatigued was I that I fell asleep. When I got home and tumbled into a fine bed, it was most luxurious.

TUESDAY 8 JANUARY. I got up very fretful, but drove off the fiend. I got my coach and *valet de louage* and went to M. Torraz, my banker, a good, brisk, civil fellow. I received a letter from my dear mother, which gave me great comfort, for I had not heard from her since I left England and had formed to myself dreary ideas of her being dead, or sick, or offended with me, which it had been thought prudent to conceal from me. I had also an exceedingly good letter from my brother David, in which he very sensibly and genteelly reproved me for yielding so much to the attacks of melancholy.

I sent a letter of recommendation from Colonel Chaillet to the Comtesse de St. Gilles. She received me at four o'clock. She was past fifty and had long been *hackneyed in the ways of men*, but, being strong, was still well enough. She talked of Duke Hamilton, who had been a great gallant of hers. She had animal spirits and talked incessantly. She carried me out in her coach to take the air. I was already then quite in the Italian mode. We returned to her house, where was a stupid *conversazione,* all men. After this we all went to a public ball at the Théâtre de Carignan. It was very handsome and gay. I danced a minuet with the Spanish Ambassadress. There was here many fine women. The counts and other pretty gentlemen told me whenever I admired a lady, "Sir, you can have her. It would not be difficult." I thought at first they were joking and waggishly amusing themselves with a stranger. But I at last discovered that they were really in earnest and that the manners here were so openly debauched that adultery was carried on without the least disguise. I asked them, "But why then do you marry?" "Oh, it's the custom; it perpetuates families." I met here a Capitaine Billon to whom I had a letter from M. de Froment. He was a blunt Frenchman, very obliging. I also met here young Gray, son to my Lord, a good, brisk little fellow.

WEDNESDAY 9 JANUARY. There was at present no minister here from our Court. But M. Dutens, who acted in his place, carried me to wait on the Comte de Viry, the Prime Minister. The Court was in mourning, so I could not be presented till I had a black coat. I trifled away the morning.

I went at five to Mme. de St. Gilles', where I tired to death. Her husband was an old shrewd fellow, who had killed his man in Poland. The room was full of young rakes, mighty stupid, and old worn-out miscreants in whom impotence and stupidity were united. I attended her to the opera, as one of her cicisbays. She had two of us. One held her gloves or her muff, and another her fan. After being heartily wearied in her box, I went down to the parterre, from whence I saw, in a high box, Mr. Wilkes. To see a man whom I have so often thought of since I left England filled me with romantic agitation. I considered he might have been dead as well as Churchill, and methought I viewed him in the Elysian fields. When I got home I sent him another note.

THURSDAY 10 JANUARY. I tried to write this morning, but could do nothing. I drove about in the environs. At three I called on M. Bartoli, the King's antiquary, whom M. Schmidt at Karlsruhe had advised me to see. I was courteously received. I found him confusedly learned and lively. He improved the more I talked with him. I gave him anecdotes of Voltaire and Rousseau. He did not approve of the writings of either of the two, for he was a man attached to the Catholic religion. I told him that Rousseau said, "I live in a world of chimeras." He replied, "Then let him keep his books there, and not be sending them out into the real world." He offered me his services while I remained at Turin.

I then went to Mme. St. Gilles'. The whim seized me of having an intrigue with an Italian countess, and, as I had resolved to stay very little time here, I thought an oldish lady most proper, as I should have an easy attack. I began throwing out hints at the opera. I sat vis-à-vis to her and pressed her legs with mine, which she took very graciously. I began to lose command of myself. I became quite imprudent. I said, "Surely there will be another world, if only for getting the King of Prussia flogged"; against whom I raged while the Imperial Minister sat by us. Billon carried me to the box of the Countess Burgaretta, and introduced me to her. She was a most beautiful woman. Billon told me I might have her. My mind was now quite in fermentation. I was a sceptic, but my devotion and love of decency remained. My desire to know the world made me resolve to intrigue a little while in Italy, where the women are so debauched that they are hardly to be considered as moral agents, but as inferior beings. I shall just mark little sketches of my attempts in that way. This night (the third of our acquaintance) I made plain addresses to Mme. St. Gilles, who refused me like one who wished to have me. But thinking me more simple than I really was, feared to trust me. I was too easy about the matter to take any pains.

FRIDAY 11 JANUARY. I had now my black clothes. My *valet de louage* told me my hair must be dressed "in a horse-tail." I was in droll bad humour and abused the fellow, saying, "Then you must get me shod too. Have you a good blacksmith at Turin? Send for him." However, I did comply with the courtly mode. I waited on Dutens, who was about publishing a complete edition of the works of Leibnitz with notes and I know not what more. *Opus magnum et ponderosum.* Will men still be plodding in this manner? Let them alone. It is as good as playing at cards. I was presented to the King of Sardinia, who, after all his Italian wars, was just a little quiet man. He only asked me whence? and whither? I looked at him as a kind of heir to the British Crown. There was a numerous Court, mostly military. I went to mass in the King's chapel, which he attends regularly every day.

This morning I was quite in love with Mme. Burgaretta. Billon certainly officiated for me as a genteel pimp. To show how corruption may prevail without shame, thus in gross flattery did I write to him this morning:

My dear Sir,—If you are a man worthy of respect, an obliging man whom one must love; in short, if you have any noble virtue in your soul, arrange for me to see Mme. B— today. You told me yesterday that it will be possible for me to enjoy the favours of that goddess in a very little time. Oh, how adorable she is! I beg of you to be at the coffee-house after the Court. I shall have the honour of finding you there.

Was not this real rascality to prostitute the praises of merit in such a manner? But when a man gives himself up to gross gallantry he must lose much of his delicacy of principle. Billon told me with great simplicity, "It's a low game." I shall only talk in general of my Turin deviations. I had Billon to dine with me, after which Bartoli and I went and saw a church. I was madly in love with Mme B—. I called on her thrice this afternoon, but did not find admittance.

At four Dutens presented me at the French Ambassador's to his Excellency's lady. I had the honour to hand her to her coach. About the middle of the stair we were met by a marquise, who of course was to turn back. But the great question was, who should be led first to her coach? *Madame la marquise! Madame l'ambassadrice!* I was simple enough to be tossed from the one to the other, as I did just what I was bid; while the rogue Dutens enjoyed my perplexity and probably studied from it something to insert among his notes on Leibnitz on determining motives. At last her Excellency of France took the *pas.* I was deeply hipped, and knew not what to make of myself. I went and lounged some time at Mme. St. Gilles'; then I returned to the drawing-room of the French Ambassadress, where I was presented to M. Chauvelin himself. I was quite loaded with gloom and stood at the back of the chairs of those who were playing, to whom I hardly gave any attention but was fixed in proud and sullen silence. This was a most sad evening.

SATURDAY 12 JANUARY. At night I sat a long time in the box of Mme B., of whom I was now violently enamoured. I made my declarations, and was amazed to find such a proposal received with the most pleasing politeness. She however told me, "It is impossible. I have a lover" (showing him), "and I do not wish to deceive him." Her lover was the Neapolitan Minister, Comte Pignatelli, in whose box she sat. He was a genteel, amiable man. He went away, and then I pursued my purpose. Never did I see such dissimulation, for she talked aloud that I should think no more of my passion, and the *piémontais* around us heard this and said without the least delicacy, "A traveller expects to accomplish in ten days as much as another will do in a year." I was quite gone. She then said to me, "Whisper in my ear," and told me, "We must make arrangements," assuring me that she had talked severely to persuade people that there was nothing between us. She bid me call upon her next day at three. This was advancing with rapidity. I saw she was no very wise personage, so flattered her finely. "Ah, Madame, I understand you well. This country is not worthy of you. That is true" (like a mere fool). "You are not loved here as you ought to be." Billon came and repeated gross bawdy. This was disgusting. When I got home I was so full of my next day's bliss that I sat up all night.

SUNDAY 13 JANUARY. By want of sleep and agitation of mind, I was quite feverish. At seven I received a letter from Mme—telling me that people talked of us, and forbidding me to come to her or to think more of the "plus malheureuse de femmes." This tore my very heart. I wrote to her like a madman, conjuring her to pity me. Billon came and went out with me in my coach. He told me I had lost her merely by being an *imprudent* and discovering my attachment to all the world. I had wrought myself up to a passion which I was not master of. I saw he looked upon me as a very simple young man; for amongst the thoroughbred libertines of Turin to have sentiment is to be a child. I changed my lodgings. She wrote to me again. I wrote to her an answer more mad than my former one. I was quite gone. At night I saw her at the opera. We were reserved. But I told her my misery. She said, "C'est impossible." I was distracted. I forgot to mention that I have paid her one visit. . . .

MONDAY 14 JANUARY. Night before last I plainly proposed matters to Mme. St. Gilles. "I am young, strong, vigorous. I offer my services as a duty, and I think that the Comtesse de St. Gilles will do very well to accept them." "But I am not that kind of woman." "Very well, Madame, I shall believe you." I thought to take her *en passant*. But she was cunning and saw my passion for Mme. B—, so would not hazard with me.

This morning I waited on Mr. Needham, who read me a defence of the Trinity which was most ingenious and really silenced me. I said, "Sir, this defence is very good; but pray what did you do before you thought of it?" He replied that he submitted to it as a mystery. He said the Catholic religion was proved as a general system, like the Newtonian philosophy, and, although we may be perplexed with partial difficulties, they are not to shake our general belief. He said the world would very soon be divided into Catholics and Deists. He threw my ideas into the orthodox channel.

But still I recalled Rousseau's liberal views of the benevolent Divinity, and so was more free. Needham said that a man whose melancholy hurt his rational powers could hardly be accountable for his moral conduct. He consoled me.

After dinner I called on Norton and Heath, two English gentlemen. I did not know what to say to them. I liked the opera much tonight, and my passion was already gone. Honest Billon said, "If you want to make love, I can find you a girl." I agreed to this by way of cooling my raging disposition to fall in love. At night Mme. St. Gilles seemed piqued that I pursued her no longer, and, suspecting that I was enchained by Mme. B——, she said, "Really, you are a little mad. You get notions, and your head turns. I'll tell you: I think you have studied a great deal. You ought to go back to your books. You should not follow the profession of gallant or you will be terribly taken in. Be careful of your health and of your purse. For you don't know the world." Although my former love-adventures are proof enough that it is not impossible for me to succeed with the ladies, yet this abominable woman spoke very true upon the whole. I have too much warmth ever to have the cunning necessary for a general commerce with the corrupted human race.

TUESDAY 15 JANUARY. I went to Billon's, who had a very pretty girl for me with whom I amused myself. I then went to another ball at the Théâtre de Carignan. I tired much. Billon had promised to have a girl to sleep with me all night at his lodgings. I went there at eleven but did not find her. I was vexed and angry.

WEDNESDAY 16 JANUARY. Billon and another French officer dined with me. We were well. I then called on Needham, who explained his philosophical opinion of transubstantiation, by which I was convinced that it was not absurd. He and I then went and waited on the French Ambassadress. After which I went to Mme. St. Gilles', where I was quite disgusted. I went home very dull. What a strange day have I had of it!

THURSDAY 17 JANUARY. All the forenoon I wrote. After dinner I took Bartoli to air in my coach. We went and saw the Bernardines' library. I was gloomy but patient. At night I was again at a ball. I was calm, pensive and virtuous. Sabbati, Secretary to the French Ambassador, talked a good deal with me, and said, "You are a man from another century." I had eyed a singular lady some time. She was very debauched. But I took a fancy to her. Sabbati presented me to her. I said, "Mme. S——, this is the fifth evening that I have tried to make your acquaintance." She seemed gay and pleased.

FRIDAY 18 JANUARY. I passed the morning at home, but was so sadly dissipated that I could do no good. While I was at dinner, an Augustine monk came and asked charity. He said he had been twenty-seven years *religious et semper contentus*.

I then went to Billon's, where I had a pretty girl. I was disgusted with low pleasure. Billon talked of women in the most indelicate manner. I then went to Mme. Burgaretta's, where I found two more swains. She grumbled and complained of a headache; and she dressed before us, changing even her shirt. We indeed saw no harm; but this scene entirely cured my passion for her. Her *femme de chambre* was very clever, and, when the Countess was dressed, carried away her morning clothes in a little barrel. At the opera I sat in the box of Mme. S——, who was soft and gentle, and seemed to like my compliments. I was at Mme. St. Gilles' in good spirits, and went home pretty much content.

SATURDAY 19 JANUARY. Here have I stayed a week longer than I intended, partly from love, partly to see a grand opera which is to be performed tomorrow. After dinner I sat some time with Needham, who told me he was in orders as a Catholic priest and had always lived with conscientious strictness. He said he had many severe struggles to preserve his chastity, but had done so, and was now quite serene and happy. He had also been distressed with a lowness of spirits which impedes devotion. Thomas à Kempis complains of a *siccitas animi*. I was amazed to find a man who had such parts and had seen so much of the world, and yet so strict as worthy Needham. I talked of the eternity of hell's torments, which he defended as the continual shade which must be in the universe, which wicked beings ought justly to form. He said too that the pains would be in proportion to the offences, and that perhaps to exist with a certain degree of pain was better than to be annihilated.

At the opera I sat in Mme. S——' box, and fairly told her my love, saying that I could not leave Turin, being entirely captivated by her. She seemed propitious. Mme. St. Gilles, deservedly balked of my services, was not a little angry. She was impudent enough to tell about that I had made a bold attack upon her. I did not like to hear this joke.

MONDAY 21 JANUARY. Never was mind so formed as that of him who now recordeth his own transactions. I was now in a fever of love for an abandoned being whom multitudes had often treated like a very woman of the town. I hesitated if I should not pass the winter here and gravely write to my father that really a melancholy man like myself so seldom found anything to attach him that he might be indulged in snatching a transient pleasure, and thus would I inform him that an Italian Countess made me remain at Turin. Was there ever such madness? O Rousseau, how am I fallen since I was with thee! I wrote a long letter to Mme. S—, entreating her pity *and all that*. Her answer was that if she had known my letter was of such a nature, she would not have opened it. She had told me plainly her mind at the opera. Pedro, my stupid *valet de place*, brought me this shocking word-of-mouth message. I saw that amongst profligate wretches a man of sentiment could only expose himself.

After dinner I went to Needham, and was consoled with learned and solid conversation. We went to the opera together, and sat in the middle of the parterre, from whence I never stirred but was quite independent. I enjoyed fully the entertainment. Needham talked of the religious orders, particularly of the Trappe, and explained them in so philosophical a manner that I had much solemn satisfaction.

After the opera Norton and Heath insisted I should go home with them and sup. I went, like a simpleton. They carried me into a low room of their inn, where they romped with two girls and gave me a most pitiful supper. This, now, was true English. I had now and then looked from the parterre to Mme. S—, but did not go to her box. I determined to set out next morning for Milan.

# Henry Miller

## *Quiet Days in Clichy*

It was in the late afternoon of a rainy day that I espied a newcomer at the Café Wepler. I had been out shopping, and my arms were loaded with books and phonograph records. I must have received an unexpected remittance from America that day because, despite the purchases I had made, I still had a few hundred francs in my pocket. I sat down near the place of exchange, surrounded by a bevy of hungry, itching whores whom I had no difficulty whatever in eluding because my eyes were fastened on this ravishing beauty who was sitting apart in a far corner of the café. I took her to be an attractive young woman who had made a rendezvous with her lover and who had come ahead of time perhaps. The *apéritif* which she had ordered had hardly been touched. At the men who passed her table she gave a full, steady glance, but that indicated nothing—a Frenchwoman doesn't avert her glance as does the English or the American woman. She looked around quietly, appraisingly, but without obvious effort to attract attention. She was discreet and dignified, thoroughly poised and self-contained. She was waiting. I too was waiting. I was curious to see whom she was waiting for. After a half hour, during which time I caught her eye a number of times and held it, I made up my mind that she was waiting for anyone who would make the proper overture. Ordinarily one has only to give a sign with the head or the hand and the girl will leave her table and join you—if she's that kind of girl. I was not absolutely sure even yet. She looked too good to me, too sleek, too well-nurtured, I might say.

When the waiter came round again I pointed her out and asked him if he knew her. When he said no I suggested that he invite her to come over and join me. I watched her face as he delivered the message. It gave me quite a thrill to see her smile and look my way with a nod of recognition. I expected her to get up immediately and come over, but instead she remained seated and smiled again, more discreetly this time, whereupon she turned her head away and appeared to gaze out the window dreamily. I allowed a few moments to intervene and then, seeing that she had no intention of making a move, I rose and walked over to her table. She greeted me cordially enough, quite as if I were a friend indeed, but I noticed that she was a little flustered, almost embarrassed. I wasn't sure whether she wanted me to sit down or not, but I sat down nevertheless and, after ordering drinks, quickly engaged her in conversation. Her voice was even more thrilling than her smile; it was well-pitched, rather low, and throaty. It was the voice of a woman who is glad to be alive, who indulges herself, who is careless and indigent, and who will do anything to preserve the modicum of freedom which she possesses. It was the voice of a giver, of a spender; its appeal went to the diaphragm rather than the heart.

I was surprised, I must confess, when she hastened to explain to me that I had made a *faux pas* in coming over to her table. "I thought you had understood," she said, "that I would join you outside. That's what I was trying to tell you telegraphically." She intimated that she did not want to be known here as a professional. I apologized for the blunder and offered to withdraw, which she accepted as a delicate gesture to be ignored by a squeeze of the hand and a gracious smile.

"What are all these things?" she said, quickly changing the subject by pretending to be interested in the packages which I had placed on the table.

"Just books and records," I said, implying that they would hardly interest her.

"Are they French authors?" she asked, suddenly injecting a note of genuine enthusiasm, it seemed to me.

"Yes," I replied, "but they are rather dull, I fear. Proust, Céline, Elie Faure . . . You'd prefer Maurice Dekobra, no?"

"Let me see them, please. I want to see what kind of French books an American reads."

I opened the package and handed her the Elie Faure. It was *The Dance over Fire and Water.* She riffled the pages, smiling, making little exclamations as she read here and there. Then she deliberately put the book down, closed it, and put her hand over it as if to keep it closed. "Enough, let us talk about something more interesting." After a moment's silence, she added: "*Ce-lui-là, est-il vraiment français?*"

"*Un vrai de vrai,*" I replied, with a broad grin.

She seemed puzzled. "It's excellent French," she went on, as if to herself, "and yet it's not French either . . . *Comment dirais-je?*"

I was about to say that I understood perfectly when she threw herself back against the cushion, took hold of my hand and, with a roguish smile which was meant to reinforce her candor, said: "Look, I am a thoroughly lazy creature. I haven't the patience to read books. It's too much for my feeble brain."

"There are lots of other things to do in life," I answered, returning her smile. So saying, I placed my hand on her leg and squeezed it warmly. In an instant her hand covered mine, removed it to the soft, fleshy part. Then, almost as quickly, she drew my hand away with an—"*Assez, nous ne sommes pas seuls ici.*"

We sipped our drinks and relaxed. I was in no hurry to rush her off. For one thing, I was too enchanted by her speech, which was distinctive and which told me that she was not a Parisian. It was a pure French she spoke, and for a foreigner like myself a joy to listen to. She pronounced every word distinctly, using almost no slang, no colloquialisms. The words came out of her mouth fully formed and with a retarded tempo, as if she had rolled them on her palate before surrendering them to the void wherein the sound and the meaning are so swiftly transformed. Her laziness, which was voluptuous, feathered the words with a soft down; they came floating to my ears like balls of fluff. Her body was heavy, earth-laden, but the sounds which issued from her throat were like the clear notes of a bell.

She was made for it, as the saying goes, but she did not impress me as an out-and-out whore. That she would go with me, and take money for it, I knew—but that doesn't make a woman a whore.

She put a hand on me and, like a trained seal, my pecker rose jubilantly to her delicate caress.

"Contain yourself," she murmured, "it's bad to get excited too quickly."

"Let's get out of here," said I, beckoning the waiter.

"Yes," she said, "let's go somewhere where we can talk at leisure."

The less talking the better, I thought to myself, as I gathered my things and escorted her to the street. A wonderful piece of ass, I reflected, watching her sail through the revolving door. I already saw her dangling on the end of my cock, a fresh, hefty piece of meat waiting to be cured and trimmed.

As we were crossing the boulevard she remarked how pleased she was to have found someone like me. She knew no one in Paris, she was lonesome. Perhaps I would take her around, show her the city? It would be amusing to be guided about the city, the capital of one's own country, by a stranger. Had I ever been to Amboise or Blois or Tours? Maybe we could take a trip together some day. *"Ça vous plairait?"*

We tripped along, chatting thus, until we came to a hotel which she seemed to know. "It's clean and cozy here," she said. "And if it's a little chilly, we will warm each other in bed." She squeezed my arm affectionately.

The room was as cozy as a nest. I waited a moment for soap and towels, tipped the maid, and locked the door. She had taken off her hat and fur piece, and stood waiting to embrace me at the window. What a warm, plantular piece of flesh! I thought she would burst into seed under my touch. In a few moments we started to undress. I sat down on the edge of the bed to unlace my shoes. She was standing beside me, pulling off her things. When I looked up she had nothing on but her stockings. She stood there, waiting for me to examine her more attentively. I got up and put my arms around her again, running my hands leisurely over the billowy folds of flesh. She pulled out of the embrace and, holding me at arm's length inquired coyly if I were not somewhat deceived.

"Deceived?" I echoed. "How do you mean?"

"Am I not too fat?" she said, dropping her eyes and resting them on her navel.

"Too fat? Why, you're marvelous. You're like a Renoir."

At this she blushed. "A Renoir?" she repeated, almost as if she had never heard the name. "No, you're joking."

"Oh, never mind. Come here, let me stroke that pussy of yours."

"Wait, I will first make my toilette." As she moved towards the *bidet* she said: "You get into bed. Make it nice and toasty, yes?"

I undressed quickly, washed my cock out of politeness, and dove between the sheets. The *bidet* was right beside the bed. When she had finished her ablutions she began to dry herself with the thin, worn towel. I leaned over and grabbed her tousled bush, which was still a little dewy. She pushed me back into bed and, leaning over me, made a quick dive for it with her warm red mouth. I slipped a finger inside her to get the juice working. Then, pulling her on top of me, I sank it in up to the hilt. It was one of those cunts which fit like a glove. Her adroit muscular contractions soon had me gasping. All the while she licked my neck, my armpits, the lobes of my ears. With my two hands I lifted her up and down, rolling her pelvis round and round. Finally, with a groan, she bore down on me full weight; I rolled her over on her back, pulled her legs up over my shoulders, and went at her slam-bang. I thought I'd never stop coming; it came out in steady stream, as if from a garden hose. When I pulled away it seemed to me that I had an even bigger erection than when I plugged in.

"*Ça c'est quelque chose,*" she said, putting her hand around my cock and fingering it appraisingly. "You know how to do it, don't you?"

We got up, washed, and crawled back into bed again. Reclining on an elbow, I ran my hand up and down her body. Her eyes were glowing as she lay back, thoroughly relaxed, her legs open, her flesh tingling. Nothing was said for several minutes. I lit a cigarette for her, put it in her mouth, and sank deep into the bed, staring contentedly at the ceiling.

"Are we going to see more of each other?" I asked after a time.

"That is up to you," she said, taking a deep puff. She turned over to put her cigarette out and then, drawing close, gazing at me steadily, smiling, but serious, she said in her low, warbling voice: "Listen, I must talk to you seriously. There is a great favor I wish to ask of you . . . I am in trouble, great trouble. Would you help me, if I asked you to?"

"Of course," I said, "but how?"

"I mean money," she said, quietly and simply. "I need a great deal . . . I *must* have it. I won't explain why. Just believe me, will you?"

I leaned over and yanked my pants off the chair. I fished out the bills and all the change that was in my pocket, and handed it to her.

"I'm giving you all I have," I said. "That's the best I can do."

She laid the money on the night table beside her without looking at it and, bending over, she kissed my brow. "You're a brick," she said. She remained bent over me, looking into my eyes with mute, strangled gratitude, then kissed me on the mouth, not passionately, but slowly, lingeringly, as if to convey the affection which she couldn't put into words and which she was too delicate to convey by offering her body.

"I can't say anything now," she said, falling back on the pillow. "*Je suis émue, c'est tout.*" Then, after a brief pause, she added: "It's strange how one's own people are never as good to one as a stranger. You Americans are very kind, very gentle. We have much to learn from you."

It was such an old song to me, I almost felt ashamed of myself for having posed once again as the generous American. I explained to her that it was just an accident, my having so much money in my pocket. To this she replied that it was all the more wonderful, my gesture. "A Frenchman would hide it away," she said. "He would never give it to the first girl he met just because she was in need of help. He wouldn't believe her in the first place. *'Je connais la chanson,'* he would say."

I said nothing more. It was true and it wasn't true. It takes all sorts to make a world and, though up to that time I had never met a generous Frenchman, I believed that they existed. If I had told her how ungenerous my own friends had been, my countrymen, she would never have believed me. And if I had added that it was not generosity which had prompted me, but self-pity, myself giving to myself (because nobody could be as generous to me as I myself), she would probably have thought me slightly cracked.

I snuggled up to her and buried my head in her bosom. I slid my head down and licked her navel. Then farther down, kissing the thick clump of hair. She drew my head up slowly and, pulling me on top of her, buried her tongue in my mouth. My cock stiffened instantly; it slid into her just as naturally as an engine going into a switch. I had one of those long, lingering hard-ons which drive a woman mad. I jibbed her about at will, now over, now under her, then sidewise, then drawing it out slowly, tantalizingly, massaging the lips of the vulva with the bristling tip of my cock. Finally I pulled it out altogether and twirled it around her breasts. She looked at it in astonishment. "Did you come?" she asked. "No," I said. "We're going to try something else now," and I dragged her out of the bed and placed her in position for a proper, thorough back-scuttling. She reached up under her crotch and put it in for me, wiggling her ass around invitingly as she did so. Gripping her firmly around the waist, I shot it into her guts. "Oh, oh, that's marvelous, that's *wonderful,*" she grunted, rolling her ass with a frenzied swing. I pulled it out again to give it an airing, rubbing it playfully against her buttocks. "No, no," she begged, "don't do that. Stick it in, stick it all the way in . . . I can't wait." Again she reached under and placed it for me, bending her back still more now, and pushing upward as if to trap the chandelier. I could feel it coming again, from the middle of my spine; I bent my knees slightly and pushed it in another notch or two. Then bango! it burst like a sky rocket.

It was well into the dinner hour when we parted down the street in front of a urinal. I hadn't made any definite appointment with her, nor had I inquired what her address might be. It was tacitly understood that the place to find her was at the café. Just as we were taking leave it suddenly occurred to me that I hadn't even asked her what her name was. I called her back and asked her—not for her full name but for her first name. "N-Y-S," she said, spelling it out. "Like the city, Nice." I walked off, saying it over and over to myself. I had never heard of a girl being called by that name before. It sounded like the name of a precious stone.

# DUNCAN FALLOWELL

## *One Hot Summer in St. Petersburg*

Cleansed, washed, combed and dressed in clean clothes, I feel thoroughly invigorated and descend to the Bar Angleterre on the ground floor. It is now 10:20 pm. The bar is beginning to fill with women of the night, those blonde stalking felines in dark suits with short skirts, long legs, slanting eyes, a cigarette maybe between glossy lips. Oh, Russian eyes . . . So many pairs of eyes in this city touching you inside. It's the eyes that kill you . . . The Bar Angleterre is small and the service confoundedly slow. I am parched, dying, but the barman continues to tot up numbers with a calculator at the far end of the bar.

"They take ages," says a voice beside me, using the English idiom. It's one in a dark suit with short skirt, by Boss or Lagerfeld, that type, slanting eyes, long straight blonde hair, because in fact they don't all look like that. Several border on the outrageous. The most floozielike among them has a backcombed beehive and a bosom like the bastion of a fortress. Another wears a black dress with too many white lace frills like a waitress from the 1950s at Lyons Corner House. But we do not have here the lycra hams of Berlin or the silicone cartoons of Paris or the junkies of New York or the cockney sparrowhawks of London. On the whole this lot are smart, fine girls.

"Do they always take ages?"

"Not always."

"Would you like a drink?"

"I'd like another coffee."

"That all?"

"A coffee would be very nice."

"I'm not staying at this hotel."

"Where are you staying?"

"With a Russian family."

"Ah."

"Can I ask you a question?"

"Anything."

"How much do you charge?"

"Oh. Are you interested?"

"No."

"$100."

"And if I'm interested?"

"$200."

"Oh."

"What are you doing in St Petersburg?"

"I'm a writer."

"I hate writers."

"Sorry."

"They never stop writing."

"I can't get started."

"That's an improvement."

"Why?"

"You are troubled."

"I'm thinking."

"The way some of them churn it out . . . ugh!"

"Yes, that's repulsive, isn't it."

"You are sweating."

"Am I?"

"Yes."

At last the barman attends to us.

"I was in the sauna."

"Did you have massage?"

"No. I'd quite like a massage."

"$50 I will do massage for you. I am no good at money. Some are good at it. Me no."

"Me no too."

"This is embarrassing . . . where do you come from?" she asks.

"I only have $30. Nothing complicated," I reply.

"OK."

"OK?"

"OK."

"Hang on . . . I have only $27. Sorry."

"Oh God, I hate writers!"

"You said that before."

"Once upon a time I had affair with a writer . . ." She stares down at the coffee, stirring it with a spoon, the memory stinging still. ". . . OK."

"OK? You will give a massage for $27?"

"OK."

"You are sweet to me."

To leave the Astoria, or indeed any of the other dollar prisons, is to pass through an air-lock of paranoia, propelled onto the streets like a potential victim, the body clenching against threat, against the 24-hour sunshine nightmare vibrating around you, quiet at this hour, uncluttered, pensive, as though the city had drawn in its breath prior to a kiss or an expectoration.

"We can walk. Do not be afraid."

She is not the first Russian to say that to me. Do I look afraid? Does it show through so clearly? She is not thin. When I think of "woman" I do not think of bones.

We climb a morose staircase on the Moika Embankment to a flat full of pink light and cuddly toys—bears, rabbits, donkeys, crocodiles, tigers, a whole zoo of nylon fluff. I must be a bloody fool coming here. They might rob me or anything—well, no, I'm handing over all my dollars as it is, but . . . The main room overlooks the canal. Shag-pile rugs cover the floor. A large square divan against the wall is heaped with cushions and animals. But it is the heavy aroma of scent which makes me chuckle uneasily—I've got myself trapped in some preposterous cliché and must somehow see it through.

"I'm sorry about all this," she says, indicating the fluffies and sweeping most of them onto the floor. "It's not my place."

"Whose is it?"

"My friend's. She's in Moscow for 3 months—in my flat."

"You are from Moscow?"

"From St. Petersburg. I work in Moscow."

"Shall I take my clothes off?"

"Do what you like."

I take the money out of my trouser pocket and put it under an ashtray. It's mostly in dollar singles. And throw my clothes onto an armchair in deliberate disarray.

"Are they all singles?" she queries. She's one of those well-to-do Russians who find single notes an irritation.

I lie face down on the bed and say "Do my back and shoulders first. You can use your fingernails a bit." I really need this.

"Do you want a whisky?" she asks. "I'm having one."

She pours it neat into a couple of vodka glasses and carefully removes her own clothes, placing the suit on a coathanger. I don't think she wants to do back & shoulders—a fingernail is running up and down the inside of my thigh. It feels delicious. I am resting the side of my face on my hands and thinking—we are like 2 people in a commercial. But the whisky and the slow relentless movement of the fingernail induce a sloughing-off of self-consciousness. The edges of personality begin to dissolve . . . turn over . . . her eyes are hidden by her hair . . . the breasts move with a slow comfortable rhythm . . . I like breasts—sssssssssslip . . . she's slipped a condom over my cock.

There is a soft click inside, like a muffled gear-change, as I shift into a different aspect of character. This is the secret of the chance encounter: to take a holiday from yourself. . . . A second before the magnesium flash I hear a kettle whistling in an adjacent flat. . . . Relaxed now, I keep chuckling. Sex without love has a purity which can lighten the heart. So long as you have love somewhere else. Sex in a loveless life can be a reminder of inner bleakness—though it is much better than nothing at all. It keeps you in shape for love. She is amused by my grin, not resentful of it. Quite often after surprise sex I have this chuckling feeling. It's the silly feeling of success. It can be resented if the other party has mixed feelings. And vice-versa.

"You are in love?" she asks.

"Er . . ."

"But you have not had her."

"Aha."

"Is she beautiful?"

"Yes."

"I think you can have her."

"How do you know?"

"Of course you can have her."

She showers.

Then I shower while she tidies the room with fleet accuracy. She helps me button up my shirt, saying "This is a beautiful shirt."

"What is your name?"

"Anya."

"Aren't you afraid of AIDS in this job?"

"Don't be childish. I love my job. I am very careful. And remember— AIDS brings the death principle into our days—which makes us more alive!"

Only a university-educated Russian prostitute could produce a remark like that. Don't believe them when they say the Russians do not have the gift of self-mockery. Giving a kiss on the cheek, a droll look and a wave, she returns with poise and relish to the Astoria.

# Katherine Mansfield

## *The Letters and Journals*

JOURNAL                                    *February 20, 1915*

The curious thing was that I could not concentrate on the end of the journey. I simply felt so happy that I leaned out of the window with my arms along the brass rail and my feet crossed and [*illegible*] the sunlight and the wonderful country unfolding. At Châteaudun where we had to change I went to the Buffet to drink. A big pale green room with a large stove jutting out and a buffet with coloured bottles. Two women, their arms folded, leaned against the counter. A little boy, very pale, swung from table to table, taking the orders. It was full of soldiers sitting back in their chairs, swinging their legs and eating. The sun shone through the windows.

The little boy poured me out a glass of horrible black coffee. He served the soldiers with a kind of dreary contempt. In the porch an old man carried a pail of brown spotted fish—large fish, like the fish one sees in glass cases swimming through forests of beautiful pressed seaweed. The soldiers laughed and slapped each other. They tramped about in their heavy boots. The women looked after them, and the old man stood humbly waiting for someone to attend to him, his cap in his hands, as if he knew that the life he represented in his torn jacket, with his basket of fish—his peaceful occupation—did not exist any more and had no right to thrust itself here.

The last moments of the journey I was very frightened. We arrived at Gray, and one by one, like women going in to see a doctor, we slipped through a door into a hot room completely filled with two tables and two colonels, like colonels in comic opera, big shiny grey-whiskered men with a touch of burnt-red in their cheeks, both smoking, one a cigarette with a long curly ash hanging from it. He had a ring on his finger. Sumptuous and omnipotent he looked. I shut my teeth. I kept my fingers from trembling as I handed the passport and the ticket.

"It won't do, it won't do at all," said my colonel, and looked at me for what seemed an age in silence. His eyes were like two grey stones. He took my passport to the other colonel, who dismissed the objection, stamped it, and let me go. I nearly knelt on the floor.

By the station stood F., terribly pale. He saluted and smiled and said, "Turn to the right and follow me as though you were not following." Then fast he went towards the Suspension Bridge. He had a postman's bag on his back, and a paper parcel. The street was very muddy. From the toll house by the bridge a scraggy woman, her hands wrapped in a shawl, peered out at us. Against the toll house leaned a faded cab. "Montez! vite, vite!" said F. He threw my suitcase, his letter bag and the parcel on to the floor. The driver sprang into activity, lashed the bony horse, and we tore away with both doors flapping and banging. "Bon jour, ma chérie," said F. and we kissed each other quickly and then clutched at the banging doors. They would not keep shut, and F. who is not supposed to ride in cabs, had to try to hide. Soldiers passed all the time. At the barracks he stopped a moment and a crowd of faces blocked the window. "Prends, ça, mon vieux," said F., handing over the paper parcel.

Off we flew again. By a river. Down a long strange white street with houses on either side, very gay and bright in the late sunlight. F. put his arm round me. "I know you will like the house. It's quite white, and so is the room, and the people are, too."

At last we arrived. The woman of the house, with a serious baby in her arms, came to the door.

"It is all right?"

"Yes, all right. Bonjour, Madame."

It was like an elopement.

We went into a room on the ground floor, and the door was shut. Down went the suitcase, the letter bag, [*illegible*] again. Laughing and trembling we pressed against each other—a long long kiss, interrupted by a clock on the wall striking five. He lit the fire. We stayed together a little, but always laughing. The whole affair seemed somehow so ridiculous, and at the same time so utterly natural. There was nothing to do but laugh. Then he left me for a moment. I brushed my hair and washed and was ready when he came back to go out to dinner. The wounded were creeping down the hill. They were all bandaged up. One man looked as though he had two red carnations over his ears; one man as though his hand was covered in black sealing-wax. F. talked and talked and talked. "When I was little I thought the sun was the most terrible thing in the world, but now it is quite pale." [*An illegible sentence*].

Then the long, long dinner. I hardly said a word. When we came out, stars were shining, through wispy clouds, and a moon hung like a candle-flame. There was a tiny lamp on the table; the fire flickered on the white wood ceiling. It was as though we were on a boat. We talked in whispers, overcome by this discreet little lamp. In the most natural manner we slowly undressed by the stove. F. slung into bed. "Is it cold?" I said. "Ah, no, not at all cold. Viens, ma bébé. Don't be frightened. The waves are quite small." With his laughing face, his pretty hair, one hand with a bangle over the sheets, he looked like a girl. [*illegible*]

The sword, the big ugly sword, but not between us, lying in a chair. The act of love seemed somehow quite incidental, we talked so much. It was so warm and delicious, lying curled in each other's arms, by the light of the tiny lamp—*le fils de Maeterlinck*—only the clock and the fire to be heard. A whole life passed in thought. Other people, other things. But we lay like two old people coughing faintly under the eiderdown and laughing at each other. We went to India, to South America, to Marseilles in the white boat, and then we talked of Paris. And sometimes I lost him in a crowd of people; and it was dark, and then he was in my arms again, and we were kissing. (Here he is. I know his steps.)

I remember how he talked of the sea in his childhood—how clear it was—how he used to lean over the pier and watch it and the fish and shells gleaming—and then his story: "Le lapin blanc." At last the day came and birds sang, and again I saw the pink marguerites on the wall. He was *très paresseux*, he lay on his stomach, and would not get up. Finally— one, two, three—and then he shivered and felt ill and had fever and a sore throat and shivers. All the same, he washed scrupulously and dressed, and at last I had the blue and red vision again—dors mon bébé—and then a blurred impression of him through the blind.

I did not feel happy again until I had been to the *cabinet* and seen the immense, ridiculous rabbits. By the time he came at 12:30, I felt awfully happy. We went off to lunch at the same little restaurant, and had eggs we dipped the bread in; and pears and oranges. The soldiers there. The garden full of empty bottles. The little boy—the same boy who had smoked the long cigarette the night before.

# ERNEST HEMINGWAY

## *A Moveable Feast*

At the Nègre de Toulouse we drank the good Cahors wine from the quarter, the half, or the full carafe, usually diluting it about one-third with water. At home, over the sawmill, we had a Corsican wine that had great authority and a low price. It was a very Corsican wine and you could dilute it by half with water and still receive its message. In Paris, then, you could live very well on almost nothing and by skipping meals occasionally and never buying any new clothes, you could save and have luxuries.

Coming back from The Select now where I had sheered off at the sight of Harold Stearns who I knew would want to talk horses, those animals I was thinking of righteously and light-heartedly as the beasts that I had just foresworn. Full of my evening virtue I passed the collection of inmates at the Rotonde and, scorning vice and the collective instinct, crossed the boulevard to the Dôme. The Dôme was crowded too, but there were people there who had worked.

There were models who had worked and there were painters who had worked until the light was gone and there were writers who had finished a day's work for better or for worse, and there were drinkers and characters, some of whom I knew and some that were only decoration.

I went over and sat down at a table with Pascin and two models who were sisters. Pascin had waved to me while I had stood on the sidewalk on the rue Delambre side wondering whether to stop and have a drink or not. Pascin was a very good painter and he was drunk; steady, purposefully drunk and making good sense. The two models were young and pretty. One was very dark, small, beautifully built with a falsely fragile depravity. The other was childlike and dull but very pretty in a perishable childish way. She was not as well built as her sister, but neither was anyone else that spring.

"The good and the bad sisters," Pascin said. "I have money. What will you drink?"

"*Une demi-blonde,*" I said to the waiter.

"Have a whisky. I have money."

"I like beer."

"If you really liked beer, you'd be at Lipp's. I suppose you've been working."

"Yes."

"It goes?"

"I hope so."

"Good. I'm glad. And everything still tastes good?"

"Yes."

"How old are you?"

"Twenty-five."

"Do you want to bang her?" He looked toward the dark sister and smiled. "She needs it."

"You probably banged her enough today."

She smiled at me with her lips open. "He's wicked," she said. "But he's nice."

"You can take her over to the studio."

"Don't make piggishness," the blonde sister said.

"Who spoke to you?" Pascin asked her.

"Nobody. But I said it."

"Let's be comfortable," Pascin said. "The serious young writer and the friendly wise old painter and the two beautiful young girls with all of life before them."

We sat there and the girls sipped at their drinks and Pascin drank another *fine à l'eau* and I drank the beer; but no one was comfortable except Pascin. The dark girl was restless and she sat on display turning her profile and letting the light strike the concave planes of her face and showing me her breasts under the hold of the black sweater. Her hair was cropped short and was sleek and dark as an oriental's.

"You've posed all day," Pascin said to her. "Do you have to model that sweater now at the café?"

"It pleases me," she said.

"You look like a Javanese toy," he said.

"Not the eyes," she said. "It's more complicated than that."

"You look like a poor perverted little *poupée*."

"Perhaps," she said. "But alive. That's more than you."

"We'll see about that."

"Good," she said. "I like proofs."

"You didn't have any today?"

"Oh that," she said and turned to catch the last evening light on her face. "You were just excited about your work. He's in love with canvases," she said to me. "There's always some kind of dirtiness."

"You want me to paint you and pay you and bang you to keep my head clear, and be in love with you too," Pascin said. "You poor little doll."

"You like me, don't you, Monsieur?" she asked me.

"Very much."

"But you're too big," she said sadly.

"Everyone is the same size in bed."

"It's not true," her sister said. "And I'm tired of this talk."

"Look," Pascin said. "If you think I'm in love with canvases, I'll paint you tomorrow in water colors."

"When do we eat?" her sister asked. "And where?"

"Will you eat with us?" the dark girl asked.

"No. I go to eat with my *légitime*." That was what they said then. Now they say "my *régulière*."

"You have to go?"

"Have to and want to."

"Go on, then," Pascin said. "And don't fall in love with typewriting paper."

"If I do, I'll write with a pencil."

"Water colors tomorrow," he said. "All right, my children, I will drink another and then we eat where you wish."

"Chez Viking," the dark girl said.

"Me too," her sister urged.

"All right," Pascin agreed. "Good night, *jeune homme*. Sleep well."

"You too."

"They keep me awake," he said. "I never sleep."

"Sleep tonight."

"After Chez Les Vikings?" He grinned with his hat on the back of his head. He looked more like a Broadway character of the Nineties than the lovely painter that he was, and afterwards, when he had hanged himself, I liked to remember him as he was that night at the Dôme. They say the seeds of what we will do are in all of us, but it always seemed to me that in those who make jokes in life the seeds are covered with better soil and with a higher grade of manure.

# Mercedes de Acosta

## *Here Lies the Heart*

After I returned to New York I received a letter from Greta, who was still in Sweden. In her letter she said jokingly, *I will meet you for dinner a week from Tuesday at eight o'clock in the dining room of the Grand Hotel.* I got this letter on a Tuesday morning. I figured that if I could get the necessary ship passage, I could then fly from Bremen to Malmo, Sweden, that same day, take the train from there to Stockholm and arrive late that night. At this time the only airfield in Sweden was at Malmo.

I was staying with Vouletti Proctor (who had married Vernon Brown) and when I told her of my plan to spend one evening with Greta and fly back to Bremen the following day to catch the *Europa's* return trip on Thursday, she encouraged me to do it. Marion Stevenson and Vouletti always encouraged me in all my wild adventures. I loved them for it. I booked my passage on the *Europa* and sailed the following day. In the meantime, I cabled Greta what I hoped would seem a casual wire: WILL MEET YOU FOR DINNER EIGHT O'CLOCK GRAND HOTEL NEXT TUESDAY EVENING AS SUGGESTED.

The trip over was very rough. This was the month of October and the gales kept portholes closed and even boarded up. But the *Europa* was a well-built ship and we made good time in spite of head winds.

Less than a week later I arrived in Stockholm at one o'clock in the morning. It was bitter cold and I was frozen and desperately tired, partly because of the nervous tension and my excitement about the whole adventure. I had wired for a room in the Grand Hotel and when the porter met me at the station and we drove there in a glacial and thick fog, I felt as though I had reached the North Pole. Seized in sudden panic I thought, What if I don't meet Greta? What if she fails to turn up for dinner? Of course, I knew her address, but she might have gone to the country or be hiding in a Viking's lair!

The manager of the hotel had stayed up to meet me and explain that it was so crowded that the only reservation he had been able to keep for me was the Royal Suite. I was too tired to object and followed him upstairs, praying it was not going to cost me all the money I had. When he switched on the lights I saw an enormous room with great ornate gold mirrors, heavy furniture, crystal chandeliers and stuffy red plush curtains. I was delighted. It was all just as it should have been—every inch a royal suite! When I remarked that I could roller skate in the bathroom as it was so large, the manager took me seriously and asked if I was a professional roller skater.

I undressed and climbed into the great bed. It seemed to me I had just gone to sleep when the telephone rang. I groped for the receiver. To my joy I heard Greta's voice. "It is not possible that you are here. You are really wonderful," she said.

"What time is it? Where are you?" I asked. She answered that it was six o'clock in the morning, that she had called the hotel to see if I had arrived and was surprised and yet not surprised when they said I was there and, in her usual way, she added "I'll be right over."

I rang off, jumped out of bed and began to dress. I looked out of the window. It was still pitch dark outside, as indeed I knew it would be for many hours yet. In winter one never sees the sun in Stockholm before tea. In a very few minutes Greta knocked on my door. She came in and burst into laughter. "You are funny. I might have known I'd find you in the Royal Suite," she said. "But hurry up! Put on your coat and heavy shoes—bundle up. Let's get out of this stuffy place." I asked her where she was going to take me. To my astonishment she answered, "To the zoo." Now it was my turn to laugh. "Imagine sane people going to the zoo in the icy cold dark at six o'clock in the morning!" She laughed again. "But who said we were sane?"

Out in the street it was freezing cold but I did not feel it. I was far too excited. Soon we reached the gates of the zoo and as we passed into it she said, "I know how you love animals so I thought you had better come and show yourself to them before going anywhere else."

We went into the zoo restaurant, which I was surprised to find open at such an early hour, and had coffee and a delicious breakfast. After breakfast and in this same mood we went into the monkey house. Moving toward a cage which held a large monkey, Greta put her hand between the bars as if to shake hands with him. At the same time she bent forward putting her face close to the cage and spoke to him. "How are you, Honey Lamb?" she said softly. He stretched out his hand, but instead of taking hers he made a gesture toward her face. If she had not moved I am sure he would only have patted it. Unfortunately, as his hand reached out of the cage she drew back. Startled by her movement he leaned far enough out to contact her face, and changing his gesture from affection to violence, scratched it. To my horror I saw blood trickling down her cheek. All the tales of people dying from monkey scratches sprang to my mind. I was petrified with fear but I tried not to show it.

"Don't touch your cheek. We must try and find a doctor," I said as calmly as I could, but she knew as well as I did the danger of such a scratch. Besides, I knew she was thinking, as I was, that this might scar her face.

Fortunately, not far from the zoo we found a chemist's shop, and he gave us the address of a doctor nearby. The doctor was an old man and very kind. He cleaned the wound and dressed it and, to our great relief, said he felt no ill effect would come of it and that he was sure it would eventually leave no scar. He also recognized Greta, but he seemed such a nice person that I felt she needn't worry about the newspapers. We left his office with a dressing on Greta's cheek and our high spirits somewhat curbed.

At Greta's apartment I tried to recover a little from my trip, the cold, and wayward monkeys. That evening we dined at eight o'clock at the Grand Hotel as planned.

The evening was a sentimental one. We sat at a table in the corner of the room which Greta had reserved and the same one she had described to me so many times in Hollywood. And we did the traditional things, ordering caviar, champagne, and our favorite tunes from the orchestra. It was a charming evening and there, in that rococo room with its pink-shaded lights, its soft string orchestra and its old-world atmosphere, I felt that I was moving in a dream within a dream.

*The White Horse Inn* was playing in Stockholm at this time and after dinner we went to see it. When we left the theatre a gang of photographers was lined up outside waiting for Greta. She saw them, lost her head, and dodging through the crowd disappeared before I could follow her. Luckily, I had had a great deal of training in Hollywood at this sort of thing and knew that when the crowd thinned out I would find her somewhere. I was right about this. Some time after the theatre was dark I found her in a small shop down the street where she had hidden behind the counter.

It was an unhappy ending to our evening. I wonder if press photographers actually realize what a thoroughly miserable time they have given Greta over all the many years of their relentless and merciless pursuit.

I stayed on in Sweden longer than I had planned. The following day Greta took me to Tistad, some hours away from Stockholm. We went to stay with two friends of hers, Count and Countess Wachtmeister. Their estate was large and they had a beautiful house there besides a model farm where the Count bred bulls and cows and ran a dairy.

It was interesting to see Greta on her native soil. We took long walks across country and through plowed fields of heavy, dark mud, and as in Hollywood we sometimes started out at the crack of dawn. When we tramped past typically Swedish red-painted farmhouses and saw the cones of fir trees piled high in their courtyards, I realized that in some mysterious way she had an affinity with them, which I, as a stranger, never could have. Something of her spirit was in the earth beneath our feet and in the very wind that whistled round us.

I was in Tistad the last days in October and the first days in November and was told it was still too early for the snow, but nevertheless I said, "I *must* see snow here in the country before I leave." To this Greta answered, "Then you had better try and do something about it." Jokingly I answered, "Tonight I will pray for snow and we will have some tomorrow." That night I did pray for snow and the next morning about seven o'clock, while it was still dark, Greta tossed a snowball through the open window at my bed. It had snowed all night.

Seeing snow made me say how much I would love to experience Christmas in Sweden. Soon after, the whole household suddenly took on an air of mystery. The servants whispered and ran to and fro in the hallways. Greta and the Countess disappeared for hours. They said they were going to the village and did not want me with them. I was rather hurt at this and I went for a walk by myself and nursed my feelings.

That evening with a look of mischief in her eyes, Greta told me to dress for dinner and make myself look as nice as possible. She said a distinguished guest was coming. She herself put on a white sweater and white slacks and twined flowers in her hair. Before dinner we went down to the library and in front of a roaring fire had several rounds of schnapps, which made us very gay. When the Count and Countess appeared in full evening dress, I knew that indeed something out of the ordinary was about to take place.

When the butler opened the doors leading into the dining room, there stood a Christmas tree as high as the ceiling, completely decorated, with brightly lighted candles on its boughs. The table was festively arranged and the whole room had a genuine air of Christmas spirit.

After a delicious dinner with many kinds of wines, everyone gave me presents. Greta gave me a pair of rubber boots which I wore all the following day tramping across the fields with her. I was tremendously touched by the whole evening.

Before I left Stockholm, Greta took me to see the house where she was born. She made no comment as we stood looking at it—nor did I. I was very much moved. I was moved because it was her birthplace and also by the fact that she had brought me there to see it. I knew that such a gesture meant much to her. As we moved away neither of us spoke.

# James Merrill

## *A Different Person: A Memoir*

One bright midday in late February, as I was passing the Albergo da Rai-
mondo on my way home, a voice in my ear began singing a popular love-
song. I looked round into the eyes of the rather dashing man, perhaps
eight years my senior, who was picking me up. But just like that, on the
street, in broad daylight! Out of simple discretion I hurried him past the
*portiere* and up to my apartment. In a half-hour we were again dressed,
and talking. His name was Franco, he worked—well, let's say that his
work kept him out of Rome a lot of the time. There was really no address
or telephone where I could reach him. He had a confident, bohemian air
and gazed at me ardently throughout this explanation, so I saw nothing
wrong with it. He told me of his good heart and sincerity as well. One in-
dispensable phrase rose many times to his lips: *io invece*—I on the other
hand—words that favorably distinguished the speaker from those thou-
sands who were using the very same formula, wherever Italian was heard,
at that exact moment. Somehow it added to Franco's credibility; had he
been play-acting, he'd have had a better script. I gave him my telephone
number, and when he called two weeks later asked him over right away.
Separation had inflamed us both. We fell into bed. *"Ti voglio bene, Dzim, ti
voglio bene,"* Franco kept breathing as he sought to turn me facedown beneath him. But this position alarmed me, for all its exciting novelty, and
besides—*ti voglio bene?* That wasn't saying very much. If Franco merely
"wished me well," as Luigi had his ugly fiancée, he had better go by him-

self to the tavern where his friends gathered and where he'd suggested on the telephone that I accompany him this evening. Obviously this Lothario had all along been trifling with an innocent boy's emotions: why should I let myself in for a lifetime at the beck and call of such a heartless person? His clothes furthermore were shabbier than I'd remembered, and he had a blackhead on his neck.

I expected Dr. Detre to applaud my mature decision. Instead he allowed himself a youthful laugh. "You have proven to my satisfaction that the only way to learn a foreign language is in bed. Do you honestly not know what *ti voglio bene* means? It is how an Italian says 'I love you.'"

I protested. *Amo* was the verb, just as in Latin. Lovers were *amanti*. "*L'amo*," confesses Violetta in Act III—I love him. "*M'ama*"—she loves me—sings Nemorino in *L'Elisir d'Amore*.

"I do not question your experience of nineteenth-century opera," said Dr. Detre, "only of the Italian language as it is spoken today."

I bit my lip. Franco loved me! But how would I ever find him again?

"Nevertheless," Dr. Detre pursued, "from your account of this admirer and the circumstances under which you met, I have to agree with your appraisal of his character."

# DOM MORAES

## *My Son's Father: A Poet's Autobiography*

I bought Frank Harris's autobiography in the five-volume Olympia Press edition, and took the Orient Express to Belgrade.

Just before the Yugoslav frontier, sudden doubts overcame me. I knew that Harris's book was banned in England. I wondered if it was also banned in Yugoslavia. There was no logical reason why it should be, but I wondered. I was not yet eighteen, so it seemed to me highly likely that if it was banned, I should spend some considerable time inside a Communist prison. I seized a moment when the compartment was empty to stuff the five volumes into the ventilator. The result of this was that for the next five hours the temperature in the compartment rose steadily, till it resembled an oven. Streaming with sweat, I climbed out of the Orient Express into a wilderness of Belgrade snow. Thickly it carpeted the ground, and thickly it fell from the sky, which was pitch dark, since it was two in the morning.

I shivered my way down the platform till I found a decrepit and toothless porter, who spoke a mixture of German and English. I demanded a hotel. There were no taxis. He heaved my case and typewriter to his shoulders, and plodded ahead of me through the arctic weather. We traversed numerous deserted, snow-covered streets, till we came to the Moskva. It was full. The porter, a phlegmatic man, led me to two more hotels. Both were full. He then conducted me to the tourist office. Despite the hour, it was open. As we entered, like two travelling snowmen, an elderly official from behind the information desk bounded forward, kissed me loudly on both cheeks, and exclaimed in English, "Ah! My African brother!" For some reason I was infuriated, but my supposed nationality seemed to work wonders. Within minutes he had found me a room in somebody's house. I paid my rent to the official. Then the porter, who was nauseatingly cheerful, and I set off on another terrible trek through wind and snow. After about half an hour, I began to feel like an icicle. Doubts assailed me as to whether I would ever thaw out. Suddenly the porter dumped my luggage in the snow. "Is it here?" I chattered, relieved. *"Ja, ja,"* said the porter. He took me by the arm and led me for some distance past faceless houses, till we arrived at the foot of a large statue entirely covered in snow. The porter pointed at this. "Tito," he said. *"Ist gut."* I restrained an impulse to hit him. "How far are we," I asked carefully, "from *das Haus?"* *"Ja, ja,"* he said. We plodded back to my luggage and the journey continued.

We reached the house at last. A cheerful Serbian maid opened the door, and whisked us into a warm kitchen, where an enormous wood stove crackled and spat. I paid the porter, and, dripping with melted snow, followed the maid to a large and handsome bedroom. Into the snowdrift of an immense bed I sank, wet, cold, and miserable, and slept heavily.

When I awoke next morning I felt very ill, but felt also that I must bestir myself. So I rose and dressed. I noted, while I was doing so, that this was obviously a woman's room. There was a dressing table littered with cosmetics, and on the bedside table stood the photograph of a very beautiful, dark-haired young woman with a child.

The originals of these photographs were seated in the kitchen. The woman was even more beautiful than in the photograph. She had very vivid violet eyes which contrasted with her raven hair, and a pearl-pale Slavonic face. Her daughter, who was about six, looked very much like her. Also in the kitchen was the maid, and to my dismay, the porter. He looked more decrepit and toothless than ever in the day.

"How do you do," said the beautiful brunette, in French. "This is my house. You are very welcome. Please have some coffee." I drank some coffee, while the porter nodded and winked conspiratorially at me. Presently I inquired what he wanted. "He says," translated the lady, "that he will show you round Belgrade." Though I could not imagine a more undesirable guide, it struck me that, since I didn't know where I was, and spoke no Serbian, he might be useful. So we departed together.

I had no idea where we were bound for, but the porter did. Half-way down the snowy street, he stopped, pointed to a bar, made repulsive drinking noises, and said, "Schnapps." I replied, *"Nein."* *"Ja, ja,"* he said. *"Ist gut."* Inside the bar he smacked down three rapid tumblerfuls of *slivovitz,* for which I paid. We then continued. But the porter's broken boots only seemed capable of leading him to bars. Utterly helpless, since I would have been lost without him, I followed him through about six. Meanwhile I began to shiver, not only because of the cold. I could feel my cheeks burning with fever, and an iron vice seemed to have fastened round my chest. Frank Harris had bequeathed me a very bad chill. Finally I said to the porter, *"Das Haus."* *"Nein,"* he replied defiantly, "schnapps." I didn't even know the address of the house, and was starting to feel as though I would collapse. In the next bar I waved a fistful of dinars in the porter's face. He put down his *slivovitz* and squinted at them. *"Raus,"* I said. *"Das Haus.* Then *sie haben* this." He appeared to understand, and we crunched back through the snow. The house, to my surprise, was only five minutes' walk away. Once there, I did collapse, and was put efficiently to bed by my hostess and the maid.

They didn't report my illness to the tourist office, which they were supposed to do, so that I could be removed to hospital. Instead, they nursed me, fed me broth, herb tea, and medicine, and supplied endless hot bricks for my feet. My hostess went into town and found some English magazines. She would sit and talk to me in a soothing husky voice. Her name was Dragika, and she had been a widow for three years. Her husband, an engineer, had been killed in an accident, and since then she had let rooms to guests to supplement her income. The room I slept in was in fact her bedroom.

Dragika's brilliant violet eyes brightened and darkened like a cat's, under her long dark lashes. One day, when they were dark, she told me that she had been raped, when she was twelve, by a dozen German soldiers. I felt sorrow and pity: her gentleness when she described the incident touched me terrifyingly. She was now about 25. I fell, naturally, madly in love with her.

At the same time, I didn't see what I could do about it. I was a stranger in transit, and very young (angrily, I realised this), and our lives, really, were utterly disparate. When, convalescent, I sat by the stove in the kitchen playing with Dragika's daughter, Nevenka the maid fetching me endless cups of coffee, my eyes followed Dragika about painfully, imprinting her upon my memory before it was too late. Finally, I was well. Dragika took me round the city. She was a much better guide than the porter, and also I was delighted to be with her. But a great guilt preyed on my mind. Returning home the first night after I was well, I said, "I know that I'm sleeping in your bed, and you sleep with Nevenka. Why don't you sleep in your own bed? I'll sleep in the kitchen." Her brows lifted above her marvellous violet eyes, and her husky affectionate laugh answered me. *"Bien,"* she said. "I'll sleep in my own bed. But you sleep there too."

So I did. Everything was suddenly very simple.

# ROBIN MAUGHAM

## *Escape from the Shadows: An Autobiography*

The following evening, after dinner, Gerald took me to the casino in Nice. He'd spilt red wine down the front of his evening dress shirt earlier at dinner. He was already drunk when we arrived. He sat down at the *chemin de fer* table. The fact that he played wildly did not worry the management—they knew that, as always, Willie would pay his debts; however, the fact that he insulted almost everyone round the table did disturb them. A French player he would address as "frog-face"; any lady he would address, with a grin, as "you silly old bitch." Presently the casino manager came up to me and told me that unless I removed Gerald he would have to call the police. To my surprise, when I told Gerald that I was tired and begged him to drive me back to the Mauresque in the Voisin Coupé we had taken out, he staggered to his feet without any argument. I took him by the arm and helped him to walk out of the casino and along the Promenade des Anglais to the car.

"I've got a surprise for you," Gerald kept saying. "I've got a wonderful surprise."

I tried to make him let me drive, but he was too drunk to listen to reason. We swerved along the coast road until we reached Villefranche where Gerald turned right and drove down towards the harbour.

"Just wait till you see what's waiting for you on the yacht," he kept saying.

I followed Gerald as he staggered over the gangplank. The aft saloon was in darkness. Gerald switched on the lights. Lying on the double bunk, naked except for a pair of shorts, was a blond boy of about seventeen. As he lay there, his hair tousled, his limbs sprawled out in sleep, his lips slightly parted, his skin glowing like bronze in the dim lights of the saloon, he looked so innocent and beautiful that I felt the same keen stab of pain in my heart that I had felt a dozen years before when I had seen the farmer's boy riding back from the hayfields.

As we came in, the boy awoke and stared at us drowsily. Then he sprang to his feet. He smiled as he greeted Gerald in French. As soon as he smiled, the look of innocence left him. His face was now transformed by a strange look of yearning—as if Gerald were the only person in the world who could grant the fulfilment of all his wishes. Gerald kissed him on the mouth, then glanced towards me.

"*Laurent,*" he said, "*je veux t' introduire mon ami—Robin.*"

Then Gerald turned back to me. "Robin," he said, "this is my little friend Laurent. Have a good time with him. He's a very sweet boy. You've nothing to fear."

Gerald poured himself a glass of brandy from a bottle on the bar. Then he opened the door which led forward.

"Goodnight, ducks," he said. "See you both in the morning."

He lurched out of the door and closed it behind him. I was left alone with Laurent.

For a moment there was silence. Laurent was staring at me solemnly. I could feel my heart thudding. I believed that both of us had been put into an awkward predicament for, though I was only twenty, the boy might not want to share the bunk with me for the night.

"*Puis-je t'offrir quelque chose à boire?*" the boy asked.

"Please," I answered. "I'd love a glass of wine."

"Red or white?"

"Whichever you prefer."

"It's very sweet of you to say that," the boy said. "But then I can see right off that you're a very sweet person."

Then he crossed the little saloon and handed me my glass, and raised his own.

"*Santé,*" he said. He took a gulp of wine from his glass and put it down on the bar. Then he turned round and faced me. He smiled, and once again the strange look of yearning transformed his face. He stretched out his arms and put them round my neck. Suddenly he leaned forward and kissed my lips.

*"N'aie pas peur,"* he whispered. "Don't be afraid."

———

At dawn, he was still lying in my arms. His face was unlined, once again his lips were faintly parted. His teeth were small and very white. He looked like a child. Presently he awoke and stared up at me for a moment without recognition. Then he smiled.

"You're very sweet. Do you know that?" he said. "But I must go. I must go to work. I work in a carpenter's shop."

"When can we meet again?" I asked.

"When you like," he answered. "Any evening, or any time Sunday."

I was so attracted to him that I could hardly bear to think of being parted from him for a whole day.

"What about tonight?" I asked.

"That's all right," he replied. "I'll meet you here at ten o'clock."

# WILLIAM BECKFORD

## The Journal of William Beckford
### in Portugal and Spain

### 1787–1788

I never passed in all my life a day more agreeably. In the morning Carency, Listenais and the young Infantado* came in and breakfasted, and we all mounted our horses and scampered along a broad level road in high glee and spirits. Verdeil and the governor, who has such an excellent opinion of my head and heart, followed at a distance. The governor let fall in confidence that the young Princess was rather too fond of talking about me. I must take care, or I shall kindle a flame not easily extinguished. I am surrounded with fires; it is delightful to be warmed, but unless I summon up every atom of prudence in my composition I shall be reduced to ashes.

Rojas and Kauffman dined with us. The latter accompanied me to the Prado and from thence to Ahmed Vassif's, whom we found in all his glory surrounded by twenty or thirty of his attendants in their most splendid dress, giving audience to the Tripolitan Ambassador,† whom he had invited to supper. He is a young man of two-and-twenty, son of the *Chaid* or First Minister of Tripoli. His brother, a boy of twelve, was seated next

---

*Pedro Alcantara de Toledo Salm-Salm (1773–1841), 12th Duke of Infantado; later President of Council of Regency, and Prime Minister.

† Madrid Court Almanac (*Kalendario Manual*) for 1788 calls him *Sidi Amora Coggia;* born 1765; eldest son of the First Minister of the Barbary State of Tripoli, which had thrown off Turkish rule. Beckford spells the brother's name variously, but I have standardised it to Mohammed.

to him, and behind the sofa stood a rank of venerable grey-bearded Africans, the most picturesque figures I ever beheld. The little boy's name is Mohammed. There is a languid tenderness in his eyes, a softness in the contour of his face, and a bewitching <      > in his smile that enchanted me. We conserved* in lingua franca. I was seated on the carpet like an Oriental, to the great delight of Ahmed Vassif, who has hopes of alluring me to Constantinople; but still more to that of little Mohammed, who kept whispering to me with a tone of voice that went to my soul, and pressing my hands with inconceivable tenderness. I thought myself in a dream—nay, I still think myself so, and expect to wake. What is there in me to attract the affections of these infidels at first sight, I cannot imagine. Mohammed and I continued drinking each other's looks, to use the phraseology of Hafiz, with such avidity that we forgot how the time passed, and were startled upon quitting one instant the contemplation of each other to find the saloon illuminated with three vast lustres, the musicians placed in due order, the pages standing in solemn rows, and Mme. de Santa Cruz, the little Villamayors and Sabatinis† with high plumed heads and streaming ribbons, taking their places to the right and left of Ahmed Vassif. Presently in came the Prince Masserano, who followed my example, and throwing himself cross-legged on the carpet at the feet of his divinity Mme. Villamayor, where he looked like a crump-backed tailor stitching the hem of her garment. Mme. de Santa Cruz looked in high beauty, her hair fell wildly over her ivory forehead, and——‡

---

* The writing of *conserved* for *conversed* shows under what emotion Beckford was labouring.

† Letter 16 of *Spain* calls them *the two little Sabatinis, half Spanish, half Italian,* so they were perhaps grandchildren of Charles III's favourite architect, an Italian who migrated to Spain in 1760, General Francisco Sabatini (1722–95).

‡ Entry unfinished.

# CHRISTOPHER ISHERWOOD

## Christopher and His Kind: 1929–1939

At the Cosy Corner, Christopher met a youth whom I shall call Bubi (Baby). That was his nickname among his friends, because he had a pretty face, appealing blue eyes, golden blond hair and a body which was smoothskinned and almost hairless, although hard and muscular. On seeing Bubi, Christopher experienced instant infatuation. This wasn't surprising; to be infatuated was what he had come to Berlin for. Bubi was the first presentable candidate who appeared to claim the leading role in Christopher's love-myth.

What was this role? Most importantly, Bubi had to be The German Boy, the representative of his race. (Bubi was actually Czech, but that could be overlooked since German was the only language he spoke.) By embracing Bubi, Christopher could hold in his arms the whole mystery-magic of foreignness, Germanness. By means of Bubi, he could fall in love with and possess the entire nation.

That Bubi was a blond was also very important—and not merely because blondness is a characteristic feature of The German Boy. The Blond—no matter of what nationality—had been a magical figure for Christopher from his childhood and would continue to be so for many years. And yet I find it hard to say why . . . John Layard would have encouraged me to invent an explanation, never mind how absurd it sounded. He would have said that *anything* one invents about oneself is part of one's personal myth and therefore true. So here is the first explanation which occurs to me: Christopher chose to identify himself with a black-haired British ancestor and to see The Blond as the invader who comes from another land to conquer and rape him. Thus The Blond becomes the masculine foreign *yang* mating with Christopher's feminine native *yin* . . . This makes a kind of Jungian sense—but I can't by any stretch of the imagination apply it to the relations between Bubi and Christopher. Bubi had been, among other things, a boxer, so he must have been capable of aggression. But with Christopher he was gentle, considerate, almost too polite.

In addition to being able to play The German Boy and The Blond, Bubi had a role which he had created for himself; he was The Wanderer, The Lost Boy, homeless, penniless, dreamily passive yet tough, careless of danger, indifferent to hardship, roaming the earth. This was how Bubi saw himself and how he made Christopher and many others see him. Bubi's vulnerability, combined with his tough independence, was powerfully attractive and at the same time teasing. You longed to protect him, but he didn't need you. Or did he? You longed to help him, but he wouldn't accept help. Or would he? Wystan wasn't at all impressed by Bubi's performance as The Wanderer. Yet, largely to please Christopher, he wrote a beautiful poem about Bubi, *This Loved One.*

Throughout Christopher's stay in Berlin, Bubi spent a few hours with him every day. For Christopher, this was a period of ecstasy, sentimentality, worry, hope and clock-watching, every instant of it essentially painful. Christopher wanted to keep Bubi all to himself for ever, to possess him utterly, and he knew that this was impossible and absurd. If he had been a savage, he might have solved the problem by eating Bubi—for magical, not gastronomic reasons. As for Bubi himself, he was the most obliging of companions; but there was nothing he could do, in bed or out of it, to make Christopher feel any more secure.

They went shopping together and bought Bubi small presents, mostly shirts, socks and ties; he refused to let Christopher be extravagant. They ate wiener schnitzels and whipped-cream desserts at restaurants. They went to the Zoo, rode the roller-coaster at Luna Park and swam in the Wellenbad, a huge indoor pool which had a mechanism for making waves. At the movies, they saw Pudovkin's *Storm Over Asia* and Pabst's Wedekind film, *Pandora's Box.* The latter was highly educational entertainment for Christopher, as Wystan unkindly pointed out, since it shows the appalling consequences of trying to own someone who is naturally promiscuous.

Christopher did indeed start to make a scene when Bubi broke a date with him. After being coached by Wystan, he painstakingly repeated a short speech which began: *"Ich bin eifersuechtig"* (I am jealous). Bubi listened patiently. Perhaps he even sympathized with Christopher's feelings; for he himself, as Wystan found out later, had a weakness for whores and would pursue them desperately, giving them all the money he had. He then answered at some length, laying his hand on Christopher's arm and speaking in a soothing tone. But Christopher's German was still scanty and he couldn't understand whatever lies Bubi was telling him.

All was soon forgiven, of course. When Christopher left for London, Bubi pulled a cheap gold-plated chain bracelet out of his pocket—probably an unwanted gift from some admirer—and fastened it around Christopher's wrist. This delighted Christopher, not only as a love-token but also as a badge of his liberation; he still regarded the wearing of jewellery by men as a daring act, and this would be a constant reminder to him that he was now one of the free. When he got home, he displayed the bracelet challengingly. But his mother Kathleen wasn't shocked, only vaguely puzzled that he should care to wear anything so common.

# JONATHAN KEATES

## *Italian Journeys*

The incident I was going to recount took place during a sultry late August when the nights were so hot that sleep became impossible and the latchkeys worked apace till dawn. Among the artistic clientele at the Pensione S—— that year, and in the room next to mine, was a bald, bespectacled Frenchman of a certain age, who kept himself very much to himself. He spent his mornings and afternoons at the beach and went out cruising at night attired as a *matelot*, the complete outfit, white bellbottoms, blue collar, red pompom, Jean Genet crossed with Pierre Loti. Far from its being decorative, there was something woefully ridiculous in such a costume which made the rest of us rather glad of his unclubbableness than otherwise. The crucial mistake made by so many visitors to Venice is to be either conspicuously underclad, like the huge frankfurter-pink German *Burschen* who lurch through the streets wearing only exiguous bathing trunks as if the place were a seaside resort, or to overdress wildly, an excess of décor intended to proclaim good taste but usually looking like fatuous exhibitionism.

Monsieur Lunette (let us call him that, since he sported a pair of them) went to the latter extreme, and in our standoffish we-got-here-before-you way, we gave a collective shudder whenever we saw him cross the *campo*, a dumpy, myopic Querelle peering anxiously after each strapping Marco or Angelo who passed by. Jean-Luc the Profile voted him, not without a certain self-gratulatory relief, *"un désastre,"* while Agi muttered mysteriously "he looks like the ghost of my second husband." The Brazilian boys giggled about what they would do if they happened to meet him on the hotel's impenetrably dark, tortuous staircase, but I don't recall the opportunity ever having presented itself.

On the night in question I'd been out to dinner with some friends at a crazy jazz restaurant in Cannaregio, full of alternative, right-on Italians being bravely bohemian. There was a not unpleasant dampness in the evening's warmth, and the notion of simply hopping aboard the *vaporetto*, and pottering up to bed was intolerable. After we'd said our *"ciaos"* and *"buona nottes"* in that infinitely prolonged ritual of leavetaking which operates in Italy, I wandered off alone through the humid darkness, half resolved on a walk to Saint Mark's and a late ice-cream, but then deciding it might be nicer, in my present mood of benign contentment, to cross the Rialto bridge and find some secluded *campiello* to sit in and listen to the water in the canal, the scrapping cats and the oddly comforting sound of some cretinous television game show gurgling out of a first-floor window.

It was half-past midnight when I let myself in at the *pensione*, and I thought it was pretty certain that nobody else was back when I heard voices on the little terrace that opened off the corridor next to the bathroom. Jean-Luc Profile and his girlfriend, the sombre, hollow-eyed Margarita, together with another woman, were talking in quietly measured tones about the recently-published work of a contemporary philosopher. Pointless as it seemed to break in upon them, I stood for a while listening on the darkened landing, until I realized that the discussion would be audible to me from my own room.

In bed I opened my copy of *Peter Wilkins and the Flying Indians*, a faded red Everyman with "T. Bussell, Angmering, 1946" on the endpaper, and started to read. The gentle French voices in the darkness and the chirping crickets were extraordinarily soothing, but I was still reluctant to switch off the light. Then, as if in answer to my demand for a pretext, there came the noise of somebody coming up the stairs. It could only be Monsieur Lunette, and evidently he was not alone.

There was an unwritten, unspoken rule at the *pensione* that you never brought anyone back for sex. Philosophy in the small hours was all very well, and some of us might now and then slip along the corridors for a little more than Althusser and Derrida, but the comfort of strangers was not what the latchkeys were for. Fancy, as they say, my surprise when I realized that Lunette had fished up not one but a brace of gentlemen callers.

I should explain at this point that the walls were of the very thinnest. The top floor of the little *palazzo* had simply been divided by primitive partitions, and we might have been in Japan for all the privacy they afforded. It was one of the occupational hazards of sleeping in the *soffitto* that you could hear every snore, every grunt, every twanging spring from the next room, so that you soon acquired a mousy discretion in getting in and out of bed or in making sure that your shoes didn't fall with too loud a thud when you took them off.

What now ensued was a demonstration of this principle of audibility to an operatically exaggerated degree. *Peter Wilkins* was consigned to the bedside table, and I sat bolt upright, mesmerized by an episode all the more vividly realized for being invisible. Lunette's two guests were—well, somehow they would be—sailors. More specifically, country boys from a village somewhere down south, doing their military service on the lagoon. They had that thick, slurred meridional speech and that vocal timbre impossible to isolate in words except by saying that it strikes resonances you never hear north of Rome. When they spoke, I could almost smell their singular southern smell—pungent, lingering, never wholly attributable but compounded of artichokes, tomatoes, rancid oil, sweat, tobacco, coffee and cheap soap.

Their voices, as they answered their host's questions, were full of a comradely innocence. It was clear that with a creditable yet wholly professional solicitude he was putting them at their ease before getting down to business. Did they miss their families? Yes, they did, but look, there were lots of southerners, really good kids, up here, so it didn't matter much. Had they ever been to France? No, they'd never been to France, it was too expensive, but one of them had an uncle who worked in a bar in Lille, so maybe one day. . . . Were they always together? Always, Mimmo and Ciccio, since the *prima media,* before that even, ask anyone back home.

This last detail obviously appealed to Lunette. There was a perceptible thickening in the intensity of the atmosphere, registered by the silence that followed. One of them offered a cigarette. "Yes," said Lunette, "let's relax a bit," and together they started to undress.

I have to admit that at this point I felt slightly annoyed. It is presumably a not unusual experience for concealed listeners or watchers to want to intervene so as to direct the occasion theatrically to make it go as they wish. Thus it seemed quite out of character that these two peasant lads from the Abruzzi, reared to due proletarian modesty, should suddenly choose to strip, however sultry the evening. A quick embarrassed jerk-off and goodnight would have been the appropriate scenario. But of course it wasn't like that at all. There was the noise of belt-buckles undoing, the thump-thump of shoes, the clumsy shucking-off of trousers and vests and then an eternity of silence, in which, above the occasional soft indrawing and expulsion of breath, I could hear a subdued *ostinato* of French conversation from the terrace—"c'est la vérité elle-même qui fait la démarche," "on demande pourquoi un tel système exige . . . ," "c'est à dire . . ."—the metallic scratching of the crickets and now and then a plash of water in the canal beneath.

Transmitted thus, the noises in the next room assumed a strange hieratic eloquence, like the sounds made by hidden worshippers. In my prurient curiosity I felt like Clodius spying on the rites of the Bona Dea or the ridiculous poet blundering in upon the celebrants in the *Thesmophoriazusae* of Aristophanes. A gentle yet insistent chorus of alternating gasps and moans signalled imminent orgasm, breaking at last in what sounded more like surprise than outright excitement as both boys came simultaneously. There was another silence, then a little embarrassed laugh or two.

"God, we've made right pigs of ourselves, haven't we?"

"Yeah, we're a couple of dirty pigs, we are. Aren't you coming too?"

The question had a good-humoured ring to it, as if they were anxious their friend shouldn't miss out on the fun.

"Er, no," answered Lunette softly, "no, I can't. Not just now."

"Never mind. Maybe later."

I heard one of them sit down on the bed and light a cigarette. "Well," he said, "that was my first time with a man, I don't mind admitting it. With a woman, it's different."

"Was it your first time too?" Lunette asked the other boy. It was exactly what I would have asked, though there was something positively anthropological in its detached tone, as if Mimmo or Ciccio, whichever, were merely a unit in a field study, to be written up in a notebook afterwards.

"Yes . . . I mean no, not really."

The ensuing pause was made significant when his friend, sounding suddenly very hurt and angry, exclaimed: "What do you mean, not really? Have you done it before?"

Another pause.

"Yes. Once or twice."

"Shit, you never told me!"

The charm of the moment (and in garrulous Italy the talk which follows sex is worth everything else for pleasure) evaporated under a shadow of guilt and betrayal. I imagined that inseparable comradeship as it might now fragment, Mimmo's mother, with grey bun and black shawl, saying anxiously that he didn't see much of Ciccio these days, they used to be such friends, the frosty salutation in the bar at evening as the old men in hats silently downed their drinks, and the perpetual twinge of ambiguous pain caused by a single revelation.

Without saying anything, the three got dressed. While they rustled and scraped into their clothes, I caught again snatches of the terrace symposium, which had now turned into a discussion of the affinity between the concept of beauty and the idea of mortality. "En effet nous nous trouvons dans le pays du néo-platonisme," "la beauté va toujours à la recherche de la mort," "oui, elle veut mourir." It was two o'clock and they had been at it since before midnight. There was something comfortable in this relentless looping and unwinding of articulated ideas, highflown Gallic poppycock though most of them were, a conceptual hot-air balloon floating serenely over a terrain of bruised illusions and shattered friendship. I longed suddenly not to have heard anything through the bedroom wall.

"Well, we'd better be off then," one of the lads was saying.

"I'll come a bit of the way with you," said Lunette.

"There's no need."

"It isn't any trouble, really." His tone was pleading, submissive. For a moment nobody moved or spoke. Then he said: "Can I see you again? Perhaps a drink or something?"

There was an embarrassed cough. "Yeah, well ... like, well, it's a bit difficult. We don't get much free time. And then there's ... well, you know."

"But don't worry, if we see you in the street and we're with our mates, we'll still say hello. It's not as if we wouldn't. Don't want to be rude or anything, but ... like I say, it's difficult. You being ..."

The implications of this were all the more devastating for their ingenuous charm and sincerity. Lunette said nothing in response, and the three of them went tumbling downstairs again. It occurred to me afterwards, in a moment of cynical reflection on the episode, that at no stage had there been any suggestion of money changing hands or of the boys intending to roll their trick.

My sleeplessness had passed into that sinister phase of bogus vitality which precedes total exhaustion. *Peter Wilkins* was worse than useless under the circumstances. I lay there staring at the gap in the shutters as the mosquitoes gathered on the ceiling to descend as soon as the light was switched off. What consumed me, I realized, was a dubious mixture of amusement and envy with a sense of the occasion's emotional nuances, heightened, as I felt, by my having been an auditor rather than a spectator. The French had by now suspended their *causerie* and sloped off to bed. A real loneliness of the hard hours was starting to grip when I heard Lunette rattle his key in the lock and let himself back into his room.

He gave a little sigh as he got undressed, and said very distinctly, as if he knew somebody could hear: "Oui, c'est ça. Vraiment c'est ça." Then, with great energy and despatch, he brought himself off, and lay there a while groaning softly. And after that he burst into tears.

The sound of him weeping softly into his pillow made me feel gross and stupid. I wanted to tell him it didn't matter, they were only ignorant clodhopping boys who couldn't have known they were wounding his dignity, that it was just a night's entertainment of the sort Venice throws up everywhere, and that next morning he'd savour the anecdotal possibilities of the experience. Only that wasn't the point. These muffled sobs were perhaps the witness of a bleak interval of self-acknowledgment, when, amid all his dwindling resources of vanity, he knew momentarily what he was. Tomorrow night he'd be bravely out again, bumfreezer, flyflap and all, desperately getting the show on the road. For now he weltered in the gloom of his apparent failure.

# Dervla Murphy

## *Wheels Within Wheels: Unraveling an Irish Past*

From Flanders I cycled to Bruges, Antwerp, Brussels, Luxemburg, Maastricht, Aachen, Bonn and so up the Rhine—which greatly disappointed me—to Mainz. There I spent a week-end with the Hilckmanns, whom we were to have visited in August 1939. Then on to Heidelberg, Rothenburg, Biberach, Regensburg, Creglingen (where Riemenschneider's Marien-altar excited me more than anything else on this trip), Munich, the Black Forest, Strasbourg and across central France. In Paris I spent four days feeling euphoric, except when I was kidnapped one night by White Slavers in the Place de la Concorde on my way back from the Opera to my left-bank doss-house.

It was midnight as I crossed the Place de la Concorde and when a large car pulled up just ahead of me I ignored it, assuming that some lustful male was in search of willing prey. Then a pleasant-looking woman beckoned me and, speaking in English with only a slight accent, warned me that it is very dangerous for girls to walk alone in Paris after midnight. "Where are you staying?" she asked. "You are taking a terrible risk. My husband and I would like to take you to your hotel." I was too touched by this solicitude to point out that I *enjoyed* walking around Paris in the middle of the night. And because it would have seemed churlish to refuse such a kind offer I slipped into the back seat, explaining that I was lodging just off the Rue St. Jacques.

It struck me as rather odd that my protectress left the front seat to sit beside me, but I became suspicious only as we passed Notre Dame. As I began to protest that we had missed our turning my companion switched on an electric torch and opened a large photograph album which she laid on my knee. "Look at those, my dear," she said. "We're just going to take you home for a little fun and a drink—some champagne, you would like? And then within an hour you shall be safely home in bed."

While she was speaking I had been staring at the album with a mixture of horror, terror and nausea. I had never before seen pornographic photographs—or, indeed, even heard of them. Noticing my expression, the woman's voice changed. "Look at me!" she said sharply. I looked up at her and she ordered, "Keep on looking—don't move!" Terrified, I kept on looking; she was pointing one finger directly at my eyes and gazing fixedly at me by torchlight. When I realised that she was trying to hypnotise me I swung away and groped for the door-handle—though we had crossed the river and were travelling at some 40 mph up the Boulevard de la Bastille. Her voice changed again. "You mustn't be afraid," she soothed. "We are going to have a nice party for only a little while. We are so fond of young people and we have no children for ourselves."

I sat for a moment, calculating fast. If I tried to escape at this speed I would probably be killed. If I waited for the car to stop at its destination I would certainly be overpowered by both my captors. How often had I put the hero of an adventure story into just such a dilemma! But always I provided someone to rescue him—or at least staged an earthquake for the purpose—and there was no one to rescue me, nor any likelihood of an earthquake in Paris.

There were, however, two policemen standing in the Place de la République refereeing an argument between a taximan and his fare. As I reached again for the door-handle my 'protectress' grabbed me by the wrists. But at that age I had the strength of a young ox and very few women could have restrained me. Here we had to slow down almost to walking pace—traffic was streaming from the nearby railway stations— and when I had made it clear that I intended to escape the car stopped. As I scrambled out it half-turned and raced away down the Avenue de la République.

Had I been able to afford it I would have taken a taxi back to the Rue St. Jacques because my legs felt extraordinarily wobbly. But I had just enough money left to keep me in food until I got home. So I walked, only pausing to buy a bottle of plonk for my nerves in an all-night lorry-drivers' restaurant.

My landlady—whose mother had been for three years my father's landlady—did not believe that the kidnappers were professional White Slavers. Had they been, she said, they would not have shown me 'dirty pix'—at least at that stage—and would have drugged me as soon as I entered the car. In her view they were one of the amateur gangs who had recently begun to operate to supply brothels in—of all places—Soviet Central Asia.

# FRANCIS KING

## *Yesterday Came Suddenly*

On my visit to Italy, undertaken in a Long Vac in order to write a book, *The Brownings in Italy,* commissioned by Home & Van Thal but never completed, I was seduced (there is no other word for it) by a gondolier. As I stepped out of his gondola—in those days even an impoverished foreign tourist could from time to time afford one—and began to walk away, he suddenly called out after me, "Hey! Hey!" I turned reluctantly, thinking that he must be dissatisfied with his tip. Then with a series of gestures— hand pointing to his mouth, as he mimed eating, then at me, then at himself, then at a trattoria on the Zattere beside us—he clearly indicated that we should eat together. I looked at my watch, worried that at six thirty I was supposed to be meeting the English friend with whom I was travelling. Then, swept up and away in a whirlwind of excitement, I thought, To hell with him!

I already knew a little Italian. With these rudiments, with recourse to a pocket dictionary, and with a use of gesture so frantic that it soon attracted the amused notice of the other diners, all Italian, in the little trattoria, we managed somehow to converse with each other, with mounting pleasure. He was called Gino, I learned. His father and his grandfather had been gondoliers before him.

From the first, without words, we seemed to apprehend what each of us wanted. Gino led me to the landing stage where we waited for the *vaporetto* to take us to the Lido. Now we did not try to converse. We merely from time to time looked at each other and smiled as though in some conspiracy about to be brought to its triumphant conclusion. At the Lido we walked out along the darkening beach, past other lovers, until we came to a narrow stretch where there was no one at all. I was pitifully maladroit, greedy, precipitate. "All these years I've lived for this," I told him. It was only the truth. But of course he did not understand my English, merely shaking his head and laughing.

For the remainder of my week in Venice I spent much of my time with him. From time to time I wondered whether to give him money. Mustn't that be the only reason why he had in the first place picked me up? But I never did so and he never asked for any. Instead, I bought him a tie, a shirt, a pullover—the latter one which I had seen in a shop window and had marked down for myself.

When I left Venice, we exchanged addresses and promised each other a swift reunion. From Oxford I wrote to him, frequently consulting my dictionary to make sure that my Italian would be intelligible, and received a barely literate letter back. I wrote again. To my amazement, the reply on this occasion came not from Venice but from Genoa. He was working there as a stevedore in the port, he explained, in order to earn the money to join me in England. At first I was thrilled by the prospect. But then, as the days passed, I began to be increasingly troubled by doubts. Would he be allowed through immigration? And if he were allowed through, what would he then *do*? I could hardly expect my mother to put him up, and I myself was in no position to support him. I wrote to the address in Genoa which he had given, attempting to express these misgivings in a manner which would not be hurtful. But at the same time I longed to see him once again. Perhaps I could come to Genoa for the Christmas vacation, I suggested. When he next wrote, it was from Marseilles. He was getting nearer and nearer. Then it was Toulon. After that, at once mercifully and devastatingly, I heard nothing more. A letter addressed c/o a shipping company in Toulon was, after many weeks, returned. What became of him? Did he return to Venice, at last realizing that he would not be welcome in England? Did he meet some other lover? Did some disaster befall him?

Three years later—by then I was working in the British Institute in Florence—a sudden impulse sent me on a weekend journey, on my own, to Venice. First I went to the address which he had originally given me. After my repeated knockings at the heavy wooden door, an elderly woman answered, squinting at me from under the cloth tied over her head and low across her seamed forehead, with what seemed to me suspicion, even hostility. *"È partito,"* she said. Where? I asked. Abroad, she replied. *"Lontano, lontano."* She raised a hand and made a weaving gesture with it, as though his travels had sent him zigzagging on and on and on across the world. Was she his mother? Or merely his landlady? I felt constrained from asking, so clear was it to me that she did not welcome my presence.

After that, I wandered for hours on end along the canals looking for him. At last I saw a gondolier to whom, when we had once been together, Gino had stopped to chat. I asked him, in my faltering Italian, if he knew where I could find Gino Neri. Gino? he queried. Gino was there, over there! He pointed to a nearby gondola. But this was another Gino, grey-haired, stout, bearded. I repeated Gino's surname. The man shook his head, shrugged his shoulders. My Gino might never have existed.

With a mixture of sadness and relief, I then gave up.

—

Soon after my return from that tumultuously happy week with Gino in Venice, I met Angus Wilson at a party in London. We were friends, but friends still wary of each other. He stared at me. Then he said, "You look different."

"Different? Different? How?" I thought that he was about to say something malicious—as he so often did at that period.

He laughed. "You've come out of your refrigerator!"

With that remarkable perspicacity of his, he had at once realized the change in me.

# LORD BYRON

## Selected Letters and Journals

EDITED BY LESLIE A. MARCHAND

[TO JOHN MURRAY]                                    *Venice Novr. 25th. 1816*

... Venice pleases me as much as I expected—and I expected much—it is one of those places which I know before I see them—and has always haunted me the most—after the East.——I like the gloomy gaiety of their gondolas—and the silence of their canals—I do not even dislike the evident decay of the city—though I regret the singularity of it's vanished costume—however there is much left still;—the Carnival too is coming.——St. Mark's—and indeed Venice—is most alive at night—the theatres are not open till *nine*—and the society is proportionably late—all this is to my taste—but most of your countrymen miss & regret the rattle of hackney coaches—without which they can't sleep.——I have got remarkably good apartments in a private house—I see something of the inhabitants (having had a good many letters to some of them) I have got my gondola—I read a little—& luckily could speak Italian (more fluently though than accurately) long ago;—I am studying out of curiosity the *Venetian* dialect—which is very naive—soft & peculiar—though not at all classical—I go out frequently—and am in very good contentment.—— The *Helen* of Canova—(a bust which is in the house of M[adam]e the Countess d'Albrizzi* whom I know) is without exception to my mind the

---

* The Countess Isabella Teotochi Albrizzi conducted the most celebrated salon, or *conversazione*, in Venice. She was a friend of Canova, the sculptor, Pindemonte, Alfieri, Ugo Foscolo, and most of the literati and artists of the day. She was called the Madame de Staël of Italy.

most perfectly beautiful of human conceptions—and far beyond my ideas of human execution.—

> In this beloved marble view
>> Above the works & thoughts of Man—
>> What Nature *could*—but *would not* do—
>> And Beauty and Canova *can!*
> Beyond Imagination's power—
>> Beyond the Bard's defeated art,
> With immortality her dower—
>> Behold the *Helen* of the *heart!*

Talking of the "heart" reminds me that I have fallen in love—which except falling into the Canal—(and that would be useless as I swim) is the best (or worst) thing I could do.———I am therefore in love—fathomless love—but lest you should make some splendid mistake—& envy me the possession of some of those Princesses or Countesses with whose affections your English voyagers are apt to invest themselves—I beg leave to tell you—that my Goddess is only the wife of a "Merchant of Venice"— but then she is pretty as an Antelope,—is but two & twenty years old— has the large black Oriental eyes—with the Italian countenance—and dark glossy hair of the curl & colour of Lady Jersey's—then she has the voice of a lute—and the song of a Seraph (though not quite so sacred) besides a long postscript of graces—virtues and accomplishments—enough to furnish out a new Chapter for Solomon's song.—But her great merit is finding out mine—there is nothing so amiable as discernment.—Our little arrangement is completed—the usual oaths having been taken—and everything fulfilled according to the "understood relations" of such liaisons. The general race of women appear to be handsome—but in Italy as on almost all the Continent—the highest orders are by no means a well looking generation—and indeed reckoned by their countrymen very much otherwise—Some are exceptions but most of them as ugly as Virtue herself. . . .

yrs ever & very truly

B

[TO JOHN MURRAY]                    *Ravenna. August 1st. 1819*

Address yr. answer to Venice however

... You have bought Harlow's drawings* of Margarita and me rather dear methinks—but since you desire the story of Margarita Cogni—you shall be told it—though it may be lengthy.——Her face is of the fine Venetian cast of the old Time—and her figure though perhaps too tall not less fine—taken altogether in the national dress.——In the summer of 1817, Hobhouse and myself were sauntering on horseback along the Brenta one evening—when amongst a group of peasants we remarked two girls as the prettiest we had seen for some time.—About this period there had been great distress in the country—and I had a little relieved some of the people.—Generosity makes a great figure at very little cost in Venetian livres—and mine had probably been exaggerated—as an Englishman's——Whether they remarked us looking at them or no—I know not—but one of them called out to me in Venetian—"Why do not you who relieve others—think of us also?"—I turned round and answered her—"Cara—tu sei troppo bella e giovane per aver' bisogno del' soccorso mio"—she answered—["]if you saw my hut and my food—you would not say so["]—All this passed half jestingly—and I saw no more of her for some days—A few evenings after—we met with these two girls again—and they addressed us more seriously—assuring us of the truth of their statement.—They were cousins—Margarita married—the other single.—As I doubted still of the circumstances—I took the business up in a different light—and made an appointment with them for the next evening.—Hobhouse had taken a fancy to the single lady—who was much shorter—in stature—but a very pretty girl also.——They came attended by a third woman—who was cursedly in the way—and Hobhouse's charmer took fright (I don't mean at Hobhouse but at not being married—for here no woman will do anything under adultery), and flew off—and mine made some bother—at the propositions—and wished to consider of them.—I told her "if you really are in want I will relieve you without any conditions whatever—and you may make love with me or no just as you please—*that* shall make no difference—but if you are not in

---

*George Henry Harlow, who had painted a portrait of Byron in England in 1815, was in Venice in 1818, and made drawings of the poet and his mistress which Murray bought when the artist returned to England. Margarita Cogni looks very demure in her portrait. Harlow's drawing of Byron shows him with long hair.

absolute necessity—this is naturally a rendezvous—and I presumed that you understood this—when you made the appointment".———She said that she had no objection to make love with me—as she was married—and all married women did it—but that her husband (a baker) was somewhat ferocious—and would do her a mischief.—In short—in a few evenings we arranged our affairs—and for two years—in the course of which I had <almost two> more women than I can count or recount—she was the only one who preserved over me an ascendancy—which was often disputed & never impaired.—As she herself used to say publicly— "It don't matter—he may have five hundred—but he will always come back to me".———The reasons of this were firstly—her person—very dark—tall—the Venetian face—very fine black eyes—and certain other qualities which need not be mentioned.—She was two & twenty years old—and never having had children—had not spoilt her figure—nor *anything else*—which is I assure you—a great desideration in a hot climate where they grow relaxed and doughy and *flumpity* in a short time after breeding.———She was besides a thorough Venetian in her dialect—in her thoughts—in her countenance—in every thing—with all their naïveté and Pantaloon humour.—Besides she could neither read nor write—and could not plague me with letters—except twice that she paid sixpence to a public scribe under the piazza—to make a letter for her—upon some occasion when I was ill and could not see her.———In other respects she was somewhat fierce and "prepotente" that is—overbearing—and used to walk in whenever it suited her—with no very great regard to time, place, nor persons—and if she found any women in her way she knocked them down.—When I first knew her I was in "relazione" (liaison) with la Signora Segati—who was silly enough one evening at Dolo—accompanied by some of her female friends—to threaten her—for the Gossips of the Villeggiatura—had already found out by the neighing of my horse one evening—that I used to "ride late in the night" to meet the Fornarina.——— Margarita threw back her veil (fazziolo) and replied in very explicit Venetian—"*You* are *not* his *wife: I* am *not* his *wife—you* are his Donna—and *I* am his *donna—your* husband is a cuckold—and mine is another;—for the rest, what *right* have you to reproach me?—if he prefers what is mine—to what is yours—is it my fault? if you wish to secure him—tie him to your petticoat-string—but do not think to speak to me without a reply because you happen to be richer than I am."———Having delivered this pretty piece of eloquence (which I translate as it was related to me by a byestander) she went on her way—leaving a numerous audience with Madame Segati—to ponder at her leisure on the dialogue between them.—When I came to Venice for the Winter she followed:—I never had any regular *liaison* with her—but whenever she came I never allowed any other connection to interfere with her—and as she found herself out to be a favourite she came pretty often.—But She had inordinate Self-love—and was not tolerant of other women—except of the Segati—who was as she said my regular "Amica"—so that I being at that time somewhat promiscuous—there was great confusion—and demolition of head dresses and handkerchiefs—and sometimes my servants in "redding the fray"* between her and other feminine persons—received more knocks than acknowledgements for their peaceful endeavours.———At the "Cavalchina" the masqued ball on the last night of the Carnival—where all the World goes—she snatched off the mask of Madame Contarini—a lady noble by birth—and decent in conduct—for no other reason but because she happened to be leaning on my arm.—You may suppose what a cursed noise this made—but this is only one of her pranks.—At last she quarrelled with her husband—and one evening ran away to my house.— I told her this would not do—she said she would lie in the street but not go back to him—that he beat her (the gentle tigress) spent her money— and scandalously neglected his Oven. As it was Midnight—I let her stay—and next day there was no moving her at all.———Her husband came roaring & crying—& entreating her to come back, *not* She!—He then applied to the Police—and they applied to me—I told them and her husband to *take* her—I did not want her—she had come and I could not fling her out of the window—but they might conduct her through that or the door if they chose it———She went before the Commissary—but was obliged to return with that "becco Ettico" (consumptive cuckold), as she called the *poor* man who had a Ptisick.—In a few days she ran away again.—After a precious piece of work she fixed herself in my house— really & truly without my consent—but owing to my indolence—and not being able to keep my countenance—for if I began in a rage she always finished by making me laugh with some Venetian pantaloonery or other—and the Gipsy knew this well enough—as well as her other powers of persuasion—and exerted them with the usual tact and success of all She-things—high and low—they are all alike for that.—Madame

---

* *Waverley,* Chapter LIV.

Benzone also took her under her protection—and then her head turned.—She was always in extremes either crying or laughing—and so fierce when angered that she was the terror of men women and children—for she had the strength of an Amazon with the temper of Medea. She was a fine animal—but quite untameable. *I* was the only person that could at all keep her in any order—and when she saw me really angry—(which they tell me is rather a savage sight), she subsided.—But she had a thousand fooleries—in her fazziolo—the dress of the lower orders—she looked beautiful—but alas! she longed for a hat and feathers and all I could say or do (and I said much) could not prevent this travestie.—I put the first into the fire—but I got tired of burning them before she did of buying them—so that she made herself a figure—for they did not at all become her.—Then she would have her gowns with a *tail*—like a lady forsooth—nothing would serve her—but "l'abito colla *coua*", or *cua,* (that is the Venetian for "la *Coda*" the tail or train) and as her cursed pronunciation of the word made me laugh—there was an end of all controversy—and she dragged this diabolical tail after her every where.——In the mean time she beat the women—and stopped my letters.—I found her one day pondering over one—she used to try to find out by their shape whether they were feminine or no—and she used to lament her ignorance—and actually studied her Alphabet—on purpose (as she declared) to open all letters addressed to me and read their contents.——I must not omit to do justice to her housekeeping qualities—after she came into my house as "donna di governo" the expences were reduced to less than half—and every body did their duty better—the apartments were kept in order—and every thing and every body else except herself.——That she had a sufficient regard for me in her wild way I had many reasons to believe—I will mention one.——In the autumn one day going to the Lido with my Gondoliers—we were overtaken by a heavy Squall and the Gondola put in peril—hats blown away—boat filling—oar lost—tumbling sea—thunder—rain in torrents—night coming—& wind increasing.— On our return—after a tight struggle: I found her on the open steps of the Mocenigo palace on the Grand Canal—with her great black eyes flashing through her tears and the long dark hair which was streaming drenched with rain over her brows & breast;—she was perfectly exposed to the storm—and the wind blowing her hair & dress about her tall thin figure—and the lightning flashing round her—with the waves rolling at her feet—made her look like Medea alighted from her chariot—or the Sibyl of the tempest that was rolling around her—the only living thing within hail at that moment except ourselves.—On seeing me safe—she did not wait to greet me as might be expected—but calling out to me—"Ah! Can' della Madonna xe esto il tempo per andar' al' Lido?" (ah! Dog of the Virgin!—is this a time to go to Lido?) ran into the house—and solaced herself with scolding the boatmen for not foreseeing the "temporale".—I was told by the servants that she had only been prevented from coming in a boat to look after me—by the refusal of all the Gondoliers of the Canal to put out into the harbour in such a moment and that then she sate down on the steps in all the thickest of the Squall—and would neither be removed nor comforted. Her joy at seeing me again—was moderately mixed with ferocity—and gave me the idea of a tigress over her recovered Cubs.——But her reign drew near a close.—She became quite ungovernable some months after—and a concurrence of complaints some true and many false—"a favourite has no friend"—determined me to part with her.—I told her quietly that she must return home—(she had acquired a sufficient provision for herself and mother, &c. in my service,) and She refused to quit the house.—I was firm—and she went—threatening knives and revenge.—I told her—that I had seen knives drawn before her time—and that if she chose to begin—there was a knife—and fork also at her service on the table and that intimidation would not do.— The next day while I was at dinner—she walked in, (having broke open a glass door that led from the hall below to the staircase by way of prologue) and advancing strait up to the table snatched the knife from my hand—cutting me slightly in the thumb in the operation.—Whether she meant to use this against herself or me I know not—probably against neither—but Fletcher seized her by the arms—and disarmed her.—I then called my boatmen—and desired them to get the Gondola ready and conduct her to her own house again—seeing carefully that she did herself no mischief by the way.—She seemed quite quiet and walked down stairs.—I resumed my dinner.—We heard a great noise—I went out— and met them on the staircase—carrying her up stairs.—She had thrown herself into the Canal.—That she intended to destroy herself I do not believe—but when we consider the fear women and men who can't swim have of deep or even of shallow water—(and the Venetians in particular though they live on the waves) and that it was also night—and dark—& very cold—it shows that she had a devilish spirit of some sort within her.—They had got her out without much difficulty or damage except the salt water she had swallowed and the wetting she had undergone.—I fore-saw her intention to refix herself, and sent for a Surgeon—enquiring how many hours it would require to restore her from her agitation, and he named the time.—I then said—"I give you that time—and more if you require it—but at the expiration of the prescribed period—if *She* does not leave the house—*I* will".——All my people were consternated—they had always been frightened at her—and were now paralyzed—they wanted me to apply to the police—to guard myself—&c. &c.—like a pack of sniveling servile boobies as they were——I did nothing of the kind—thinking that I might as well end that way as another—besides—I had been used to savage women and knew their ways.—I had her sent home quietly after her recovery—and never saw her since except twice at the opera—at a distance amongst the audience.—She made many at-tempts to return—but no more violent ones.—And this is the story of Margharita Cogni—as far as it belongs to me.—I forgot to mention that she was very devout—and would cross herself if she heard the prayer-time strike—sometimes—when that ceremony did not appear to be much in unison with what she was then about.—She was quick in reply—as for instance;—one day when she had made me very angry with beating somebody or other—I called her a *Cow* (*Cow* in Italian is a sad affront and tantamount to the feminine of dog in English) I called her "Vacca" she turned round—curtsied—and answered "Vacca *tua*—'Celenza" (i.e. Ec-celenza) *your* Cow—please your Excellency.—In short—she was—as I said before—a very fine Animal—of considerable beauty and energy—with many good & several amusing qualities—but wild as a witch—and fierce as a demon.—She used to boast publicly of her ascendancy over me—contrasting it with that of other women—and assigning for it sundry reasons physical and moral which did more credit to her person than her modesty.——True it was that they all tried to get her away—and no one succeeded—till her own absurdity helped them.—Whenever there was a competition, and sometimes—one would be shut in one room and one in another—to prevent battle—she had generally the prefer-ence.——

yrs. very truly and affectly

B

# BEN SONNENBERG

## Lost Property:
## Memoirs and Confessions of a Bad Boy

In my memoirs I tried to write about losing my virginity. That had happened the summer before with a maid-of-all-work at a hotel in the south of France. I'd have preferred Hazel Scott. The great jazz pianist Hazel Scott had once danced a fox trot with me at an Urban League Ball when I was ten. Hazel Scott! Hazel Scott! *She'd* have known what to do. My virginity would have slipped from me with her. And afterwards, light-hearted, *déniaisé*, I'd have gone back to the Savoy and danced with the Cotton Club girls.

But to have had my virginity *taken:* and by the maid (her name was Raimonde): left me feeling angry and cheated. (*N'est-ce que ça?* That's it? says Julien Sorel after his first time.) With no time to memorize the sights upstairs of Raimonde's tiny room (smelling doubtless of urine and sex and Gitanes), with no time to prepare an attitude, I left the next morning for Paris. Acting world-weary and newly wise, I spoke to my mother and Helen in a jaded, superior voice, meant to sound like Herbert Marshall's, if I spoke to them at all. From my own room at the hotel, which was called Chez Paquay, three floors below Raimonde's, I'd looked down on the terrace every night, and heard the umbrellas being shut up one by one, *plok! plok!* an epoch ending each night. An epoch had ended for me indeed. But who was there to tell?

\* \* \*

The summer after . . . I started an obscure love affair in Málaga. . . . One day I went into the Italcable office. I was carrying a record. The cable clerk, a girl in her late twenties, a little overweight, told me she was studying singing. Her name was Pilár. Or Linda. After she got off work we went to a café and a day or two later I took her out for lunch. Pilár (or Linda) told me that her favorite composers were Granados, Falla and Berlioz; and after lunch we went into the woods on the hill where the Moorish castle is. There she sang for me the Berlioz song *"La Captive"* (words by Victor Hugo). She sang very badly, it seemed to me. "Let me pay for your singing lessons," I said. Her eyes filled with tears. *Io cangiero tua sorte,* I'll change your fate, as Don Giovanni sings to Zerlina.

I took her to the Pez Espada Hotel in Torremolinos. I saw her once or twice again, each time at a different hotel, each time (I now realize) attended by excruciating shame for her. Her subsequent pain and humiliation I can but imagine, for I dropped her. In another way, though, I went on with her intensely. I imagined meeting her parents and brother, who was doing his military service in Salamanca, or who had been killed while doing his military service, I didn't know just how. I imagined walking out with her in the evenings, holding hands like *novia y novio.* I imagined our looking at a house in a suburb of Málaga. There I imagined telling her I'd set her up, get her a maid and a piano and give her an allowance.

I remember reading, perhaps in Unamuno, that Spanish men tend to enact three myths: the first is El Cid, the second is Don Juan and the third is Don Quixote. Here was I, after only a year in Spain, corrupting and seducing a young woman, with easygoing passion and casual villainy, and abandoning her like Don Juan, and dreaming about it all afterwards, like Don Quixote. I wrote a story, in intimation of either Galdós (*Tristana*) or Machado de Assis (*Dom Casmurro*) or Pirandello. In my story the hero dreams of setting up house with a young woman like Pilár (or Linda) and at the end of the story he is killed by the young woman's brother who, in the story, is both imaginary and dead.

* * *

One afternoon I passed a shape, large, active and white, in the bushes. It made a funny noise. My mind was on Sabina's best friend. LeAnne lived across the Isar. Mostly we met at LeAnne's house before her small son got home. However, on that day we were to meet in Schwabing at my pension.

"*Frau* Göhmann, a lady is coming for tea."

"Very well, *Herr;* I'll change the sheets."

Munich, Germany, Europe: all so well made for adultery.

# GEORGE MELLY

## *Belle de Jour*

FOR J. B.

Strolling vaguely after luncheon through the streets of Amsterdam
Plants and lace in every window, dodging motorbike and tram,
John and I in some confusion, turning left instead of right
Crossed a bridge and round a corner glimpsed, above a door, a light.
Near extinguished by the sunbeams yet it bravely glimmered red.
In a window sat a lady and behind her stretched a bed
In the next room sat another, yet another 'cross the way
No detective needs to ponder where we'd wandered yesterday.
Bars and porno-shows and sex-shops lined both banks of a canal
(I'd been here an earlier summer, drinking with another pal).
Paid for lust in many cities—had to as my girth increased.—
But I'd never knocked and entered at the portals of the East.
Said to John I'd like a woman. Didn't say what I'd espied.
Standing in a sunlit doorway, raven-haired and almond-eyed.
White skirt split to show a lemon slice of thigh above the knee,
Brought back thoughts of adolescence. In the nursery after tea,
Scorning halma, snap or ludo, how my little willy grew,
As I, pressed against the lino, read *The Bride of Fu Manchu.*
John announced that he'd be going, strode away without a glance.
Minutes later found me paying fifty guilders in advance.
Curtain drawn and rubber ready, gazing into slanted eyes
Ask her name to aid tumescence, "It is Linda," she replies.

Jolly nearly my undoing. "Linda" is a name that should
Grace a typist in the rush hour swaying home to Cricklewood.
Not that I'm averse to typists. Lusted after quite a few,
Pressed against them in the tube trains bound for Hendon, Neasden, Kew.
"Pam" or "Christine," "Pat" or "Maureen"; names to stir me in the dark,
Dreaming of them playing tennis on the courts of Finsbury Park.
I could love a girl called Linda. I could yield my ageing heart,
But it's not a name to conjure up a Dutch East-Asian tart.
Still although she says I'm heavy and asks me if I'm drunk,
In the end I find I'm standing with a letter full of spunk.
She is busy at the bidet, my 7-minute bride,
But she indicates a "tidibin," a pedal by its side.

# THE MIDDLE EAST
## AND
# NORTH AFRICA

# T. E. LAWRENCE

## *The Seven Pillars of Wisdom*

The men were young and sturdy; and hot flesh and blood unconsciously claimed a right in them and tormented their bellies with strange longings. Our privations and dangers fanned this virile heat, in a climate as racking as can be conceived. We had no shut places to be alone in, no thick clothes to hide our nature. Man in all things lived candidly with man.

The Arab was by nature continent; and the use of universal marriage had nearly abolished irregular courses in his tribes. The public women of the rare settlements we encountered in our months of wandering would have been nothing to our numbers, even had their raddled meat been palatable to a man of healthy parts. In horror of such sordid commerce our youths began indifferently to slake one another's few needs in their own clean bodies—a cold convenience that, by comparison, seemed sexless and even pure. Later, some began to justify this sterile process, and swore that friends quivering together in the yielding sand with intimate hot limbs in supreme embrace, found there hidden in the darkness a sensual co-efficient of the mental passion which was welding our souls and spirits in one flaming effort. Several, thirsting to punish appetites they could not wholly prevent, took a savage pride in degrading the body, and offered themselves fiercely in any habit which promised physical pain or filth.

# Pierre Loti

## *Aziyadé*

About four o'clock one fine spring afternoon I happened to halt by the closed door of an old mosque to watch two storks fighting. It was not long since the massacres, three bare days since the executions, and leave to go on shore had only recently been granted. The scene was a street in the old Mussulman quarter. Tumbledown houses stood on either side of narrow winding alleys, which were overhung to half their breadth by *shaknisirs,* a kind of balcony, shuttered and barred, used as a private outlook post, with tiny invisible peep-holes for spying upon the passers-by. Tufts of wild oats were springing up between the dark cobble-stones and fresh green branches waved above the housetops. I caught glimpses of clear blue sky, and the balmy air of May pervaded every corner. The population of Salonica still manifested towards us a constrained and hostile attitude, while we had orders to drag our swords and a whole panoply of war through the streets. Here and there a turbaned form would slip past, hugging the wall. Not a single woman showed her head behind the protecting bars of the *haremliks.* It seemed a city of the dead.

I had supposed myself so utterly alone, that I was strangely moved on noticing close to me, at the level of my head, behind thick bars of iron, a pair of eyes intent upon my own. The eyebrows were brown and met in a slight frown. Courage and candour were mingled in that glance, which was like a child's, all innocence and youth.

The lady of the eyes rose and showed herself down to the girdle, in the long stiff folds of a Turkish *fereje* (mantle) of green silk embroidered in silver. A white veil was arranged with care over her head, revealing only her forehead and her enormous eyes. The irises were of a vivid emerald, that sea-green hue celebrated by the Eastern poets of old.

That is how I first saw Aziyadé.

\* \* \*

"Portia, heaven-lit torch! Portia, thy hand. 'Tis I."

(*Portia, Alfred de Musset.*)

Two hours after sunset, one last, solitary caïque, coming from Azar-Kapu, drew towards the jetty. Samuel was at the oars. On the cushions in the stern reclined a veiled form. I saw that it was she! When the boat came alongside, the square surrounding the mosque was deserted and the night had turned cold. Without a word I seized her hand and ran with her to the house, giving no thought to poor Samuel, who was left outside.

When at last the impossible dream had come true, and she was there in the room I had prepared for her, alone with me, behind the ironbound doors, all I could do was to throw myself at her feet and clasp her knees. I realised how desperately I had longed for her. I was drowned in ecstasy.

And then I heard her voice. For the first time she spoke and I could understand—rapture hitherto unknown! But I myself could not utter one syllable of all the Turkish I had learnt for her sake; I could only stammer in English, as before, incoherent words I did not understand myself.

"*Severim seni,* Loti," she said. (Loti, I love you, I love you.)

Aziyadé was not the first to murmur these never-dying words to me. But never before had the exquisite music of love been wafted to my ears in the Turkish language. Delicious, half-forgotten music, can it be that I hear it again, gushing with such passion from the pure depths of a woman's heart, with such enchantment that I seem never before to have listened to it, that it thrills my disillusioned soul with the music of the spheres.

I lifted her in my arms, and held her so that the lamplight fell upon her face and I could gaze at her.

"Speak again," I said, like Romeo. "Speak again."

I murmured in her ear many things that I felt she could not but understand. My powers of speech had returned and with them my Turkish, and I asked her question after question, imploring her to answer. But she only gazed at me in ecstasy. I saw that she had no idea of what I was saying, and that my voice fell upon deaf ears.

"Aziyadé," I cried, "don't you hear me?"

"No," she replied.

Then in her grave voice, she uttered these sweet, wild words: "*Senin laf yemek isterim!*" ("I wish I could devour the speech of your lips, Loti, and the sound of your voice.")

*Eyoub, December 1876.*

Aziyadé seldom speaks, and, though she often smiles, she never laughs. Her step is without sound; her movements are supple, sinuous, unhurried and inaudible.

This is a true picture of that mysterious little creature, who almost always slips away at dawn, to return at nightfall, the hour of phantoms and genii.

There is a dreamlike quality about her and she seems to cast a radiance whithersoever she goes. You look to see an aureole floating above that serious and childlike countenance. Nor do you look in vain, when the light catches those ethereal, rebellious, little curls, that cluster so deliciously about her cheeks and forehead. She thinks them unbecoming, and spends an hour every morning in unsuccessful efforts to plaster them down. This labour and the business of tinting her nails a brilliant orange are her two principal occupations. She is idle, like all women brought up in Turkey. But she can do embroidery, make rose-water and write her name. She scrawls it all over the walls, as solemnly as if it were a matter of vital importance, and she sharpens all my pencils for the task.

Aziyadé conveys her thoughts to me not so much with her lips as with her eyes. Their expression has extraordinary variety and eloquence. She is so expert in this language of the eyes, that she might use the spoken word less than she does or even dispense with it entirely. Sometimes she replies with a stave or two from a Turkish song. This trick of quotation, which would be tiresome in a European woman, has on Aziyadé's lips a curious Oriental charm. Her voice, though very young and fresh, is grave and its tones are always low pitched, while the Turkish aspirates lend it at times a certain huskiness.

This girl of eighteen or nineteen is capable of forming, on a sudden impulse, some desperate resolve, and of carrying it through in defiance of everything, even death itself.

———

In the early days at Salonica, when I used to risk both Samuel's life and my own for the sake of one short hour with her, I had nursed this insane dream: to live with her in some remote corner of the East, where my poor Samuel could join us. This dream of mine, so contrary to all Mussulman ideas, so utterly impossible from every point of view, has come true in almost every detail.

Constantinople is the only place where such a scheme could have been attempted. It is a genuine wilderness of men, of which Paris was once the prototype, an aggregate of several large towns, where every man can lead his own life without interference, and assume as many different characters as he pleases—Loti, Arif and Marketo.

Blow, blow, thou winter wind! Let the squalls of December shake the bars on doors and windows.

Safe behind our massive iron bolts, with a whole arsenal of loaded guns to protect us, and yet more secure in the inviolable sanctuary of a Turkish dwelling—warming ourselves at the copper brazier—is it not well with us, my Aziyadé, in this home of ours?

# GUSTAVE FLAUBERT

## *Flaubert in Egypt: A Sensibility on Tour*\*

*Soirée chez la Triestine.* Little street behind the Hôtel d'Orient. We are
taken upstairs into a large room. The divan projects out over the street; on
both sides of the divan, small windows giving on the street, which cannot
be shut. Opposite the divan, a large window without frame or glass;
through it we see a palm-tree. On a large divan to the left, two women sitting cross-legged; on a kind of mantelpiece, a night-light and a bottle of
raki. La Triestina comes down, a small woman, blonde, red-faced. The
first of the two women—thick-lipped, snub-nosed, gay, brutal. *"Un poco
matta, Signor,"* said La Triestina; the second, large black eyes, straight nose,
tired plaintive air, probably the mistress of some European in Cairo. She
understands two or three words of French and knows what the Cross of
the Legion of Honor is. La Triestina was violently afraid of the police,
begged us to make no noise. Abbas Pasha, who is fond only of men, makes
things difficult for women; in this brothel it is forbidden to dance or play
music. Nevertheless she played the *darabukeh* on the table with her fingers, while the other rolled her girdle, knotted it low on her hips, and
danced; she did an Alexandrian dance which consists, as to arm movements, in raising the edge of each hand alternately to the forehead. Another dance: arms stretched out front, elbows a little bent, the torso

---

\* *A Narrative Drawn from Gustave Flaubert's Travel Notes and Letters,* translated and edited by
Francis Steegmuller.

motionless; the pelvis quivers. Preliminary ablutions of *ces dames.* A litter of kittens had to be removed from my bed. Hadely did not undo her jacket, making signs to show me she had a pain in her chest.

Effect: she in front of me, the rustle of her clothes, the sound made by the gold piastres of her snood—a clear, slow sound. Moonlight. She carried a torch.

On the matting: firm flesh, bronze arse, shaven cunt, dry though fatty; the whole thing gave the effect of a plague victim or a leperhouse. She helped me get back into my clothes. Her words in Arabic that I did not understand. They were questions of three or four words, and she waited for the answer; our eyes entered into each other's; the intensity of our gaze doubled. Joseph's expression amid all this. Love-making by interpreter.

*       *       *

Speaking of bardashes, this is what I know about them. Here it is quite accepted. One admits one's sodomy, and it is spoken of at table in the hotel. Sometimes you do a bit of denying, and then everybody teases you and you end up confessing. Traveling as we are for educational purposes, and charged with a mission by the government, we have considered it our duty to indulge in this form of ejaculation. So far the occasion has not presented itself. We continue to seek it, however. It's at the baths that such things take place. You reserve the bath for yourself (five francs including masseurs, pipe, coffee, sheet and towel) and you skewer your lad in one of the rooms. Be informed, furthermore, that all the bath-boys are bardashes. The final masseurs, the ones who come to rub you when all the rest is done, are usually quite nice young boys. We had our eye on one in an establishment very near our hotel. I reserved the bath exclusively for myself. I went, and the rascal was away that day! I was alone in the hot room, watching the daylight fade through the great circles of glass in the dome. Hot water was flowing everywhere; stretched out indolently I thought of a quantity of things as my pores tranquilly dilated. It is very voluptuous and sweetly melancholy to take a bath like that quite alone, lost in those dim rooms where the slightest noise resounds like a cannon shot, while the naked *kellaas* call out to one another as they massage you, turning you over like embalmers preparing you for the tomb. That day (the day before yesterday, Monday) my *kellaa* was rubbing me gently, and when he came to the noble parts he lifted up my *boules d'amour* to clean them, then continuing to rub my chest with his left hand he began to pull with his right on my prick, and as he drew it up and down he leaned over my shoulder and said *"baksheesh, baksheesh."* He was a man in his fifties, ignoble, disgusting—imagine the effect, and the word *"baksheesh, baksheesh."* I pushed him away a little, saying *"làh, làh"* ("no, no")—he thought I was angry and took on a craven look—then I gave him a few pats on the shoulder, saying *"làh, làh"* again but more gently—he smiled a smile that meant, "You're not fooling me—you like it as much as anybody, but today you've decided against it for some reason." As for me, I laughed aloud like a dirty old man, and the shadowy vault of the bath echoed with the sound.

. . . A week ago I saw a monkey in the street jump on a donkey and try to jack him off—the donkey brayed and kicked, the monkey's owner shouted, the monkey itself squealed—apart from two or three children who laughed and me who found it very funny, no one paid any attention. When I described this to M. Belin, the secretary at the consulate, he told me of having seen an ostrich trying to violate a donkey. Max had himself jacked off the other day in a deserted section among some ruins and said it was very good.

Enough lubricities.

*   *   *

*Dance.* The musicians arrive: a child and an old man, whose left eye is covered with a rag; they both scrape on the *rebabah,* a kind of small round violin with a metal leg that rests on the ground and two horse-hair strings. The neck of the instrument is very long in proportion to the rest. Nothing could be more discordant or disagreeable. The musicians never stop playing for an instant unless you shout at them to do so.

Kuchuk Hanem and Bambeh begin to dance. Kuchuk's dance is brutal. She squeezes her bare breasts together with her jacket. She puts on a girdle fashioned from a brown shawl with gold stripes, with three tassels hanging on ribbons. She rises first on one foot, then on the other—marvellous movement: when one foot is on the ground, the other moves up and across in front of the shin-bone—the whole thing with a light bound. I have seen this dance on old Greek vases.

Bambeh prefers a dance on a straight line; she moves with a lowering and raising of one hip only, a kind of rhythmic limping of great character. Bambeh has henna on her hands. She seems to be a devoted servant to Kuchuk. (She was a chambermaid in Cairo in an Italian household and understands a few words of Italian; her eyes are slightly diseased.) All in all, their dancing—except Kuchuk's step mentioned above—is far less good than that of Hasan el-Bel-beissi, the male dancer in Cairo. Joseph's opinion is that all beautiful women dance badly.

Kuchuk took up a *darabukeh*. When she plays it, she assumes a superb pose: the *darabukeh* is on her knees, or rather on her left thigh; the left elbow is lowered, the left wrist raised, and the fingers, as they play, fall quite widely apart on the skin of the *darabukeh*; the right hand strikes flatly, marking the rhythm. She leans her head slightly back, in a stiffened pose, the whole body slightly arched.

*Ces dames*, and particularly the old musician, imbibe considerable amounts of *raki*. Kuchuk dances with my tarboosh on her head. Then she accompanies us to the end of her quarter, climbing up on our backs and making faces and jokes like any Christian tart.

At the café of *ces dames*. We take a cup of coffee. The place is like all such places—flat roof of sugarcane stalks put together any which way. Kuchuk's amusement at seeing our shaven heads and hearing Max say: *"Allah il allah,"* etc.

Second and more detailed visit to the temple. We wait for the effendi in the café, to give him a letter. Dinner.

We return to Kuchuk's house. The room was lighted by three wicks in glasses full of oil, inserted in tin sconces hanging on the wall. The musicians are in their places. Several glasses of *raki* are quickly drunk; our gift of liquor and the fact that we are wearing swords have their effect.

Arrival of Safiah Zugairah, a small woman with a large nose and eyes that are dark, deep-set, savage, sensual; her necklace of coins clanks like a country cart; she kisses our hands.

The four women seated in a line on the divan singing. The lamps cast quivering, lozenge-shaped shadows on the walls, the light is yellow. Bambeh wore a pink robe with large sleeves (all the costumes are light-colored) and her hair was covered with a black kerchief such as the fellahin wear. They all sang, the *darabukehs* throbbed, and the monotonous rebecs furnished a soft but shrill bass; it was like a rather gay song of mourning.

*Coup* with Safia Zugairah ("Little Sophie")—I stain the divan. She is very corrupt and writhing, extremely voluptuous. But the best was the second copulation with Kuchuk. Effect of her necklace between my teeth. Her cunt felt like rolls of velvet as she made me come. I felt like a tiger.

Kuchuk dances the Bee. First, so that the door can be closed, the women send away Farghali and another sailor, who up to now have been watching the dances and who, in the background, constituted the grotesque element of the scene. A black veil is tied around the eyes of the child, and a fold of his blue turban is lowered over those of the old man. Kuchuk shed her clothing as she danced. Finally she was naked except for a *fichu* which she held in her hands and behind which she pretended to hide, and at the end she threw down the *fichu*. That was the Bee. She danced it very briefly and said she does not like to dance that dance. Joseph, very excited, kept clapping his hands: *"La, eu, nia, oh! eu, nia, oh!"* Finally, after repeating for us the wonderful step she had danced in the afternoon, she sank down breathless on her divan, her body continuing to move slightly in rhythm. One of the women threw her her enormous white trousers striped with pink, and she pulled them on up to her neck. The two musicians were unblindfolded.

When she was sitting cross-legged on the divan, the magnificent, absolutely sculptural design of her knees.

Another dance: a cup of coffee is placed on the ground; she dances before it, then falls on her knees and continues to move her torso, always clacking the castanets, and describing in the air a gesture with her arms as though she were swimming. That continues, gradually the head is lowered, she reaches the cup, takes the edge of it between her teeth, and then leaps up quickly with a single bound.

She was not too enthusiastic about having us spend the night with her, out of fear of thieves who are apt to come when they know strangers are there. Some guards or pimps (on whom she did not spare the cudgel) slept downstairs in a side room, with Joseph and the negress, an Abyssinian slave who carried on each arm the round scar (like a burn) of a plague-sore. We went to bed; she insisted on keeping the outside. Lamp: the wick rested in an oval cup with a lip; after some violent play, *coup*. She falls asleep with her hand in mine. She snores. The lamp, shining feebly, cast a triangular gleam, the color of pale metal, on her beautiful forehead; the rest of her face was in shadow. Her little dog slept on my silk jacket on the divan. Since she complained of a cough, I put my pelisse over her blanket. I heard Joseph and the guards talking in low voices; I gave myself over to intense reverie, full of reminiscences. Feeling of her stomach against my buttocks. Her mound warmer than her stomach, heated me like a hot iron. Another time I dozed off with my fingers passed through her necklace, as though to hold her should she awake. I thought of Judith and Holofernes sleeping together. At quarter of three, we awake—another *coup*, this time very affectionate. We told each other a great many things by pressure. (As she slept she kept contracting her hands and thighs mechanically, like involuntary shudders.)

I smoke a *sheesheh,* she goes down to talk with Joseph, brings back a bucket of burning charcoal, warms herself, comes back to bed. *"Basta!"*

How flattering it would be to one's pride if at the moment of leaving you were sure that you left a memory behind, that she would think of you more than of the others who have been there, that you would remain in her heart!

In the morning we said goodbye very calmly.

* * *

That night we returned to Kuchuk Hanem's: there were four women dancers and singers—*almehs.* (The word *almeh* means "learned woman," "blue-stocking," or "whore"—which proves, Monsieur, that in all countries women of letters...!!!)... When it was time to leave I didn't leave... I sucked her furiously—her body was covered with sweat—she was tired after dancing—she was cold—I covered her with my pelisse, and she fell asleep with her fingers in mine. As for me, I scarcely shut my eyes. Watching that beautiful creature asleep (she snored, her head against my arm: I had slipped my forefinger under her necklace), my night was one long, infinitely intense reverie—that was why I stayed. I thought of my nights in Paris brothels—a whole series of old memories came back—and I thought of her, of her dance, of her voice as she sang songs that for me were without meaning and even without distinguishable words. That continued all night. At three o'clock I got up to piss in the street—the stars were shining. The sky was clear and immensely distant. She awoke, went to get a pot of charcoal and for an hour crouched beside it warming herself, then she came back to bed and fell asleep again. As for the *coups,* they were good—the third especially was ferocious, and the last tender—we told each other many sweet things—toward the end there was something sad and loving in the way we embraced.

* * *

Kuchuk dances. Movement of the neck leaving the body, like Azizeh; and her charming, old style step, one foot in front of the other.

The walls of her bedroom on the ground floor are decorated with two labels, one a picture of Fame bestowing wreaths and the other covered with Arab inscriptions. My moustache still displeases her: since I have a small mouth I shouldn't hide it. We take our leave, promising to return to say goodbye.

In the courtyard, a tall rascal with one eye covered by a scarf; he holds out his hand, saying *"ruffiano"*\*—I give him three piastres.

The result of all this—infinite sadness; like the first time, she had perfumed her breasts with rosewater. This is the end; I'll not see her again, and gradually her face will fade from my memory.

* * *

At Esna I saw Kuchuk Hanem again; it was sad. I found her changed. She had been sick. I shot my bolt with her only once. The day was heavy and overcast; her Abyssinian servant was sprinkling water on the floor to cool the room. I stared at her for a long while, so as to be able to keep a picture of her in my mind. When I left, we told her we would return the next day, but we did not. However, I intensely relished the bitterness of it all; that's the main thing, and I felt it in my very bowels. At Kena I had a beautiful whore who liked me very much and told me in sign language that I had beautiful eyes. Her name is Hosna et-Taouilah, which means "the beautiful tall one"; and there was another, fat and lubricious, on top of whom I enjoyed myself immensely and who smelled of rancid butter.

---

\* *i.e.* he claims to be Kuchuk Hanem's pimp.

# ROBERT TEWDWR MOSS

## Cleopatra's Wedding Present: New Travels Through Syria

That evening I went to the café in Martyrs Square, more than half hoping that I would find Jihad. He was sitting there talking to a group of shifty-looking North Africans. He was wearing a faded denim shirt, unbuttoned down to his navel, making visible a smooth olive chest with a dramatic gash across it. "Hello. How's the earring?" I asked. He turned his head and I could see that the area surrounding it was red and becoming infected. "You must get some disinfectant," I explained, but he looked uncomprehending.

We left the café. He was determined that I should visit his house, and by dint of not refusing I had consented to go with him. Darkness was falling, the soft light making everything seem even older and more mysterious than it already was. Jihad's house was near the now nearly empty Jewish area, Haret-Yehud, and he led me on a wonderfully serpentine route through alleyways, under archways, behind the Great Mosque and past the less well-preserved remains of the Roman gateway at the rear. I realized that this was a route that people had taken for hundreds of years. If you came to a flyover or a dual carriageway you simply walked under or over it and carried on regardless.

I was always intrigued at this time of evening by the barbers' shops— little islands of Victorian anachronism, with cloaked customers enthroned in great silver chairs, heads tilted back, being shaved with a cut-throat razor before vast, speckled Belle Epoque mirrors.

As we were walking it struck me rather belatedly that I ought to have found out more about Jihad before I went back to his house. I was, after all, carrying over a thousand dollars in cash in the little canvas money belt secreted beneath my shirt, which might prove too great a temptation to resist in a society where the average wage was fifteen dollars a week. I asked Jihad if he lived with his family, as I had presumed. "No, I never talk to my father or my mother. They live near by and send food to me. But they think I am crazy," he replied. This was hardly reassuring. I seemed to remember from various newspaper articles I had read in recent years that one of the signs of the serial killer is that he lives alone and has no bonds with any members of his family or the community. What if Jihad knocked me out cold when we got back to his place? It was pitch black now, and I had no idea where we were. I must be off my trolley, I thought in mounting panic. This man is clearly a nut, a loner, an outsider. But of course, that was precisely why I had agreed to go with him. The whole evening was overlaid with the familiar excitement that risk never fails to induce.

We eventually plunged into a dark alleyway. I looked over my shoulder. No one had seen us. If anything happened to me now I was a goner: Jihad was much more powerful than me. We crossed an ancient courtyard with uneven flags on the floor, heading for the far corner. Before us was a battered old doorway with most of the paint peeling off. Jihad took out his keys and undid the padlock and chain. The door was off its hinges, and he grasped it firmly, picked it up and deposited it to the side, as if he were King Kong. "Come," he said gruffly, and took hold of my hand. I followed. There was a mad scrabbling noise and a skeletal cat jumped onto the window ledge and squirmed through a little hole in the frame. "Ah, Beebee, Beebee," Jihad called.

"Who's Beebee?" I asked, as much for the sake of making conversation as anything else.

"My cat," said Jihad. If a man is nice to a cat he can't be all bad, I reasoned desperately. He switched on the light. The room was a dark, poverty-stricken hovel with dirty pale blue walls and a black ceiling where the chimney from the stove in the middle petered out and had belched out its fumes. There was a rickety metal-framed bed with a table beside it. Above the bed was a built-in cupboard, full of pots and pans. On the door and the wall above the bed, as on a GI's locker, were pasted pictures of mouth-watering young girls, cut out from magazines. At the foot of the bed, covered in dark brown army blankets, was a dilapidated couch. In a far corner there was a pile of rags and old newspapers. This, it would appear, was Jihad's home.

"Do you live here alone?" I asked him, not quite knowing what I wanted the answer to be. In any event, he replied simply, "Sometimes." He gestured for me to sit down, which I did, and disappeared from the room carrying a tray of glasses and a teapot. The only source of water appeared to be the tap in the loo in the courtyard outside.

Jihad returned and, pulling a selection of live wires from a socket and substituting them for some others, connected up an electric ring onto which he placed a tin kettle. He sat near by on the bed, and when the kettle had boiled I noticed that he lifted his feet up before handling the kettle.

"Why do you lift your feet up like that, Jihad?" I asked him.

"Electricity," he said. "From here to here to here." He pointed from the metal bedstead to the metal bedside table to the electric ring to the tin kettle and finally to his heart. "If I wear shoes with *zeldj*... What is *zeldj* in English?"

"Leather."

"OK, leather. If I wear with leather, no problem. If I don't I get... what do you say in English?"

"You get a shock."

"*Tamanan.* A shock."

"Could it kill you?"

He pulled a long maybe-yes-maybe-no sort of face. "Who cares?" he said, with his odd, slightly mad smile.

He reached for his packet of evil Hamara cigarettes and offered me one.

"No, look, let me buy you some," I said. "I need some myself. I can't smoke those. I have to have a special sort with mint. You know, menthol."

I knew that according to Arab etiquette I would not be allowed to buy anything myself as a guest. He would have to go to the shop, and I suddenly thought that I could go with him and see how he was greeted. If he did turn out to be the mad axeman at least there would be witnesses to my visit. At the same time I felt guilty, for I instinctively trusted and liked him.

"We go after tea," said Jihad, handing me a glass.

He sat down next to me. His presence was comforting rather than threatening, so close that I could see the scar on his pectoral muscle. "Jihad, what is that?" I couldn't resist asking.

"What?"

"That scar."

"What is scar?" he asked.

"Look, here." I touched the fine line which was intersected with little crosses where the stitches had once been, wondering if he would slug me in the mouth as an Englishman would probably have done.

"From the commandos."

"What commandos?"

"All of us. We are all commandos. Aged sixteen, seventeen, eighteen. A long time ago. We were in Lebanon, fighting Israelis." Half a lifetime ago (he was now thirty-three, I later learned).

He undid the rest of his shirt and pulled it open so that I could see the full extent of the scar. Then he shrugged the shirt off. He had a smooth olive torso, now a little out of condition but with large groups of muscles: a broad sweep of pectorals crowned with fleshy, square-tipped nipples, a long, narrow stomach, broad and meaty shoulders. His arms were strong and sinewy. When he pointed at his chest I could see a powerful bicep moving beneath the glossy skin.

"Here too." He pointed to two small scars in the middle of his sternum. These he said were knife wounds. "And here." He twisted round so that his back was facing me. "More scars." His back had two weals across it. "And here." He took my fingers and placed them under his wavy hair at the base of his skull where it joined the neck. There was a hard lump where some shrapnel had lodged and had never been removed. He was a beaten-up old thing, like a battle-torn but friendly old tomcat. I suddenly reflected that I had got myself into a very intimate position with this man, but I felt perfectly comfortable and relaxed. I would never have believed that an ex-Palestinian terrorist could be so gentle and sweet-natured.

He lifted up my glass of tea and offered it to me, then put his arm around me. He looked so vigorous and attractive, yet his life had to some extent petered out. What was he doing trapped in this dead end in life? And here was I, a voyeur, a tourist.

"Come on," I said, "let's go to the shop."

He put on his small black vest and guided me to the door. In the street he linked arms with me and we strolled along contentedly. I thought, Why do I never feel like this with English people? But the Middle East is a great place for misfits, people who cannot relate to their own kind.

There was a little square near by. We went into the shop and, to my relief, Jihad was greeted as a regular. I bought a couple of packets of Marlboro and some chocolates, then we wandered down to the ruined Roman arch and ordered sandwiches and juice in a bar. As we stood eating, a young man came in. His eye fell on Jihad's blue earring. A look of incredulity and disapproval, if not horror, suffused his face. Jihad noticed and looked at me, raising his eyes briefly to the ceiling, but continuing coolly to eat his sandwich. I wondered what made him want to draw attention to himself and set himself apart from the conventions of Syrian society. It showed a degree of self-confidence and independent thought that the average Arab would find threatening. Fortunately he was too powerfully built for anyone to tangle with him. And it was precisely this combination which the man in the bar could not deal with. Here was an obviously tough, macho guy, with an earring. It did not make sense.

"Are there many Jews in this area still?" I asked as we wandered back through the dark alleyways.

"Many of them left a few years ago. Now all their houses are empty. This one Jewish house—and this one. All empty now. All gone. And here, this is church for Jews." He jerked his head at a building across the alleyway. It had chicken wire over the windows and looked neglected. I reflected that it was strange that Syrian Jews and Palestinians, both in a sense outcasts, should live side by side in this poor area. Jihad's own family had come from Akko, now part of Israel, and he was living right next to the Jewish area. "What do you think of the Jews?" I asked him.

"They are very nice people. We get on well with them," he replied simply, and to my surprise. I had been expecting a tirade. Until the mid-fifties there were communities of Jews living successfully all over the Middle East, but the founding of Israel had put an end to that. Many times in Syria people, young and old, would say to me, shaking their heads, "Ah, Robert. Why? Why did you do it?," referring, I assumed, to the governments of the Western powers, but making it sound as though it was I who was personally responsible for the establishment of the Israeli state. Their tone implied: "You seem such a nice person. How *could* your government have done this to us?" Jihad, though, was different. He never asked why the world had turned out this way. He just chuckled dryly, not wanting explanations, or involvement. He got on with mending his watches.

We were back near Jihad's house. He told me that there was a shop near my hotel that was run by the leader of the Jewish community. The owner, Mr. Jayati, employed a Palestinian assistant. I found this notion very strange, and cynically wondered if the shop-owner did so to enhance his credibility. But then why should we assume that all Jews have the same political thoughts? Many Armenians who were pro-Western, like Baby Shoes, were strongly anti-American. Some Jews were presumably sympathetic to the Palestinian situation. In Syria the Jews had been heavily oppressed until fairly recently. They understood the nature of dispossession and discrimination if anyone did.

Jihad twiddled the dial on his radio. A warm gush of classical music swept over the room. "Ah, Dvořák," he sighed, and lay back on his bed like a connoisseur. As the music ebbed away, a male announcer with a chocolatey voice gabbled in soft Arabic and Chopin came over the airwaves. It was getting late.

"Jihad, thank you for tea. I must go now," I said.

"Go? Where? Where are you going? Stay here with me."

"That's very kind, but I think I should go back to the hotel."

"Why hotel? Hotel is stupid. Stay here with me."

"What do you mean? Where?" I said hopelessly, casting my eyes around the room.

"Here!" He banged the bed. "Sleep here with me. Please. Don't go now." He looked at me soulfully with beseeching brown eyes, making me feel mean and unreasonable.

Suddenly we were plunged into darkness. The Chopin stopped. It was a power cut. I felt Jihad very close by. He whispered into my ear: "You see, *habibi. Maktub.*" It was written.

# ISABELLE EBERHARDT

## *Prisoner of the Dunes*

*Marseilles, 16 May 1901*

Sensations of evening during Ramadan, at El Oued: leaning on the parapet of my dilapidated terrace, I gazed out at the wavy horizon of the static, desiccated ocean, which from the rocky plains of El M'guebra extends towards the waterless wilderness of Sinaoun and Rhamades. And under the twilit sky, sometimes blood-stained, bruised or blushing, sometimes dark and drowned in sulphurous beams, the great, monotone dunes seem to draw nearer, to gather round the grey town of countless domes, round the peaceful quarter of the Ouled-Ahmed, and round the closed, silent abode of Salah ben Feliba, as if to seize us and, inexplicably, to guard us for ever. Oh, fanatical, scorching land of the Souf! Why haven't you guarded us, who have loved you so, who love you still, whom you ceaselessly haunt with nostalgia and troubling visions?

———

In the south-east quarter of El Oued, at the end of a blind alley off Ouled-Ahmed street leading to the cemetery of the same name, there was a vast, terraced house, the only one in the town of cupolas. An old, unsteady door of loosened planks guarded the entrance. This door, always closed, signalled the inhabitants' desire to be cloistered from the world and its agitation. The house, already ancient, was built like all Souf dwellings of limestone covered thickly with yellowish grey plaster, and possessed a huge interior court where pale sand from the surrounding desert would constantly turn up.

Salah ben Feliba was the dwelling's original owner, and in this house I passed days which were at first the most tranquil, and finally the strangest, most troubling of my stormy existence.

———

First there were the quiet times of Chaaban and Ramadan days spent at humble housework or on excursions to the holy *zawiyas*, riding my poor, faithful Souf; nights of love and absolute security in one another's arms; enchanted dawns, calm and pink, after nights of Ramadan prayers, fiery or pale sunsets, when from my terrace I would watch the sun disappear behind the enormous dunes along the Taibeth-Gueblia road where I became lost one morning....

I used to wait, first for the market's grey dome, then the dazzling white minaret of Sidi Salem, to lose their colour, for the pink glow of sunset to fade on their western faces. At that moment, first from the far-off Ouled-Khelifa mosque, then from the Azezba mosque, the drawling, raucous wail of the *mueddin* called out "God is great!" and every breathless chest relaxed with a sigh. Immediately the market-place emptied, becoming silent and deserted.

Below in the large open room, seated facing one another, cigarettes in hand, with the wooden case between them serving as a table, Slimane and Abdelkader waited in silence for this instant. And I'd often have fun frustrating them, crying down to them that Sidi Salem was still red. Slimane would curse the nearest *mueddin* for prolonging the fast unfairly. Abdelkader teased me as usual, calling me "Si Mahfoudh." Khelifa and Ali waited with their pipes ready, one packed with *kif* and the other with *ar'ar*, and Tahar poured the soup into a dish, to save time.

And I, fascinated by the incomparable sight of El Oued, watched it turn from purple to pink, then violet, and finally a uniform grey. Thus was my melancholy and my fast prolonged.

Other times, going out at sunset to await my "redcoat," I'd sit down on the boundary stone near *spahi* Laffati's door. This was at the back of the huge rectangle separating the military quarter and Arab Bureau from the town, and facing the desert that began at the low dune of the limestone kilns, and continued along the cone-shaped dunes bordering the Allenda road. Out there, against the blazing horizon, dark silhouettes appeared on top of the limekiln dune, and as I watched them, profiled there against the purple sky, they grew deformed, became giants....

Then, from the ever-guarded door where the little rifleman in blue was patrolling, bayonet fixed, came the figure in red whose appearance I never beheld without a rush, without a tug at my heart—a pleasant feeling, even sensual, and, yet strangely sad. Why? I'll never know.

I was seated on that stone one evening soon after dark, when out of the shadows nearby appeared strange little Hania, Dahman's daughter, with her unmistakable laugh—polished and ambiguous—and the voluptuous sadness of her eyes. Wrapped in the dark-blue and red rags worn by Souf women, she was carrying wood to Ahmed ben Salem's house.

The last night I was destined to pass under my own roof was the mad night of 28 January, which was spent in furious love-making. Next day, from the peaceful dwelling of Salah ben Feliba, I departed sadly—knowing I was already exiled, yet still calm—for sinister Behima, whose fatal silhouette has remained graven in my memory just as it appeared to me from the height of the last dunes. At the end of a desolate plain sown with graves, like the one at Tarzant, low grey walls and an immense, solitary palm tree overlooking all. Everything was etched against the sooty grey horizon of that winter afternoon through which the violent sirocco raged, filling the dunes with vapours, stirring up the shifting sand.

\* \* \*

Sometimes gay, sometimes irritable and acerbic, an observer and thinker, a spiritual seeker, Dr. Taste was amazed by me, yet brotherly, admiring and often aggressive—especially on the subject of religion. He very quickly became my friend, an even closer one than Domerg had been—calmer, more down to earth, simpler too. Taste, passionate before all else, often poured out his soul to me, telling me of his mistresses and his ideas, his adventures and dreams. Curious in particular about the sensual world, a seeker of rare sensations, of exotic experiences, he sounded me out on my past, especially the most recent, perceiving accurately that, whatever I might know, the only true and honest knowledge must have been imparted heedlessly by the one person I had truly loved and who had loved me as well; for the miracle of love—one could say the sacrament—is accomplished only when love is shared, and not one-sided.

Taste sought to know Slimène's emotional and sensual characteristics as a way of deducing my own. But he began by completely fooling himself about Slimène, owing to his prejudices about caste, rank and above all race. For the Frenchman imagines the Arab to be instinctive and animalistic, for whom love means the brute act, with nothing to elevate it or refine it. The officer habitually casts the subordinate in the role (and still believes it is too indulgent) of the sentimental musketeer who sprinkles the dubious rosewater of high-flown declarations (in the style of Abdelaziz) over the stench of animal lust. The doctor's interest in these matters, and his sincere admiration for me, increased from the day he saw in Slimène what Slimène even failed to see in himself—the foreignness of his exceptional nature, resembling none other, either for good or ill.

Despite the bitterness of separation from my beloved and the ongoing struggle to defend myself against the prowling wolves, which depressed me and confused me by turns—my time in hospital was one of the most bearable among the recent periods of my life in Africa; I have good and comforting memories of this asylum, this refuge from pain lost in a far-off oasis.

# JOE ORTON

## *The Orton Diaries*

TANGIER                                                    *Sunday 7 May, 1967*

We got up early; a grey morning, drizzle. We'd done most of the packing last night. We had only to pack shaving materials and clothes-brushes. We had one medium-sized suitcase each, and I carried a canvas bag, originally intended for fishermen. At London Airport terminal I bought a Mickey Spillane* detective novel from the Smith's bookstand, Kenneth bought the paperback edition of *A Case of Human Bondage* by Beverley Nichols.† We neither of us read them on the plane.

We had an uneventful journey. We saw Bill Fox, an acquaintance from last year, on the plane and chatted to him. He had a woman with him. "She's some silly whore I picked up at the customs," he said. "You didn't think I was a convert, did you?" "I wondered," I said. "Good God no!" he said, "I shall be taking it up the arse as usual during the next fortnight." We talked a little more and he went back to his seat. We waved goodbye at the airport at Tangier.

We were driven into town to the flat which is actually half a villa in an alley way called the Rue Pizzarro.‡ The actual owner—a gentle French

---

*Mickey Spillane, the pen-name of Frank Morrison (1919–   ), author of hard-bitten detective thrillers.

†Beverley Nichols (1898–1983). English journalist and novelist.

‡The flat—No. 2 Rue Pizzaro—is where Tennessee Williams wrote *Suddenly Last Summer* which dealt, in part, with cannibalism and the barbarity of sexual promiscuity, of which Orton got a glimmering on this Tangier visit. One of Williams's last plays, *The Blonde Europeans,* is ded-

homme-femme—showed us around the place. It is furnished in a most "luxurious" manner—antique furniture and mirrors, gilded chandeliers—awful shit, but comfortable. The kind of taste I abhor, but as I am staying in Tangier for two months I want privacy, comfort and quiet. If I have to have a flat decorated by a gentle French queer it's a small price to have to pay. The main advantage the flat has is a terrace overlooking an enclosed garden and so when the hellish Tangier wind blows—as it is sure to do—we have a sheltered spot out of the way. We have to lock the place securely when we go out, including pulling shutters over the windows because "the Moroccans get in."

After changing we went down to The Windmill, a beach place run by an Englishman (Bill Dent) and an Irishman (Mike). The Windmill is right along the beach and so it is very quiet. Bill D. gave us a long talk about his health—he has shaking fits, he looks thinner than last year. Kenneth Halliwell says, with some truth, that what most of the Tangier regulars suffer from is drink. "He's got cirrhosis of the liver, I bet," K.H. said darkly. Mochtzar—who I had briefly last year—is now a sort of waiter at The Windmill. "He's going into the army in June," Bill Dent said. "I'll have to have him quick then," I said. We had tea and went out on the terrace, which is by the railway line. As I was sitting half-asleep, a small voice said "Hallo." It was a little boy. I had a little conversation. He asked my name. "Joe," I said. He nodded. "Joo," he said, "yes." "Are you going home now," he said. "No," I said, lying. "I'm staying with friends." He spoke then of how he was at school and was learning English. After more conversation, during a lull, he said, wistfully, "Do you like boys?" "Sometimes," I said. He nodded. "You fuck him?" he said, nodding at Kenneth. I shook my head and he said, conspiratorially, "He is asleep." And then, "You will be here many days?" "Yes," I said. "Goodbye," he said, with a smile and stopped. "I am Hassan," he said. After he had gone, K. said, "You can't have him—he is about ten." "It'll have to be a cabin job," I said. "They won't allow him in the cabins," he said. "Along the beach then," I said.

We came home and Kenneth said, "You go for some tea, bread, sugar, etc. They think you are poor and are nicer to you." So I went to the corner shop and a fat, very friendly boy served me with provisions. When I got back, I had a cup of tea and two of Kenneth's librium tablets. They are excellent and make me feel wonderfully relaxed and confident. We had

---

icated to Orton. "Tennessee Williams has been to see it twice," Orton wrote to Halliwell in October 1965, about the Broadway previews of *Entertaining Mr. Sloane.* "And, so I'm told, is wild over it. Says it's the funniest play he's ever seen."

dinner at a small French restaurant. We had a pleasant stroll along the boulevard and down to the Petit Socco. We bought two coffees and spoke to a youth. He seemed a nice bit of rough—though he had clearly been on the Kif. "I'm much too tired for anything tonight," I said to Kenneth. We said goodbye, drank our coffee and strolled past the Hotel Mamora which, from being a semi-brothel two years ago, is now a "tours" hotel with fat women and children sitting eating and drinking under pink lighting. When we were at the steps leading from the casbah, three very beautiful boys approached. "You English?" "Yes." "You like to come for a ride in a taxi?" the prettiest one said. We were too wise to be caught in that trap and we said "no." "I'll take a single one back sometime," I said to Ken. "But not three and not in a taxi." "The taxi driver is probably in the act," Ken said. We walked on and met a couple of Moroccans we knew from previous years. The effect of the librium was wonderful, so calming. We were able to carry on perfectly warm, friendly conversation in a most un-English way. "The funny thing is," Kenneth said, "they're so surprised by the complete lack of nervousness on our parts that they don't try to pester us at all." When one of them suggested that we come and smoke Kif I was able to say "no" in a firm, yet friendly way. I was really tired, and went to sleep having no sex, no inclination for any.

*Monday 8 May*

Kenneth worried about changing money. The £50 allowance simply won't take us to the end of June. We must find someone who will cash sterling and travellers' cheques of which we have £400 worth. We went to Kents (the Moroccan Woolworth) and bought shaving cream. The morning was cloudy. No sign of the sun, but it was pleasant and relaxing to stroll in the warm air. We saw Bill Fox sitting and drinking coffee at a café. He said, as we sat down, that he's had a little chicken who'd sucked his cock. "He said he loved it," he laughed. "I thought of you immediately Joe, though he's too small to fuck, I'm sure." I asked him his name. "Hassan," he said. "That's the one I spoke to at the Windmill," I said. "I must have him, only I can't take him back to our place. Not after last year, and we are staying the summer." "You can have him at my flat," Bill said. "I'll fix it up for you." He then took us to a woman who changed all Kenneth's cheques on the black market, and so that problem was settled. We all went to The Windmill for lunch. Met a nice ex–Merchant Navy man called Alan. Seems a good, decent type. "I like doing anything," he said. "I've tried women and I have come to the conclusion that two men in bed together can enjoy themselves ten times more than with a bird." We're meeting him tonight for a meal. We've locked the main salon of the flat, which is enormous and gives an impression of millionaire elegance. We'll just pretend that the flat consists of the kitchen bathroom and two bedrooms. Kenneth worried. "It's so dangerous," he says. "Look," I've said perhaps rashly, "if there's a real nastiness we can just sling him out. We're never having more than one in at a time, our money is locked away, and, up to date, I've *never* had any trouble with a boy." "There's always a first time," Ken said darkly, with which I can't argue.

We had dinner at a restaurant called Nino's. A notorious Italian runs it. When we asked what had become of Abdul-Kador, the waiter he employed last year, he pursed his lips in disapproval and said simply, "A prostitute." Kenneth gave me four librium tablets and then gave Bill Fox two, and the ex-navy man called Alan two also. They seemed to have an alarming effect on Bill, who was drinking wine with his meal. "I simply *must* take it up the arse tonight," he said, "or there will be no doing anything with me tomorrow." He said he had been a miner when he was fourteen. "I was first fucked down a mine," he announced to Nino. "Yes?" Nino said, not understanding. "Among the coal," Bill said, trying to explain. "A miner did me." Nino shook his head. "Another prostitute, yes?" "She thinks I did it for a bucket of coal," Bill said.

*Tuesday 9 May*

We went down to the beach early today. It had cleared up. Clouds passing over the sun, but enough heat to be pleasant. We were hailed with "Hallo" from a very beautiful sixteen-year-old boy whom I knew (but had never had) from last year. Kenneth wanted him. We talked for about five minutes and finally I said, "Come to our apartment for tea this afternoon." He was very eager. We arranged that he should meet us at The Windmill beach place. As we left the boy, Kenneth said, "Wasn't I good at arranging the thing?" This astounded me. "I arranged it," I said. "You would have been standing there talking about the weather for ever." K. didn't reply.*

---

*Sir Terence Rattigan: "It was perfectly plain to me—and this isn't being clever after the event—that Halliwell was wildly jealous of Joe's sexual escapades, and it was perfectly clear that Joe didn't give a fuck. Halliwell lied about his age. For every erotic triumph that Joe described, Halliwell described five of his own. That was obviously phoney. I think I got as far as asking Halliwell: 'Don't you mind when Joe goes and does these things?' He may well, but he wouldn't be doing it with any success. He resented Joe's success in that sphere as well as the other. That was one part of Joe's life he couldn't collaborate in."

I borrowed the keys of Bill Fox's flat—(because I thought I must test the boy out in less grand surroundings than the flat we've taken) and went over to the boy. He was standing under a tree in the rain. He smiled, I nodded in the direction of the waste ground opposite the beach. He took my hand and we ran across the wasteland in the rain. We reached the flat and I had difficulty in finding how to open it. Fortunately nobody came up. I was dressed poorly myself in a pair of ordinary trousers and a polo-necked jumper—now wet with rain. I got the door open and we went inside—I pissed. The boy stood in the centre of the room. I tried to explain that this apartment belonged to a friend. He seemed to understand neither French, English or Spanish. I took him to the bed. Kissed him. He was shy and didn't open his mouth. He got very excited when I undressed him. I undressed myself and we lay caressing each other for about ten minutes. He had a heavy loutish body, large cock, but not so large as to make me envious or shy. I turned him over. He wouldn't let me get in so I fucked along the line of his buttocks which was very exciting. He'd wiped his spit on his bum. When I'd come a great patch on Bill Fox's coverlet, I went and fetched a towel—then we kissed some more, neck, cheeks, eyes—he still wouldn't open his mouth—strange for an Arab boy—he must be about fifteen, surely he'd have learned (I later was told that he had only recently come up from the country). He then turned me over and came along the line of my buttocks in the same way. Suddenly he stopped and said, "How much you give me?" "Five dirham," I said. "No, please, fifteen." "No," I said, "five." He grinned. "OK," he said and went on. He took a very long time to come. We lay together for an hour afterwards while the rain poured down outside and the thunder roared. His name is Mohammed. We then took a shower together. I then gave him five dirhams, slipped it into his pocket. He said, "Please, one more." Because he was sweet, and even on a matter of one dirham, they like to gain a victory, I gave him an extra. He kissed my cheek, I hugged him and said I'd see him again. He left the flat first. I wiped up the floor in the bathroom, which was swimming, and left. Alan, who had had a most unsatisfactory experience with a drunken English sailor the night before, said, "Well I don't really mind," and laughed. He went off with a very attractive but very young boy later, after inviting Bill Fox, Kenneth and I up to his flat for a glass of wine before dinner. Bill Fox told me that the Baron Favier (from whom we rent our flat) likes to dress young men up in military uniform. "One night," Bill said, "he picked up a sailor in uniform, he took him back, made him take off his naval uniform and put on a military uniform before he could have him." Bill went off with a waiter, a nice Moroccan in his twenties. Not pretty but a good, friendly man. "Lovely sex, dear," Bill said. "He's promised to make me some hashish cakes." These are cakes made with hash—they look the same as ordinary confectionery but are greatly superior to anything sold at Fullers . . .

# JOHN HAYLOCK

## *Eastern Exchange*

One of the things I hated most about the job of teaching was having at the beginning of the term to face a class of fifty or sixty boys who were without books, pencils or even scraps of paper; on the first day they just brought themselves to class and looked as if they expected to be entertained. Unlike my Iraqi and Egyptian colleagues I never possessed the ability to extemporize for an hour to a class who understood about forty per cent of what was said to them.

When from my desk I looked at my first class, I blushed and tingled all over with embarrassment, because sitting in the back row was Rashid, a male whore whose services I had but recently engaged. In my confusion I rose and walked about the room uttering inane remarks about the English course, now and then casting sidelong glances at the back row to see if it really was the Rashid who had taken me to a *maison de passe*. He would be sure to tell his classmates and the scandalous information would be broadcast all over the place; or Rashid might blackmail me into buying his silence and I would have to pay out regular, ruinous sums. I got up onto the dais and boldly regarded the back row with an unblinking gaze, but still I wasn't sure—did Rashid have such curly hair? Yes, of course it was he. So disturbed was I that I seriously thought of dashing out of the classroom, out of the college, out of Baghdad, out of Iraq then and there.

"What is your name?" I dared to ask. "Khaleel," the young man said, smiling in rather a supercilious way, but when he smiled he did not show gapped teeth, and Rashid had gapped teeth, or hadn't he? The fact that the boy said his name was Khaleel and not Rashid meant nothing; he would hardly attend the college under his *nom de guerre*. I struggled on with the period, improvising wildly, talking about anything that came into my head—the mosques of Isfahan, the mosaics of Sancta Sophia to the boredom of fifty Arab youths from villages all over Iraq, most of whom were paying their first visit to Baghdad and had never been inside a museum in their lives. I knew I was making a bad impression and I had heard that one's reputation depended on the first class. Although the pupils were supposed to be country boys, farmers' sons, in their suits and moustaches many of them looked both grown-up and worldly-wise; they were not, of course, but they looked so. I felt a complete idiot after that first lesson. I knew I had given a lamentable performance.

That evening I loitered outside the Sindbad Hotel, where Rashid had his beat. He appeared after a while.

"Hellow, Mister Joan. You want enjoy?" Rashid's smile showed a row of gapped teeth.

The next day books were issued and I faced the class with more confidence.

# Wyndham Lewis

## *Journey into Barbary:*
## *Morocco Writings and Drawings*

To demonstrate, in the physical field, how the battle of land-rights must result in trisecting, throwing off its axis, mutilating and scattering to the four winds, the future city of Agadir, I had intended to describe how the hills, ravines and flats lay, of which the potential city is composed. But when an attempt is made to tell one how the rooms and passages of a house occur (in the murder story this is often done) most readers, it is quite certain, cannot follow, most only skip. Language is not suited for that abstract map-making. What is the use of saying—There's a big hill upon the left, then there's a lower one, to the right, flatter on the top, and so forth? None whatever—Agadir is a hilly spot. There are big sands, covered with seagulls at low water, where they are wet—enamelled and glittering. Like a white cock's comb, with heavily milled edges, there is a Kasbah upon a mountain—"véritable nid d'aigle" the French writers always call it. There are a lot of uncouth and often filthy ravines: the "front" is overgrown with cactus and the spiked candelabrum of the *Euphorbium,* and what I suspected to be juniper, and all sorts of thorny bushes—it is a wilderness of sandy gashes, steep mule and camel tracks leading to the sea; garages and impromptu one-storey hotels present their untidy backyards to the shore. But there are many wide level gaps too in the road-line and big sandy playgrounds for tethering animals or ones squatting for want of something to do—these are accounted for by the stout bulldog claims of our passionate compatriot, on behalf of other Bulldogs in the background—bigger and wickeder Bulldogs than he.

At the foot of the mountain, in a wild disordered gully, is the brothel, the *bousbir,* the *quartier réservé* (the whore-shop, the lupanar, the mud-nests of official love). Sitting on a stone, upon the opposite hill, looking down into the brothel, I could see all its alfresco mud cubby-holes. A weather-rotted curtain was fixed over the openings to the miserable dens of the females of this sad menagerie. "Deep-throated" German chanting came from a mud-cell stuck onto the nearer wall. So I could not see this choir of the Legion. The queen of the colony—a girl of about fifteen—was holding a reception at the opposite end.

One brothel inland which I met with was more peculiar even than this: it was like a large mud-built pig-sty; or like the empty many-celled Souks you come upon in the *bled,* only made of adobe instead of stone. It was quite open, or seemed so. Each cell contained a woman—I saw it about noon, I walked down this repulsive tropical lane, full of fierce houseflies: a stout snore came from each sty. This was in the mountains. The stable for loose women in Agadir was scarcely fit for mules, but it was better than the Tenderloin of the *bled.*

To the *bousbir,* the love-Souk of Agadir, I went one night, in the company of three Italians—it was the day after that I drew it. There was a tent at the gate, with an armed policeman in it. He let us in, and we found ourselves in a large empty court of mud. This was unlighted, but there were lamps behind the curtains of the women's cells, occupying three sides of it. There must have been thirty women in it. Each cell was about seven foot every way, except from roof to floor, which was under six foot. Against the inner wall was the bed. We all crept in at the hole or door on all fours. We sat on the floor of beaten mud, with our backs against the mud-wall.

We were visiting the queen of the brothel. She was a bright Berber girl, with good features, with eyes like a squirrel's, good teeth and a little chin. Her face was painted and tattooed. (There was a row of vertical spots where in a man the chin-cleft would be.) As she was so young probably her eyelids had less kohl than those of her older mates, whose eyes oozed ink; they kept crawling in and out (she usually drove them away with a harsh indignant shout). Two Foreign Legion non-coms crept in and sat down. They were German. Although drunk they were very quiet. The Roman Legionaries at Volubilis must have had much the same square countenances.

Our hostess was extremely grave and the small cell was oppressive with her matter-of-factness: with an attentive frown she made the green tea and mint, and handed everybody present a small glass—not small enough, for it is extremely sickly.

The senior of the three Italians, an ex-Foreign Legion sergeant (or commissariat non-com), was talkative, he wanted the girl to undress at once. She ignored this pointless suggestion. We all drank our tea and talked of one thing and another—no one except the Italian who had brought us paid much attention to the girl. When several cups of tea had been drunk, the chief Italian again commanded her to undress *tutti nue.* She frowned and then gave a few Berber giggles. "Oui met-toi tutti nue, Doho!" At length she went to the two beds (like ships' bunks against the wall) and took off her clothes and stood looking at us like a squirrel—showing after much coaxing its winter *cachette* of nuts. Everybody looked: when I remarked upon the stoutness of the belly, at fifteen, an Air-force non-com who had crawled in said:

"Evidemment! *C'est le ventre colonial!*"

"Elles ont toutes des bedons? Quel dommage!" I said.

"Evidemment!" he said. "Que voulez-vous! C'est bien le ventre colonial!"

She soon covered up her "colonial stomach" again, and when all harnessed up in leaden and silver bric-à-brac, sat down. She poured out more green tea with much mint.

"Eh bien, je m'en vais me coucher!" said the Air-force corporal. He crawled out.

"Moi aussi!" exclaimed one of the Foreign Legion visitors.

They crawled out—one rolled out, the other crouched and charged out through the hole head first.

We all crawled out into the pitch-black yard. There were a few white figures moving down the sides of the cells. Several Foreign Legion privates moved listlessly up and down, smoking. The other women we had seen were savage blousy bundles of grey rags—battered old flowers of the *bled,* a fat Jewess, with beady eyes in a mask of pallid dough.

"She is the best!" one of the Italians said, meaning the one we had been with. "She is the only one here."

The senior Italian remained inside; the curtain fell violently over the hole by which we had issued on all fours. We went out of the gate, *bon-soired* off the premises by the police-guard in the tent outside.

This brothel is not unknown; a book by Joseph Kessel (in its fiftieth thousand) has an account of it: he writes that in going to have a look at it he knew "that there could be nothing comparable to Casablanca," but that he was not prepared for this, that he "was stupefied by its miserable aspect.... At the bottom end of a squalid, dirty, and stinking lane, a wall of *pisé* enclosing a court more cramped than a farmyard, hid the sensual joys of Agadir. Even at Dar-es-Zor, on the Euphrates, even at Palmira, in the Syrian desert, I had found more room to move about at least, more gaity, than in this place set aside for prostitution."

It is the large, muddy farmyard without even a street lamp in the middle—the high walls and the rows of squalid niches the size of a small lavatory, built into the wall itself, that calls forth these exclamations of disgust especially from the Parisian traveller. Even if a rough pavement existed (it would cost nothing—the women could beat into the mud the flat stones required—most of these women have worked on the new highways with a hammer, stone-breaking—it is not as though they had had no practice)—if there were a hut or two in which you could stand up, or even if, covered with bugs and reeking of stale rose-water, one of the women were a credit to her down-trodden people—with a couple of bold black eyes, or an uncolonial stomach! It is such things that make people write about the *bousbir* of Agadir, especially if Parisians.

I write about it mainly because its brothel does demonstrate the extent to which Agadir is still the wild frontier township—"*Here* we are in the *bled*! In the *bled*!" as someone shouted at me when he asked me if I liked his langoustes and I did not answer quickly enough to please him—though I knew the Breton fishing-boats came all this way—and as far as St.-Louis-du-Sénégal—for such langoustes: and of course therefore the *bled* in that respect was the *bled* and not the *bled*—since we were where the luxury fish of the cities come from.

It is the *bled* (you cannot translate *bled* champaign or countryside, nor yet quite wilderness. It is what is not *city* in Maghreb—it is the steppe with its cactus, and its mud-concrete fortresses, its donkeys and well-wheels, argans, walnuts and palms—but nine-tenths wilderness, sand or tufa steppe).

Many talks with the men who look after the "reserved quarter" tended to crystallize my notion of prices. A virgin costs round about fifty or sixty francs three years out of the four. The fourth is invarably a bad year, then she is cheaper. She goes for as low as twenty-five francs. (These are all girls of about thirteen or fourteen—there are no virgins much after that of course.) There are years when—oh, anything will do it: a franc, a Hassani peseta. The father gets the money. (This is in the *douar*—in the *bled*.) There is a great deal of extreme misery, which I am sure is no fault of the French, though they naturally are blamed—even the *bled* is not worse than the Middle West (U.S.A.) in that respect (*cf.* reports *re* the starvation in the cotton-belt). Numbers of Mauresques work on the road, breaking stones. After some months of breaking stones on the road it can be readily understood that a woman does not stand on her dignity or sniff at a two-franc piece, even if she would before, which in Morocco is scarcely likely.

Under such conditions it is not surprising that the *quartiers réservés* are besieged with women of all sorts (mostly no oil-paintings, you can be sure) imploring admittance.

The Foreign Legion are the chief patrons of the *bousbir* of course. But wherever they are quartered there are women who are only too willing for a few francs to do anything: a legionnaire takes a bottle of wine and a blanket and retires into the privacy of the *bled;* others follow suit, and so it is that, in spite of every regular prostitute *passant la visite* daily, there is much venereal disease.

# SARAH HOBSON

## Through Persia in Disguise

Perhaps unfairly I felt I had seen enough, for the Turkmen could be monotonous, rather like their carpets. Giving my dictionary to Mohammad and a book to Meshed, I left that afternoon for Gurgan, a town some sixty miles away which once had been the base of the Qajar dynasty, and a stronghold against the Turkmen. But the inhabitants then seemed no better than their enemies, for "one of them had enticed an aged uncle into the desert, and there sold him for eight kurrauns to a Toorcoman ... the Khan had heard of this, and by good luck managed to seize both the buyer and seller ... he proposed, on the morrow, to boil the [seller] in a cauldron, and then kill the Toorcoman, having first made him breakfast on a boiled leg of the nephew!"*

Now Gurgan has an air of modernity, with its avenues, banks, and a cinema. But as I found mainly farm equipment to look at, I took a bus to Pahlevi Dez where the Turkmen hold a market of their products, from carpets and hats, to shovels and horses. We drove over a corrugated track between hedges of rushes and myrtle, crossed the deeply-gorged Gurgan river by a single-track humped bridge, and arrived in the village. Two streets led at right angles from each other and petered out on the plain; three shops had few goods and no customers. Everything seemed dirty

---

* W. R. Holmes, *Sketches on the Shores of the Caspian,* London 1845.

and depressed: the houses had rotting balconies and shutters, rusted roofs and drainpipes; the earth, a grey-tinged sienna, was baked into grooves after winter rains.

An aspiring linguist called 'Umar offered to show me the local crafts: carpets knotted in dark rooms; bread baked in ovens sunk into the street; and felt, where strands of wool were applied in scrolls to half-compacted wool.

"I'll take you to see some Turkmen tents tomorrow," he said, as it grew dark. "And you can stay with me."

His home was a tiny hut about ten feet square. He flung his jacket on the ground and stretched out on the rug.

"Horribly small, isn't it? But my father's building a huge house right next door."

His father arrived, a white-haired man, half-blind. He lit a candle and laid some bread and cheese on the floor.

"My mother's dead," commented 'Umar, not helping.

"I'm sorry."

"Yes, so I'm really the head of the family." He rubbed the pile of the carpet. "It's very old, this rug."

"I can see. It's beautiful."

"Yes. A professor wanted to buy it, but I said no. Of course you can have it, for a thousand *toman*."

"I'm very honoured, but . . ."

"All right, nine hundred."

He reduced the price to five hundred before he realised I would not buy it.

Towards eleven o'clock, someone rapped on the door. 'Umar opened it and called me to come.

"The gendarme's here. He wants you to go and have your passport checked."

"Oh, of course. I should have done it before."

We walked into the street, and the gendarme peered at me.

"What's his name?" he asked 'Umar.

"John. He's from England."

"Football in England is good, Mr. John?"

"Oh yes, I play twice a week."

"Do you play for England?"

In the gendarmerie, we went to the office.

"Good evening," said the man behind the desk. "Your passport please. Only a routine check."

I unzipped my pocket, and he asked: "You like our little town, sir?"

"I haven't been here long, you know."

"Yes, I know."

I handed him the passport and started to laugh. He came to the photograph and laughed as well, pointing to the photograph and then at me. 'Umar went to look.

"This is really you?"

"Yes, and nobody guessed."

"No, nobody," laughed the officer, slapping his thigh in delight. Then suddenly his face snapped into anger. "Why didn't you report here before? The Russian border is only fifty kilometres. And why are you here?"

"But—"

"You must be a Russian spy," he shouted. "You filthy boy, I shall have to arrest you."

"Arrest me? No, no I'm not a Russian spy."

"You must be, else why would you wear a disguise? I must arrest you and send you to Gurgan tomorrow." He stood up, his face tightening with emotion. "They'll send you to Tehran, and there"—he leaned forward, glaring with contempt—"you'll be thrown into prison."

At the sound of his shouting, a gendarme rushed in. The officer pointed at me and hissed: "Russian spy."

I stood up and said, with control: "I . . . am . . . not . . . a Russian spy. Look," and I snatched the passport from his desk. "Look, it says here 'British Passport'."

"This man is a Russian spy," he bawled at the others.

"I AM NOT A MAN." Then, more quietly: "Do Russians write in English?" and I pulled out my diaries and books. This made the officer think for a moment before he resumed his accusations.

For some reason, 'Umar took my side and tried to pacify the officer, who eventually left the room to discuss with the other gendarmes. Alone with me, 'Umar pushed himself against me, trying to kiss me and put his hand down the front of my shirt. I thrust him away.

"But you're a woman. So beautiful," he murmured. "Just let me touch you," and his hand slid up my thigh. I hit his arm hard and crossed the room where I leant against the wall, my legs crossed and my arms protecting my chest. He followed me.

"Aaah, tonight, what joy we can have. And you can have my carpet." He assumed a nonchalant air. "I know influential people—*they* wouldn't let you go to prison."

The officer returned and the argument started again, until finally I burst into tears. He looked puzzled.

"Well is she just a woman then?" he asked, and after some consideration, began to take down my passport details.

"It's all right, now," he said. "We won't do anything. You can go home with 'Umar now."

I did not relish the idea, so asked: "Couldn't I sleep here? I mean, now that I'm a girl, it's a bit difficult."

"Certainly, certainly, we have a roomful of bunks." He pointed to one of the gendarmes. "You. Show her where they are."

I found some sheets on my bunk, and folding them round me I started to fall asleep. The door opened, and 'Umar crept in, feeling his way towards my bunk.

"I'd never harm you," he whispered. "I just want to kiss you."

"Well I don't want to kiss you. Please go away," and after a struggle he went to lie on the bunk beside mine.

The door opened again, and a gendarme sprang onto the bunk above 'Umar. Then the officer came in with another gendarme and they lay down to my left. There was silence. Then:

"I'll give you a hundred *toman*," said the officer.

The soldier on the top bunk leant over, swinging a tin pendant which hung round his neck.

"Real silver," he said. "A hundred *toman* and this."

"I'm not interested."

"One hundred and fifty," said a third voice, threateningly.

"I tell you I'm not interested."

'Umar intervened. "Don't you need the money?"

"I've got a thousand *toman* in Tehran."

"Oh."

Silence.

"I'll give you three hundred, now," said the officer.

"Three fifty."

"Four hundred."

The bidding finally reached twenty-five pounds, but I could not determine if it was a joint offer, and any enquiry, I felt, might compromise me.

By now I was sitting up angrily, and extremely frightened, clutching the flimsy sheet round me. 'Umar came over once more to persuade me to accept the offer. I drew a knife from my pocket, though it was only a rusty penknife which would not have cut a melon rind. Someone whispered to my left.

"The officer says you can go to his house if you'd prefer privacy with him," explained 'Umar.

"I prefer nothing. And tell that . . . that officer that when I get to Tehran, I'll report him to the head of the Military Police."

Immediately the officer began to apologise. "We thought you'd want to," he said. "I mean most European girls do that *we've* met."

Soon I heard three people snoring, but 'Umar tiptoed across to my bunk. "I've got a very rich friend in Gurgan. He likes English women. He'll give you five hundred *toman*—and a carpet of your own choice."

After a few hours' uneasy sleep, I got up at five o'clock and went to fetch my bag from 'Umar's house. Near one of the shops we saw an old man leaning against a wall. 'Umar ran forward.

"Father," he cried. "What's the matter?"

"In the night. A pain. Here." He tapped his heart. "I'm dying," and he raised his eyes to heaven. "I waited for you, and waited. Oh, the pain." And he hit his head again and again against the wall.

"Run," said 'Umar, taking hold of my hand, and we raced to his home. He hurriedly changed his shirt, at the same time trying to kiss me. Then we banged on the door of a neighbouring house, and a man in pyjamas came sleepily out. We begged him to drive us to Gurgan, and he started an old Austin Cambridge, while 'Umar pushed me onto the front seat, climbing in beside me. We stopped for the old man who stretched himself on the back seat, panting, and the car went over the bridge, moving slowly towards Gurgan.

"She's nearly twenty years old," said the driver proudly, patting the steering wheel.

"*Jan*," gasped the old man behind us, each time we went over a bump. "Ah, *jan*, life."

"*Jan*," whispered 'Umar into my ear. "Darling, we can go and see my rich friend while my father's at the doctor."

We parked in the main street of Gurgan, and supported the old man to the doctor's house. He was given an injection and a prescription, and by the time we returned to the car, he had stopped his heavy breathing.

'Umar went to buy the pills, and rather than face further assaults, I left the old man and ran to the nearest bus station to go back to Tehran.

I slept most of the way, but woke intermittently to look at the passing countryside. On the right was the Caspian, grey and lifeless, reminding me more of Bournemouth on an overcast day than the exotic breeding ground of sturgeon. On the left, like a wall against the road, forest soared up the hills. Then came sorrel-coloured mountains with one snow-covered peak, for the land was changing itself to face the Iranian plateau.

I felt a sense of relief when we reached Tehran, for it seemed like security. But I was still confused about the Turkmen, for they had shown much hospitality and their jewellery was magnificent; yet at the same time they seemed to have a somewhat brutal disregard for human-beings. And it was strange, I thought, how when I was a boy I could fall in with their callousness, but the moment I was a girl, I felt humiliated and powerless.

# ANDRÉ GIDE

## *If It Die: An Autobiography*

We stayed at Sousse only six days. But on the dreary background of those monotonous days of waiting, there stands out a little episode which was of great importance in my life. And if it is indecent to relate it, it would be still more dishonest to pass it over.

At certain hours of the day, Paul left me to go and paint; but I was not so poorly as to be unable sometimes to go and join him. For that matter, during the whole time of my illness, I did not keep my bed, nor even my room, for a single day. I never went out without taking a coat and a rug with me: as soon as I got outside, some boy would appear and offer to carry them. The one who accompanied me on that particular day was a young brown-skinned Arab whom I had already noticed on the previous day among the troop of little rascals who loitered in the neighbourhood of the hotel. He wore a chechia on his head like the others and nothing else but a coat of coarse linen and baggy Tunisian trousers that stopped short at the knee and made his bare legs look even slenderer than they were. He seemed more reserved or more timid than his companions, so that as a rule they were beforehand with him; but that day, I don't know how it was, I went out without any of them seeing me, and all of a sudden it was he who joined me at the corner of the hotel.

The hotel was situated in a sandy district on the outskirts of the town. It was sad to see the olive-trees, so fine in the surrounding country, half submerged here by the drifting sandhills. A little further on one was astonished to come upon a stream—a meagre water-course, springing out of the sand just in time to reflect a little bit of sky before reaching the sea. A gathering of negresses squatting over their washing beside this trickle of fresh water was the subject Paul had chosen before which to plant his easel. I had promised to meet him there, but when Ali—this was my little guide's name—led me up among the sandhills, in spite of the fatigue of walking in the sand, I followed him; we soon reached a kind of funnel or crater, the rim of which was just high enough to command the surrounding country and give a view of anyone coming. As soon as we got there, Ali flung the coat and rug down on the sloping sand; he flung himself down too, and stretched on his back, with his arms spread out on each side of him, he looked at me and laughed. I was not such a simpleton as to misunderstand his invitation; but I did not answer it at once. I sat down myself, not very far from him, but yet not very near either, and in my turn looked at him steadily and waited, feeling extremely curious as to what he would do next.

I waited! I wonder to-day at my fortitude ... But was it really curiosity that held me back? I am not sure. The secret motive of our acts—I mean of the most decisive ones—escapes us; and not only in memory but at the very moment of their occurrence. Was I still hesitating on the threshold of what is called sin? No; my disappointment would have been too great if the adventure had ended with the triumph of my virtue—which I already loathed and despised. No; it was really curiosity that made me wait ... And I watched his laughter slowly fade away, his lips close down again over his white teeth and an expression of sadness and discomfiture cloud his charming face.

"Good-bye, then," he said.

But I seized the hand he held out to me and tumbled him on to the ground. In a moment he was laughing again. The complicated knots of the strings that served him for girdle did not long trouble his impatience; he drew a little dagger from his pocket and severed the tangle with one cut. The garment fell, and flinging away his coat, he emerged naked as a god. Then he raised his slight arms for a moment to the sky and dropped laughing against me. Though his body was perhaps burning, it felt as cool and refreshing to my hands as shade. How beautiful the sand was! In the lovely splendour of that evening light, what radiance clothed my joy! ...

In the meantime it was getting late. I had to join Paul. No doubt my countenance bore traces of my rapture and I think he guessed something; but as—out of discretion, perhaps—he did not question me, I said nothing.

\* \* \*

Another evening, immediately after Douglas had left for Blidah, Wilde asked me to go with him to a Moorish café where there was music to be heard. I agreed and called for him after dinner at his hotel. The café was not very far off, but as Wilde had some difficulty in walking, we took a carriage which dropped us in Rue Montpensier, at the fourth terrace of the Boulevard Gambetta, where Wilde told the coachman to wait for us. A guide had got up beside the coachman and this man now escorted us through a labyrinth of small streets inaccessible to carriages, until we came to the steep alley in which the café was situated. As we walked, Wilde expounded his theory of guides, and how important it was to choose the vilest, who was invariably the cleverest. If the man at Blidah had not succeeded in showing us anything interesting, it was because he wasn't ugly enough. Ours that evening was a terror.

There was nothing to show it was a café; its door was like all the other doors; it stood ajar, and there was no need to knock. Wilde was an habitué of this place, which I have described in my *Amyntas*, for I often went back to it afterwards. There were a few old Arabs sitting cross-legged on mats and smoking kief; they made no movement when we took our places among them. And at first I did not see what there was in this café to attract Wilde; but after a time I made out a young *caouadji* standing in the shadow near the hearth; he was busy preparing us two cups of ginger tea over the embers—a drink Wilde preferred to coffee. Lulled by the strange torpor of the place, I was just sinking into a state of semi-somnolence, when in the half-open doorway, there suddenly appeared a marvellous youth. He stood there for a time, leaning with his raised elbow against the doorjamb, and outlined on the dark background of the night. He seemed uncertain as to whether he should come in or not, and I was beginning to be afraid he would go, when he smiled at a sign made him by Wilde and came up and sat down opposite us on a stool a little lower than the mat-covered raised floor on which we were sitting, Arab fashion. He took a reed flute out of his Tunisian waistcoat and began to play on it very exquisitely. Wilde told me a little later that he was called Mohammed and that "he was Bosy's"; if he had hesitated at first as to whether he should come in, it was because he had not seen Lord Alfred. His large black eyes had the languorous look peculiar to hashish smokers; he had an olive complexion; I admired his long fingers on the flute, the slimness of his boyish figure, the slenderness of his bare legs coming from under his full white drawers, one of them bent back and resting on the knee of the other. The *caouadji* came to sit beside him and accompanied him on a kind of *darbouka*. The song of the flute flowed on through an extraordinary stillness, like a limpid steady stream of water, and you forgot the time and the place, and who you were and all the troubles of this world. We sat on, without stirring, for what seemed to me infinite ages; but I should have sat on for longer still, if Wilde had not suddenly taken me by the arm and broken the spell.

"Come," said he.

We went out. We took a few steps in the alley, followed by the hideous guide, and I was beginning to think our evening was to come to an end there, when at the first turning, Wilde came to a standstill, dropped his huge hand on to my shoulder, and bending down—he was much taller than I—said in a whisper:

"*Dear,*\* would you like the little musician?"

Oh! how dark the alley was! I thought my heart would fail me; and what a dreadful effort of courage it needed to answer: "Yes," and with what a choking voice!

Wilde immediately turned to the guide, who had come up to us, and whispered a few words in his ear which I did not hear. The man left us and we went on to the place where the carriage was waiting.

We were no sooner seated in it, than Wilde burst out laughing—a resounding laugh, more of triumph than of pleasure, an interminable, uncontrollable, insolent laugh; and the more disconcerted I seemed to be by his laughter, the more he laughed. I should say that if Wilde had begun to discover the secrets of his life to me, he knew nothing as yet of mine; I had taken care to give him no hint of them, either by deed or word. The proposal he had just made me was a bold one; what amused him so much was that it was not rejected; it was the amusement of a child and a devil. The great pleasure of the debauchee is to debauch. No doubt, since my adventure at Sousse, there was not much left for the Adversary to do to complete his victory over me; but Wilde did not know this, nor that I was vanquished beforehand—or, if you will (for is it proper to speak of defeat when one carries one's head so high?), that I had already triumphed in my

---

\* In English in the text.

imagination and my thoughts over all my scruples. To tell the truth, I did not know it myself; it was only, I think, as I answered "yes," that I suddenly became aware of it.

Wilde interrupted his laughter from time to time to apologise.

"I beg your pardon for laughing so; but I can't help it. It's no good." And he started off again.

He was still laughing when we stopped in front of a café in the Place opposite the theatre, where we dismissed the carriage.

"It's too early yet," said Wilde. And I did not dare ask him what he had settled with the guide, nor where, nor how, nor when, the little musician would come to me; and I began to doubt whether anything would really come of his proposal; but I was afraid to question him lest I should show the violence of my desire.

We only stayed a moment in this vulgar café, and I supposed that if Wilde did not at once get driven to the little bar of the Hôtel de l'Oasis where we went next, it was because he did not want the people of the hotel where he was known to have any inkling of the Moorish café, and that he devised this intervening stage in order to put a little more distance between the above-board and the clandestine.

Wilde made me drink a cocktail and drank several himself. We lingered for about half an hour. How long I thought it! Wilde still went on laughing, but not so convulsively, and when from time to time we spoke, it was about any trifle. At last I saw him take out his watch:

"It is time," said he, getting up.

We took our way towards a more populous quarter of the town, further than the big mosque at the bottom of the hill (I have forgotten its name) which one passes on the way to the Post Office—the ugliest part of the town now, though once it must have been one of the most beautiful. Wilde preceded me into a house with a double entrance, and we had no sooner crossed the threshold, than there appeared in front of us two enormous policemen, who had come in by the other door, and who terrified me out of my wits. Wilde was very much amused at my fright.

"Oh, no, dear, on the contrary; it proves the hotel is a very safe place. They come here to protect foreigners. I know them quite well. They're excellent fellows and very fond of my cigarettes. They quite understand."

We let the policemen go up in front of us. They passed the second floor, where we stopped. Wilde took a key out of his pocket and showed me into a tiny apartment of two rooms, where we were soon joined by the vile guide. The two youths followed him, each of them wrapped in a burnous that hid his face. Then the guide left us and Wilde sent me into the further room with little Mohammed and shut himself up in the other with the *darbouka* player.

Every time since then that I have sought after pleasure, it is the memory of that night I have pursued. After my adventure at Sousse, I had relapsed wretchedly again into vice. If I had now and then snatched a sensual joy in passing, it had been, as it were, furtively; one delicious evening there had been, however, in a boat on the lake of Como, with a young boatman (just before going to La Brévine) when my rapture was encompassed by the shining of the moon, the misty magic of the lake, the moist perfumes breathing from its shores. And after that, nothing; nothing but a frightful desert, full of wild unanswered appeals, aimless efforts, restlessness, struggles, exhausting dreams, false excitement and abominable depression. At La Roque, the summer before last, I had been afraid of going mad; I spent nearly the whole time I was there shut up in my room, where I ought to have been working, and where I tried to work in vain (I was writing *Le Voyage d'Urien*), obsessed, haunted, thinking to find perhaps some escape in excess itself, hoping to come out into the fresh air on the other side, to wear out my demon (I recognise his wile), when it was only myself I wore out, expending myself crazily to the point of utter exhaustion, to the verge of imbecility, of madness.

Ah! what a hell I had been through! And without a friend I could speak to, without a word of advice; because I had believed all compromise impossible, and because I had begun by refusing to surrender, I came near sinking to perdition . . . But what need is there to recall those lugubrious days? Does their memory explain that night's ecstasy? My attempt with Meriem, my effort after "renormalisation," had not been followed up because it had not been in consonance with my nature; it was now that I found my normal. There was nothing constrained here, nothing precipitate, nothing doubtful; there is no taste of ashes in the memory I keep. My joy was unbounded, and I cannot imagine it greater, even if love had been added. How should there have been any question of love? How should I have allowed desire to dispose of my heart? No scruple clouded my pleasure and no remorse followed it. But what name then am I to give the rapture I felt as I clasped in my naked arms that perfect little body, so wild, so ardent, so sombrely lascivious?

———

For a long time after Mohammed had left me, I remained in a state of passionate jubilation, and though I had already achieved pleasure five times with him, I renewed my ecstasy again and again, and when I got back to my room in the hotel, I prolonged its echoes until morning.

I know well enough that one of these details may provoke a smile; it would be easy for me to omit or to modify it so as to make it seem more likely; but it is not likelihood I am in quest of, but truth; and ought not the truth to be told more especially then, when it appears least likely? Why else should I mention it?

As I was simply giving my measure, and as I had been reading Boccaccio's *Nightingale* into the bargain, I had no idea there was anything surprising about it, and it was Mohammed's astonishment that first made me suspect there was. Where I went beyond my measure was in what followed and that is what seems to me really strange: glutted and exhausted as I was, I had no rest nor respite till I had pushed exhaustion further still. I often experienced later how vain it is for me to try to be moderate, in spite of what reason and prudence advise; for whenever I attempted it, I was obliged afterwards, and in solitude, to labour after that total exhaustion which alone afforded me respite, and which I obtained at no less cost. For the rest, I am not undertaking to explain anything; I know I shall have to depart this life without having understood anything—or very little—about the functioning of my body.

At the first glimmer of dawn, I got up; with sandals on my feet I ran, yes, actually ran, as far as Mustapha and further, feeling no fatigue after my night, but on the contrary, a joyfulness, a kind of lightness of body and soul which did not leave me all day long.

I saw Mohammed again two years later. His face had not changed much. He looked hardly less young; his figure had kept its grace; but the languor of his eyes had gone; I felt something hard, anxious and degraded in them.

"Don't you smoke hashish any longer?" I asked him, certain of his answer.

"No," he said, "I drink absinthe now."

He was still attractive; oh! more attractive than ever; but he was not so much lascivious now as shameless.

Daniel B. was with me. Mohammed led us to the fourth floor of a disreputable hotel; on the ground floor there was a bar at which some sailors were drinking. The bar-keeper asked our names; I wrote *César Bloch* in the book. Daniel ordered beer and lemonade, "for the sake of appearances," he said. It was night. The only light in the room we went into was the candle we had been given to go upstairs with. A waiter brought us the bottles and glasses and put them on the table beside the candle. There were only two chairs. Daniel and I sat down; and Mohammed sat on the table between us. He pulled up the haïk, which he was wearing now instead of his Tunisian costume, and stretched out his bare legs to us.

Then, while I remained sitting beside the half-empty glasses, Daniel seized Mohammed in his arms and carried him to the bed which was at the other end of the room. He laid him on his back on the edge of the bed, cross-wise, and soon I saw nothing but two slim legs dangling on either side of Daniel, who was labouring and panting. Daniel had not even taken his cloak off. Standing there in the dim light beside the bed, with his back turned, his face hidden by the curls of his long black hair, his cloak falling to his feet, he looked gigantic. As he bent over the little body he was covering, he was like a huge vampire feasting on a corpse. I could have screamed with horror.

It is always very difficult to understand the loves of others and their way of practising love. And even those of animals (that *and even* should be kept for those of men). One can envy birds their song, their flight; say with the poet:

> *"Ach! wüsstest du wie's Fischlein ist*
> *So wohlig auf dem Grund!"*

I can even give the dog devouring a bone some sort of bestial assent. But nothing is more disconcerting than the act, so different from species to species, by which each one takes his pleasure. In spite of Monsieur de Gourmont, who tries to make out disturbing analogies in this respect between man and animals, I hold that this analogy exists only in the regions of desire; and that, on the contrary, it is perhaps in what Monsieur de Gourmont calls "the physics of love"* that the differences are most marked, not only between man and animals, but often from one man to another—so much so that, if we were able to see our neighbour's practices, they would often seem as strange to us, as outlandish, and indeed, as monstrous, as the mating of batracians, of insects—and, why go so far afield?—as that of dogs and cats, or as the onanism of fish.

---

* *La Physique de l'Amour* by Remy de Gourmont.

No doubt this is the reason why failures of understanding on this point are so great, and prejudices so ferocious.

For myself, who only take my pleasure face to face, and who am often, like Walt Whitman, satisfied with the most furtive contact, I was horrified both by Daniel's behaviour and by Mohammed's complacent submission to it.

# SUB-SAHARAN AFRICA

# GEOFFREY GORER

## *Africa Dances:*
## *A Book About West African Negroes*

As far as I am concerned negroes are halfway between human beings and statues (in the Greek naturalistic tradition). With Europeans my appreciation of human beauty is falsified by my personal standards of desirability; if a person is not my type I can only approve without appreciating his qualities. With negroes the difference in surface—uniform colour, the absence of contrasting hair, the smooth texture of their skin which affects the eye like worked marble or bronze (my fingers were always surprised to find negro bodies warm and yielding)—makes them appear as much "objects" as "people," and my attitude is consequently far more detached, at any rate with strangers; after I have been talking to people for a little while I forget what colour they are.

# FRANK HARRIS

## *My Life and Loves*

This trek to the Zambesi was the most extraordinary adventure of my life. It altered my whole conception of life. Up to that year, about my fortieth, I had always tried to believe in a Divinity

> . . . that shapes our ends,
> Rough-hew them how we will.*

Now I began to put the comma after "rough" instead of after "ends."

As soon as we got into Bechuanaland to the north-east of the Transvaal, Negro tribes, men and women, came constantly to visit us; they begged bright cloths from us and knives, and naturally my Boers, who knew them intimately, had provided me with all sorts of things with which to barter for furs, etc. I soon found that the younger of the brothers was fond of gratifying his lust with any young Negro girl who took his fancy, and I had to acknowledge that the girls were anything but reserved. Karl was a fine, big man, fully six feet in height and perhaps thirty years of age, and his brother was even bigger and burlier, perhaps ten years older, and altogether more brutal: we always spoke of him as the "Doctor."

One morning, I remember, we were late in starting and some of the

---

* *Hamlet*, Act V, scene 2.

Negro leaders were laughing because Karl was not ready, having been occupied with a Negro girl in his tent. As soon as the "Doctor" learned this, he strode to the tent, and tearing up the fastenings, overthrew it and exposed his brother, half-dressed, who was packing his valise. The young Negro girl who had been helping him started up when the tent fell, and smiling, held out her hands to the "Doctor." Red with rage, he caught her by the left breast and flung her from him. She shrieked and began to cry: Karl expostulated with him; but I was furious.

"I want you to know once for all," I cried, "that I won't have these colored people ill-treated."

"*Bestie!*" he replied.

"They may be beasts, in your opinion," I went on, "but I insist that they shall be treated decently. To kiss a girl first and then maltreat her is shameful! And I won't stand for it!"

Karl nodded agreement with me while the "Doctor" went off muttering and scowling.

It was Karl who gave me at our next stopping place a lesson in Negro morality. A small tribe had come to our camp to beg: he and I got out some colored stuffs and showed them to the women and girls, who went crazy with delight. One of the prettiest of them and best formed, a girl of perhaps fifteen, took up a piece of bright blue. She was, of course, naked, except the little apron that half-covered her nudity. Karl at once threw the cloth about her shoulders: she laughed gleefully and strutted about with it; he went over and kissed her, saying she could have it. At once she threw her arms about him and then, saying something, lifted her apron.

"What does she say?" I asked.

"That she's ready for a man!" said Karl.

"What does she mean?" I asked, and Karl set himself to explain to me a custom which I found was almost universal.

"As soon as half a dozen girls in a tribe reach puberty," Karl said, "they are taken by a couple of old women to the nearest stream. There the old crones, with great ceremony, break the girls' maidenheads and then declare them fit and ready, in a week or so, to give pleasure to men and bear children."

The whole affair seemed astonishing to me: I had always imagined that the maidenhead was a result, or at least an indication, of the proprietary instinct of the male, and if it were thus gradually developed by natural selection, why do away with it in such a coarse way? But Karl assured me that the girls were all delighted to be rid of it and free to devote themselves to the higher uses of maturity. After a month's trekking we were visited one evening by a tribe which possessed a young girl almost completely white. The heads of the tribe assured Karl that she was the product of a white missionary, who fifteen years ago had journeyed far, far to the north across the great river. Some time later I told Stanley the story and wondered whether by a new sort of paper-chase, he had tracked Livingstone by parti-colored offspring across Africa. But Stanley had no sense of humor and seemed to resent the imputation. Still, I must record one fact in regard to this girl: she was extraordinarily proud of her white blood and begged Karl to find her some white man to whom she might give herself and so have done with colored men forever. Curiously enough, though of sufficient age, she had refused to submit to the ministry of the old colored women and therefore still preserved her maidenhead. She wanted white children, she declared, and would never yield herself to a Negro.

It was the Doctor who undertook to content her desire and was gratefully accepted, though I always thought there was more than a little Negro blood in his veins; still, he was at least half-white.

In the course of the next month or so we came upon three similar instances, and in every case the same insensate pride in the mulatto. It grew to be a joke with us that we were following in the missionary's footsteps!

When we were nearing the Zambesi, we spent a whole day trekking through a dense forest, and there towards midday discovered a troop of baboons. The Doctor happened to be a little ahead of us, and almost at once a huge female baboon picked him out and began, with unmistakable gestures, to show him that he had taken her fancy and that she was more than willing to be his love. Naturally the incident amused me highly and I induced the brothers to let the game go on. To cut a long story short, that female kept close to the Doctor to the edge of the forest and beyond it. The grotesque obscenity of the exhibition, the unmistakable passion of the animal, gave me a new understanding of the intimate ties that bind us men to our simian ancestors.

> However we brazen it out
> We men are a little breed.*

---

*From Tennyson's *Maud*, Part I: iv. "However we may brave it out, we men are a little breed."

I never took any part in the nightly orgies that went on between the members of our caravan and the girls of the various tribes that visited us to beg and to barter. I was content with my Kodak to take snapshots of the prettiest girls and the finest young men, and here I made some remarkable discoveries. None of the girls objected to stand for me, and not one hesitated to take off the little apron of hide they usually wore; but underneath the apron there was a small covering, perhaps two fingers broad, which they all objected to removing. They regarded their sex as ugly and would not willingly expose it.

Another curious fact: I soon found that these girls did not recognize themselves in their photos. One of our leaders was a Negro with perfectly white hair. When we showed the girls this Negro and his photoed likeness, they all exclaimed with delight: they could recognize him, but not themselves. I have often noticed that a dog does not recognize his likeness in a glass; perhaps it needs a certain amount of intelligence to know even what we look like.

Some of these young colored girls had very beautiful figures: it is usually thought that their calves are too thin and their breasts too flaccid. Naturally, taking into consideration their early maturity, they soon show these signs of age, but from ten to fifteen they are often perfectly made.

Why didn't they tempt me? I can't say; the half-white girls appealed to me much more; but the pure Negro type left me completely unmoved.

I loved to take their photographs in the most lascivious attitudes, enjoyed draping them in a pretty piece of stuff and thus bringing out their ever-present coquetry; but when they sought to excite me, I would slap their bottoms and turn away. I never could understand the attraction they possessed for most white men. I had known the fact from my varsity days in Lawrence, Kansas, where all my comrades used to hunt regularly in the Negro quarter; but even then I never went with them, not out of any moral scruple, but simply because the black girl, however well made, did not excite in me what Dr. Johnson called his "amorous propensities."

Yet I was told by Karl and the Doctor that the Negro girls were far more passionate than the white ones. "There is no comparison," Karl used to declare: "Negro girls, and boys, too, feel the sex thrill far more intensely than any whites."

It may be true. I have seen Parisian cocottes making heroes of Negro lovers; they have told me time and again just what Karl asserted; but it is not only the vigor of the Negro, but also the size of his sex which causes him to be so esteemed by the French prostitutes. On the other hand, the

Negro girl, too, is far larger than the white and that certainly detracts from the man's pleasure. Besides, the mousey smell is always present, and that was enough to choke my desire. But the want of intelligence is the chief deterrent; for Hindu girls are often very dark and have the mousey odor, yet their brains or higher spiritual understanding make them eminently desirable.

Yet my virtue was destined to suffer one defeat. One evening, a girl we had met, who was almost completely white, was encouraged by Karl to come nude to my bed. I was tossing about asleep in the night when she came and laid down beside me, or rather on me. The heat of her body had excited me before I even awoke, and before I was fully conscious I was enjoying her. I felt no disappointment when I saw her: I have seen Italian girls with darker skins and coarser features; but I cannot say that she gave me any extraordinary thrill. Yet, she did her best and the game of love to her was the best game in the world. She delighted in teaching me all the Swahili terms for the sex and for sensual pleasures. And when I used them she would scream with enjoyment.

This girl was rather intelligent, and so I asked her about sexual perversions. She seemed to think there was nothing in them, that naturally all human beings took what pleasure they could get whenever they could get it. There was no shadow of moral law in the matter. She even told me that most of the colored girls didn't know how to kiss until they were taught and were quite astonished at any extension of kissing.

I would have forgotten all about this girl, had she not begged me to take her with me on my expedition. I could not do this, but some bright cloths and beads soon consoled her for my defection, and one day I saw her making up to the big Doctor, which at once chased away any lingering scruples I may have had.

# André Gide

## *So Be It; or, The Chips Are Down*

In addition to the obligatory escort of our porters, Sultan Reï Bouba, without warning us, had added to them two young pages as mere extras. The fact was unprecedented, but probably justified the great reputation for kindness that earlier travelers' accounts had passed on to us. Nevertheless, that kindness had a quite different basis. Sultan Reï Bouba's benevolence, constantly guided by a superior intelligence, had managed to make of his Sultanate a sort of favored state, an enclave in the midst of a region converted to Islam but still rather primitive. That the considerable moral and social arrangements instituted by the Sultan were always approved by our French authorities, I am in no position to assert (besides, what I saw goes back to 1925, and many things may have changed since). But I can state that felicity and exhilaration could be read on the faces of the citizens of that little country when we went through it. We regretted not being able to tarry there. Having taken leave of the Sultan in the evening, we set out for N'Gaoundéré rather early the next day, and were keenly surprised to notice soon among our porters two youths whose sole function seemed to be to escort us. Let me add at once that they were as handsome as possible, real luxury creatures. Certainly the Sultan had chosen them. Each of them walked along at a little distance, as if belonging to our troop and yet not mingling with it, as if not deigning to mingle with it. Moreover, hardly conversing with each other. Less to burden him than to give him a semblance of justification, we had decided to entrust to the younger one Dindiki's empty cage.* In addition to that, he bore, as his elder did, an almost childish bow slung over his shoulder and, on his back like Cupid, a quiver with several arrows. Both of them wearing a sort of toque on their heads. A leather belt kept the younger one's smock from falling below mid-thigh length. Both of them looked as if they had stepped down from the fresco in the Campo Santo of Pisa, ready to take part in Benozzo Gozzoli's grape harvest. Their gait, especially that of the younger one, had something of the dancer's spring; he was Nijinsky, for the muscle's joy became apparent and we, spectators, took part in it. Surely it was not exclusively for our eyes' pleasure that the Sultan had lent us his two pages. This is what I did not cease repeating to myself for three days. Finally I made up my mind to talk freely to my faithful Adoum. But, before going farther, it is well to insert a parenthesis.

It scarcely seems possible to me that Reï Bouba was informed of my tastes. Had they been different, as Marc's were, would the Sultan have been inclined to take out of his private harem two women to accompany us on our long marches? Allow me to doubt it. And to run the risk of complications of all sorts! These two adolescents didn't commit the Sultan or us to anything. We were free to pay no attention to them, as my companion did. But inasmuch as I saw this as a most gracious attention on the part of the Sultan, it didn't seem to me right to appear to scorn it. The pages themselves appeared to be hurt by our lack of attention, by not being noticed more, for their good spirits decreased from day to day. What? Was this all we thought of them? So that the fourth morning, giving up my resistance and swallowing my shame, I asked Adoum how to go about it, for, after all, I was never alone, and the least thing I did was seen by the whole troop of porters. . . . Adoum found my embarrassment hard to understand. He asserted that every one of the porters would consider it quite natural that some evening I should ask one of the two pages to "come and wield the punkah" under my mosquito net. Let it be quickly added that it is impossible to see through the fabric of a mosquito net. It should also be added that the heat was stifling, so that the desire to have one's sleep fanned by a punkah could seem almost natural. And finally let it be added that what seemed most natural was what the expression "come and wield

---

* *Le Retour du Tchad* (which forms part of *Travels in the Congo*) describes Mala more briefly but similarly. Dindiki was a small lemur that Gide tamed in the Congo and hoped to bring back to the zoo, but unfortunately the creature died before this stage of the journey.

the punkah" signified in reality, so that no one in our group was struck by it. And in order to destroy completely any attempt at dissimulation, Mala (that was the boy's name) began by ridding himself in a hot tub of the sweat and dust of a long march, as I had just done myself. Sweet little Mala! On my deathbed I should like to see again your elfin laugh and your joy.

Little do I care if these words shock some, who will consider them impious. I have promised myself to override that. But I should like to be more sure than I am that, if I should happen to reread them, I shall not be embarrassed by them myself. Is it really around the least spiritual in me that my final thoughts will collect? When it might still be time, perhaps, to offer them to the God awaiting me, as you say, in whom I refuse to believe? In a moment the game will be up, without possible retouching. All will be over, and for all eternity! Why! all *has* been over for some time now, I am tempted to reply, and to disown in advance any recantation brought about by the confusion of the death agony. But I should like to protest also against any excessive limitation one might be tempted to see in this profession of materialism. I do not intend thereby to confine myself to mere carnal pleasure; it invites me to melt into and merge with surrounding nature. This is why my most perfect memories of sensual delight are those enveloped in a landscape which absorbs it and in which I seem to be swallowed up. In the one I have just evoked of those transports with Mala, it is not only the beautiful swooning body of the child I see again, but the whole mysterious and fearful surrounding of the equatorial forest.

# PAUL THEROUX

## *My Other Life*

The mass was sung in Latin, the hymns in Chinyanja, the drumming too was African—filling the gaps of the ritual. The drumming seemed to unnerve Father Touchette again. His mask of sadness grew tighter on his face as the drumming banged louder, echoing against the walls of whitewashed plaster, while incense rose from the thurible, drifting past the glitter of the monstrance. Then the smoky incense curled as thick as drug fumes in the shafts of sunlight that pierced it.

Amina sat in one of the rear pews with her blind granny. I watched Amina closely, the way she followed the priests with her eyes, the passing back and forth, the sudden chants and sung prayers, my spoken responses, the jostling at communion.

In her eyes this must have seemed strange, even frightening, like a ritual of magic, the kind of sorcery that went on in a village to cast a spell, drive out devils, making a person whole again. In a sense this sort of purification was the aim of the mass—the holy sacrifice of the mass, as I had been taught to call it.

Afterwards I put out the candles and gathered the cruets and tidied the sacristy while Father DeVoss whispered to Father Thomas. And I knew exactly what he was saying—practical things, like the mood of Father Touchette and the time of the train to Balaka and Blantyre.

Lunch was a long silence. We sat eating *nsima* and chicken in the heat while Father Touchette paced the verandah. Then Father Thomas led the weakened priest to the Land Rover, and helped him in, taking him by the arm. Father Touchette climbed in slowly, like someone elderly or ill, and without a word he folded his arms, seeing no one, waiting to go. His eyes were sunken and dark, he looked haunted, his mind was elsewhere. I heard someone in the watching crowd of lepers say the word *mutu,* referring to Father Touchette's head—something wrong with it. Talking louder than the others, Amina's blind granny was asking questions: Who is it? Where is he going? Will someone else come to take his place? Is he sick?

With the old blind woman monopolizing the attention of the crowd, I sidled over to Amina and was glad when she did not move away.

"I saw you in church, Amina."

"Yes."

"But you are a Muslim."

"I went because of my granny. To help her. She is a Christian."

"Did you see me watching you?"

"Yes." She sniffed nervously. "I did not know why."

"Because looking at you makes me happy."

She sniffed again, she blinked. What I had said embarrassed her.

"How did you know I was looking at you?"

"Because I was looking at you," Amina said.

This touched me, and though she spoke with her eyes averted, out of shyness, she was bolder than I had expected. And perhaps she was not looking away out of shyness, for there was confusion in the dusty road, as Father Touchette's big trunk, hoisted by dirty ropes was slung into the back of the Land Rover. Already Father DeVoss was gunning the engine and beside him Father Thomas had the grim resignation and grumpiness of a parent who has been inconvenienced by his son's expulsion from school. Father Touchette was in the rear seat, looking defeated, watched by lepers who seemed stimulated, even thrilled by the sight of this ruined mzungu.

Father DeVoss had tried to play it down, but in a place where very little changed from year to year this departure counted as momentous, an event that would be remembered and distorted in the years to come.

*"Alira,"* someone muttered. He is weeping.

It was so odd to see this grown man sitting in the vehicle with his face in his hands, tears running through his fingers. The crowd of lepers and others simply gaped at him—they were skinny, crippled, crooked, barefoot, ragged. So many of them wore large dirty bandages. They watched impassively, with hardly a murmur. It was the lepers' pitiless curiosity that made Father Touchette especially pathetic.

I had always disliked the way Father Touchette carried his breviary around with him, consulting it and seeming to wrestle with its verses. I resented his saying, "I have baptisms," when I needed help carrying bricks. The book seemed like a talisman against his ever having to work. He used it the way the lepers used their mutilation as an excuse. The young priest wore socks with his sandals, which made him look silly. I thought how madness is often a way of dressing.

"He is your friend?" Amina asked.

"No."

"But he is a mzungu."

"I would rather talk to you."

I wanted to tell her that I was glad to see him go. He was a worrier, a baptizer, a converter, a scold. "That's savage," he had said of the drumming almost every night. Perhaps I had alarmed Amina by being forthright, for after the Land Rover had driven off she disappeared as the dust settled over us.

———

The drumming was louder that night, there were shouts and yells, a kind of whooping, like panic. In my fever that same drumming had filled my imagination with vivid images of Amina dancing—her slender body gleaming, her mouth open, her glazed eyes looking drugged.

Desire for me was always the fulfillment of a fantasy—not a surprise or a shock, but something studied in advance, dreamed and premeditated. It was pleasure prepared, the completion of a thought begun in a vision. Desire was familiar and fixed; not something new, but an older, deeper wish, with a history, an embrace that had already shadowed forth in my mind. It was something specific, like a gift I yearned for. And later, when it seemed to be granted—flickering into reality and becoming attainable—I seized it.

I had heard that same drumming many nights before, rattling through the heat to reach me in my bedroom where I lay alone on my cot. It was also the sound the village women made when they pounded corn into flour, thumping a heavy pestle into the mortar. When there was more than one woman pounding, it set up a syncopation in the trees, and a chorus of grunts and thuds.

"No cards tonight," Father DeVoss said. He did not have to explain that this was out of respect for Father Touchette, who hated our card playing. Among other things, the sight of us flipping cards and collecting tricks had driven him crazy. Never mind, we would play tomorrow.

"No cards," Brother Piet exclaimed, taking up his sewing. *"Pepani— palibe sewendo!"* Sorry, no games!

It was as though we were respecting the memory of someone who had just died. And leaving Moyo was like death: life outside it bore no resemblance to life here.

"I hope he gets better," I said.

Guessing what was in my mind, Father DeVoss said, "He won't come back."

There was a great cry from the village and a surge of brightness, as though a mass of dry straw or corn shucks had been dumped in the fire and exploded into flames.

"They never come back," Father DeVoss said.

At just that moment it seemed that the only life in the place was down in the leper village—the drumming like a faulty heart beating; not wood at all, but the racing pulse of the place.

Brother Piet was sewing by the light of the pressure lamp, while Father DeVoss sat near him, with shadows on his face. In any other place they would have been reading, writing a letter, looking at pictures. But this was Moyo, as stark as anything else in the bush. They were like an old married couple.

I said good night and went to my room, where I stood by the window. I was restless, impatient, ready to leap into the darkness. The trees beyond that darkness were lighted by the fire in the village. Because of the flames each branch was distinct and black.

Slipping down the back stairs, I went outside, avoiding the path but following the firelight and the sounds of the drumming.

—

Though there was a thin circle of spectators, almost the whole village was dancing in the clearing, women on one side, men on the other, shuffling and stamping their feet, nodding their heads, raising their arms, calling out. Their heavy tread echoed in me as though they were moving flat-footed through my body.

The men clapped their hands and the women yodeled in a shrill ululation that was both fearful and triumphant—a sort of war whoop. There were no carved masks, but there were painted faces, none more frightening than the man whose face was dusted with white flour. He was a leper and he was wearing a bed sheet and carrying a crucifix. A woman opposite him was also wrapped in a bed sheet. Priest and nun, writhing in a suggestive dance that was riotous sexual mockery or a ritual, or both. The lepers danced on their dead feet that were swollen with bandages, making the sound of clubs. Small boys dressed as dogs or monkeys, naked except for the mangy pelts flapping on their backs, moved on all fours through the chanting, stamping crowd.

Another group, entering from the shadows of the huts, lifted an image on a set of poles. It was a small building like a doll's house and I guessed from its cupola, a crude steeple, that it was meant to be the representation of a church. It rested on the middle of a little platform that was set on poles as though they were carrying a stretcher.

I had missed the preliminaries, I knew. The dance had been going on for an hour or more. I had been listening to it throughout dinner and afterwards, while I had sat in silence with the two priests. The dance had now grown to a pitch of excitement that had bystanders jumping in and joining. It was impossible to tell the dancers from the spectators, there was so much movement, the stamping, the drumming, the clapping, the flapping rags.

The man dressed as the priest and the woman as the nun were at the head of a frenzied procession. Just behind them was the fragile little church building made of sticks and paper. This was either exaggerated respect or elaborate mockery.

I recognized many of the dancers as the people I had come to know since my arrival in Moyo. It was strange to see them so active, in motion. The leper dressed as a priest looked like Johnson from my English class. He carried a book—not a Bible nor a breviary, but the message was clear enough. This was Father Touchette and for their own reasons, because he had just left, they were dramatizing what they knew of him. He performed a baptism on one of the dog boys. He read his book with rolling eyes. He pranced, looking haughty. He rebuffed a flirtation from the nun. And the drumming was both music and hoarse, hectic commentary.

Among all the moving bodies it was easy for me to pick out Amina. She stood to one side, in the shadow of a hut's eaves, the firelight on her face, watching while the rest of the leper village worked themselves into a state of hysteria. And her granny seemed to be made of stone, while just in front of her Amina nodded at the dancers and clapped to the stamping rhythm.

The risen dust floated in the firelight and the moving bodies cast shadows in the trees that were broken and made more frantic by the picked-out branches. Some of the dancers looked tearful, almost tormented, with heavy faces. I saw how the lepers' dance was not many individuals but a mass of people that had one will and one shape, a swelling organism. This trembling creature filled the clearing.

Amina remained apart. If she had been among the dancers I would not have been able to get near her. But because she was next to the hut, watching—nodding to the beat of the drums—I approached her. I touched her arm. All the physicality of the dance seemed to make this touching permissible. Amina did not draw away. That meant a great deal.

"I want to visit you at your hut."

She faced the throng of dancers, the dust, the lighted smoke, the dog children, the dirty feet, the drummers beating on logs and skins, the swaying image of the church. She was too demure to speak the word. Her silence meant yes, all right.

"But what will your granny say when she sees me?"

"She will not see you," Amina said. "She is blind."

Now there was so much noise that I could not hear Amina clearly. I had been hearing those drums since the night of my arrival, when I had lain awake in my bare, whitewashed room, wondering why I had come here and what would happen to me. The drums had been part of my fever, they had been a feature of our card games, always pulsing in the background. I was certain that they had driven Father Touchette out of his mind.

That was understandable. The drums of Moyo had penetrated me too, but they had energized me. It was a physical sensation, like a drug or a drink. It was brainless, it whipped into my blood, it made me dumb and incoherent. It removed any desire in me to write—poetry or anything else.

I was trying to speak to her. What next? I wondered. But I could tell from Amina's expression that it was no use. She could not hear me either. Perhaps that was for the best. It was sensible here to be silent, no more than shadows.

Without a word, but touching her grandmother's hand, as though giving a command, Amina led the way, granny right behind her, with her leprous hand gripping Amina's shoulder. I followed, and I was glad for all these shadows, for the crowd and the confusion and the fire and the drums. How could they notice me? But even if they could, I thought, they were so dazed and heated by the dance that I did not matter.

Amina's hut—more likely her granny's—was in the outer circle of older huts, the ones nearest to the bush that surrounded Moyo. It had its own tree—I could just make out its shape in the rising firelight, and it was larger than the other stunted trees. The smell of the old trampled corn shucks in the nearby garden was an odor that was linked in my mind with snakes and scorpions and biting spiders, which lurked in the warm, broken rubbish of the shucks.

Squinting down so that I would not stumble I banged my head against a heavy pole that served as a rafter for the thatched roof.

"What is that noise?" the old woman said, and reached for me. I guessed that was what she said: the meaning was clear enough from her gesture.

*"Fisi,"* Amina said. Hyena.

The old woman had muttered in a dialect that was probably Yao. It was a bush language associated with Muslims and Mozambique that I did not understand. But I could translate Amina's replies. Perhaps she was speaking Chinyanja for my benefit—but it was not odd for the Africans at the leprosarium to converse in several languages. The granny was still talking.

"Because I am very tired," Amina said in Chinyanja. She lit a candle and placed it in a large tin can, which had holes punched in it.

To the old woman's croak, Amina said, "I want to keep the hyenas away."

Gabbling again, her granny seemed to be praying. She was at the far end of what was by Moyo standards a spacious hut, rectangular, a large single room, with two mats on the floor. She lowered herself to the distant mat and faced in our direction. She was at home in the darkness.

Except for the two mats, the exposed floor was hard, packed dirt, and the walls were mud, and dust trickled from the straws in the thatch bundles of the roof. The room stank of dirt and termites, and on the looser and untrodden part of the floor there were worm casts. The only furniture were cardboard cartons and lanterns and among this assortment a sturdy wooden crate shoved against the wall had the look of an heirloom.

I held my breath while the old woman gazed with white eyes, and then murmured.

"I am moving my mat," Amina replied. She motioned me to her mat and I sat down next to her, carefully pulling my legs under me.

Amina's face in profile was as smooth and simple as a carving with the candlelight behind it. She had long lashes and her lovely mouth looked solemn in silhouette. She sat very straight, her neck upright and seeming so fragile that I could not help reaching and touching it. She hardly moved, not even when I touched her, and when I stroked her cheek she became motionless. That was not fear or even submission, it was pleasure. I passed my fingers across her lips and she opened her mouth and bit them with her pretty teeth. She was swift, and I could feel her hunger in the sharpness of her bite.

The old woman grunted several words, her face on us, and I watched her closely as I slipped my hand under Amina's cloth, feeling for her breasts.

The dance had grown louder. Was that what the old woman was saying? Now I could recognize some of the dancers' chanting.

*"Sursum corda! Habemus ad Dominum!"*

Cupping Amina's breast, loving its warmth and its contours, I moved nearer, and she sighed and moved towards me to make it easier for me. This thrilled me.

*"Agnus Dei, qui tollis peccata mundi!"*

I kissed her and although I could smell the dirt floor, the ants, the sweat, the mice, the dust sifting out of the thatch, there was a sweetness on her lips that was like syrup, with the tang of ripe fruit, and her skin had the heavy sensuality of freshly turned earth. She received my kiss and moved nearer still, shifting to face me, the candlelight flickering in her eyes.

Had we made any noise? The old woman uttered another remark.

"It is the *zinyao*," Amina said.

The old woman grumbled as I leaned over and whispered to Amina, "Let's go outside."

She shook her head: no.

I clutched her as though questioning.

"The people will see us," she whispered, as she stared at the blind old woman.

Then we lay on the mat, side by side, while I went on stroking her breasts and breathing in shallow gasps, afraid that I might be heard. The old woman's face was fixed on us. She was still muttering, but nothing she said was clearly audible. I wanted her to sleep, yet she sat upright, her eyes unblinking.

The drumming was so loud it made the thatch bundles tremble in the roof. The voices of the dancers cried out, *"Christe, eleison! Kyrie, eleison!"* and other snatches of the mass responses, as though they were incantations.

Amina's breasts were small, her body was hard and thin. It made me think of the saplings at Moyo, their long, narrow branches and small leaves. And my fingers found parts of her body that felt like the healed scars of a young tree. Amina was so small I could caress her easily with one hand. And she was so smooth.

I put my lips against her ear and said, "When I saw you at the English class I wanted to touch you."

My face was so near to hers I could feel the change in her expression on her face. She was smiling, I knew. But she did not reply.

"So why did you come to the class?"

"To see you," she said.

"Did you want to touch me?"

She hesitated, and then she sniffed. It was her shy way of saying yes, a kind of modesty.

"Tell me." I moved so that her mouth was at my ear.

"I wanted to play with you," she said at last. The word for playing was also the word for dancing and foolery.

I stroked her arm and when my fingers touched the leprous patch, the disc of dead skin, I was not alarmed. I had been here long enough to know there was no danger to me. I slipped my hand into hers and guided it against my body, so that she would touch me. I did not have to go any further. She knew what to do, without my suggestion, and her knowledge excited me, because it showed she was a woman not a girl. Then she took possession of my whole body with the nimble fingers of her small hands. Leaning towards the little lamp she pursed her lips as though kissing the candleflame.

Just then the old woman grunted again.

"I am putting out the light," Amina said, and her one sigh against the flame killed it and brought darkness down on us.

Seconds later, when my sight returned, there was moonlight making angular shadows in the room. There was also the glow from the *zinyao* dance shining on us. It was as though this light made us want to be smaller, and so we embraced, and touched and kissed, and moved our bodies closer. Yet even in this wonderful hug I could sense the other person in the room, the restless presence of the blind woman.

She spoke again, sounding irritable.

Amina, with a grip on my hand, said, *"Ndiri ndi mphere kwabasi."* I have a serious itch. Kwabasi. Brother Piet had taught me that word. It was one of the sexiest things I had ever heard, and as she said it she moved my hand between her legs and helped me, working my fingers on what felt like the lovely pulp of a ripe fruit.

Amina was smiling at me as I touched her. The moonglow lighted her and her face became even more beautiful, animated with desire. Her mouth was open in silent rapture as the old woman spoke a whole rattling sentence as though uttering a proverb.

Amina put her mouth against my ear again and spoke breathlessly. "She says, 'Then scratch it.'"

She slipped her leg over me and clumsily steadied herself. I propped myself up on my elbows. And she opened her cloth as I fumbled with my shorts. Then she was on top of me, straddling me.

The old woman had started moaning to the drumming and the yelling outside, while Amina shut her eyes and strained not to make a sound, as she rocked back and forth.

*"Sursum corda!"*

*"Deus meus!"*

Amina hitched herself forward and moved her hands to my face and held me as she drove her body against me, riding me. I could still see the old woman at the far end of the room, the light and shadow broken over her body like patches of liquid. It was like being in the presence of an old African idol, a great impassive lump that might spring to life at any moment and become a demon.

Yet I had no fear. I took Amina by her hips and jammed her against me and she threw her head back as though convulsed. And when she bowed down and clutched me again I thought I heard her say, "I am not crying." I could not hear her cry, yet her tears were running down my face, and I tasted them to make sure.

She was pressed so hard against me it was as though we were not two people anymore, but were so penetrated that we were like one wild tearful creature. She tore at her breasts and then clamped her mouth over the fingers of one hand and wept. I was intent on one drumming rhythm. If sex was knowledge, and I believed it was, I was on the verge of knowing everything.

It was heat and noise and skin and drums and fire and smoke, and the feeling of silk in every opening of her body. It was also the growl of the crowd, and it was our old blind witness. I struggled with Amina and held her tight gorging on her like a cannibal. Soon my body was sobbing, caught in a desperate panic of possession that made me reckless. And then we too were blind.

———

After this singular act of love we turned into two people and I knew I had to get out of her hut. It was not easy for me to leave, for as soon as I got up, the old woman mumbled, saying to Amina, "Don't go," or something like it, because she too stood up and began shambling to the door.

I could not go out alone or the old woman would hear. The only way I could avoid detection and not rouse her suspicions was to stay so close to Amina, so that we would sound like one person.

In all the clatter of the drumming there was another snorting noise.

*"Fisi,"* the old woman said.

"Yes. A hyena," Amina said, as a big, bristling and humpbacked dog blundered out of the darkness next to the hut.

That was how I left, startling the slavering creature and covered by its noise. We were the noise, the hyena and me. The thing was alert but did not seem afraid. It was mangy and misshapen, and it snarled at me, not angry but annoyed, as though I was the intruder.

# ISAK DINESEN

## Out of Africa

But when we had driven a further two miles there was no more road. The tools of the road-labourers lay here; on the other side of them was the wide stony land, just grey in the dawn, all unbroken by any touch of man. We looked at the tools and at the country, we would have to leave Denys's friend to take his chance with the rifle. Afterwards, when he came back, he told us that he had never had an opportunity to use it. So we turned back, and as we turned we got our faces to the Eastern sky, reddening over the plains and the hills. We drove towards it and talked all the time of the lioness.

The Giraffe came within view, and by this time we could see him clearly and distinguish,—where the light fell on to his side,—the darker square spots on his skin. And as we came near to him we saw that there was a lion standing on him. In approaching we were a little lower than the carcass; the lion stood straight up over it, dark, and behind him the sky was now all aflame. *Lion Passant Or.* A bit of his mane was lifted by the wind. I rose up in the car, so strong was the impression that he made, and Denys at that said: "You shoot this time." I was never keen to shoot with his rifle, which was too long and heavy for me, and gave me a bad shock; still here the shot was a declaration of love, should the rifle not then be of the biggest caliber? As I shot it seemed to me that the lion jumped straight up in the air, and came down with his legs gathered under him. I stood, panting, in the grass, aglow with the plenipotence that a shot gives you, because you take effect at a distance. I walked round the carcass of the Giraffe. There it was,—the fifth act of a classic tragedy. They were all dead now. The Giraffe was looking terribly big, austere, with his four stiff legs and long stiff neck, his belly torn open by the lions. The lioness, lying on her back, had a great haughty snarl on her face, she was the *femme fatale* of the tragedy. The lion was lying not far from her, and how was it that he had learned nothing by her fate? His head was laid on his two front paws, his mighty mane covered him as a royal mantle, he too was resting in a big pool, and by now the morning air was so light that it showed scarlet.

Denys and Kanuthia pulled up their sleeves and while the sun rose they skinned the lions. When they took a rest we had a bottle of claret, and raisins and almonds, from the car; I had brought them with us to eat on the road, because it was New Year's Day. We sat on the short grass and ate and drank. The dead lions, close by, looked magnificent in their nakedness, there was not a particle of superfluous fat on them, each muscle was a bold controlled curve, they needed no cloak, they were, all through, what they ought to be.

*　*　*

Denys and I had another dramatic adventure with lions. It happened, in reality, before the other, in the early days of our friendship.

One morning, during the spring-rains, Mr. Nichols, a South African, who was then my Manager, came to my house all aflame, to tell me, that in the night two lions had been to the farm and had killed two of our oxen. They had broken through the fence of the oxen's fold, and they had dragged the dead oxen into the coffee plantation; one of them they had eaten up there, but the other was lying amongst the coffee-trees. Would I now write him a letter to go and get strychnine in Nairobi? He would have it laid out in the carcass at once, for he thought that the lions would be sure to come back in the night.

I thought it over; it went against me to lay out strychnine for lions, and I told him that I could not see my way to do it. At that his excitement changed over into exasperation. The lions, he said, if they were left in peace over this crime, would come back another time. The bullocks they had killed were our best working bullocks, and we could not afford to lose any more. The stable of my ponies, he reminded me, was not far from the oxen's enclosure, had I thought of that? I explained that I did not mean to keep the lions on the farm, only I thought that they should be shot and not poisoned.

"And who is going to shoot them?" asked Nichols. "I am no coward, but I am a married man and I have no wish to risk my life unnecessarily." It was true that he was no coward, he was a plucky little man. "There would be no sense in it," he said. No, I said, I did not mean to make him shoot the lions. But Mr. Finch-Hatton had arrived the night before and was in the house, he and I would go. "Oh, that is O.K." said Nichols.

I then went in to find Denys. "Come now," I said to him, "and let us go and risk our lives unnecessarily. For if they have got any value at all it is this that they have got none. *Frei lebt wer sterben kann.*"

We went down and found the dead bullock in the coffee plantation, as Nichols had told me; it had hardly been touched by the lions. Their spoor was deep and clear in the soft ground, two big lions had been here in the night. It was easy to follow through the plantation and up to the wood round Belknap's house, but by the time that we came there it had rained so heavily that it was difficult to see anything, and in the grass and the bush at the edge of the wood we lost the track.

"What do you think, Denys," I asked him, "will they come back to-night?"

Denys had great experience with lions. He said that they would come back early in the night to finish the meat, and that we ought to give them time to settle down on it, and go down to the field ourselves at nine o'-clock. We would have to use an electric torch from his Safari outfit, to shoot by, and he gave me the choice of the rôles, but I would rather let him shoot and myself hold the torch for him.

In order that we might find our way up to the dead ox in the dark, we cut up strips of paper and fastened them on the rows of coffee-trees between which we meant to walk, marking our way in the manner of Hanzl and Gretl with their little white stones. It would take us straight to the kill, and at the end of it, twenty yards from the carcass, we tied a larger piece of paper to the tree, for here we would stop, sweep the light on and shoot. Late in the afternoon, when we took out the torch to try it, we found that the batteries of it had been running down and that the light it gave was only faint. There was no time to go in to Nairobi with it now, so that we should have to make the best of it as it was.

It was the day before Denys's birthday, and while we dined, he was in a melancholic mood, reflecting that he had not had enough out of life till now. But something, I consoled him, might still happen to him before his birthday morning. I told Juma to get out a bottle of wine to be ready for us when we should come back. I kept on thinking of the lions, where would they be now, at this moment? Were they crossing the river, slowly, silently, the one in front of the other, the gentle cold flow of the river turning round their chests and flanks?

At nine o'clock we went out.

It rained a little, but there was a moon; from time to time she put out her dim white face high up in the sky, behind layers and layers of thin clouds, and was then dimly mirrored in the white-flowering coffee-field. We passed the school at a distance; it was all lighted up.

At this sight a great wave of triumph and of pride in my people swept through me. I thought of King Solomon, who says: "The slothful man saith, There is a lion in the way; a lion is in the streets." Here were two lions just outside their door, but my school-children were not slothful and had not let the lions keep them from school.

We found our marked two rows of coffee-trees, paused a moment, and proceeded up between them, one in front of the other. We had moccasins on, and walked silently. I began to shake and tremble with excitement, I dared not come too near to Denys for fear that he might feel it and send me back, but I dared not keep too far away from him either, for he might need my torchlight any moment.

The lions, we found afterwards, had been on the kill. When they heard us, or smelt us, they had walked off it a little way into the coffee-field to let us pass. Probably because they thought that we were passing too slowly, the one of them gave a very low hoarse growl, in front and to the right of us. It was so low that we were not even sure that we had heard it, Denys stopped a second; without turning he asked me: "Did you hear?" "Yes," I said.

We walked a little again and the deep growling was repeated, this time straight to the right. "Put on the light," Denys said. It was not altogether an easy job, for he was much taller than I, and I had to get the light over his shoulder on to his rifle and further on. As I lighted the torch the whole world changed into a brilliantly lighted stage, the wet leaves of the coffee-trees shone, the clods of the ground showed up quite clearly.

First the circle of light struck a little wide-eyed jackal, like a small fox; I moved it on, and there was the lion. He stood facing us straight, and he looked very light, with all the black African night behind him. When the shot fell, close to me, I was unprepared for it, even without comprehension of what it meant, as if it had been thunder, as if I had been myself shifted into the place of the lion. He went down like a stone. "Move on, move on," Denys cried to me. I turned the torch further on, but my hand shook so badly that the circle of light, which held all the world, and which I commanded, danced a dance. I heard Denys laugh beside me in the dark.—"The torch-work on the second lion," he said to me later, "was a little shaky."—But in the centre of the dance was the second lion, going away from us and half hidden by a coffee-tree. As the light reached him he turned his head and Denys shot. He fell out of the circle, but got up and into it again, he swung round towards us, and just as the second shot fell, he gave one long irascible groan.

Africa, in a second, grew endlessly big, and Denys and I, standing upon it, infinitely small. Outside our torchlight there was nothing but darkness, in the darkness in two directions there were lions, and from the sky rain. But when the deep roar died out, there was no movement anywhere, and the lion lay still, his head turned away on to his side, as in a gesture of disgust. There were two big dead animals in the coffee-field, and the silence of night all around.

We walked up to the lions and paced out the distance. From where we had stood the first lion was thirty yards away and the other twenty-five. They were both full-grown, young, strong, fat lions. The two close friends, out in the hills or on the plains, yesterday had taken the same great adventure into their heads, and in it they had died together.

By now all the school-children were coming out of the school, pouring down the road to stop in sight of us and there to cry out in a low soft voice: "Msabu. Are you there? Are you there? Msabu, Msabu."

I sat on a lion and cried back to them: "Yes I am."

Then they went on, louder and more boldly: "Has Bedâr shot the lions? Both two?" When they found that it was so, they were at once all over the place, like a swarm of small spring-hares of the night, jumping up and down. They, then and there, made a song upon the event; it ran as follows: "Three shots. Two lions. Three shots. Two lions." They embroidered and embellished it as they sang it, one clear voice falling in after the other: "Three good shots, two big strong bad kali lions." And then they all joined into an intoxicated refrain: "A.B.C.D.,"—because they came straight from the school, and had their heads filled with wisdom.

In a short time a great number of people came to the spot, the labourers from the mill, the squatters of the near manyattas, and my houseboys, carrying hurricane-lamps. They stood round the lions and talked about them, then Kanuthia and the Sice, who had brought knives, set to skin them. It was the skin of one of these lions that, later, I gave to the Indian High Priest. Pooran Singh himself appeared on the stage, in a negligée which made him look unbelievably slight, his melliferous Indian smile shone in the midst of his thick black beard, he stuttered with delight when he spoke. He was anxious to procure for himself the fat of the lions, that with his people is held in high esteem as a medicine,—from the pantomime by which he expressed himself to me, I believe against rheumatism and impotence. With all this the coffee-field became very lively, the rain stopped, the moon shone down on them all.

We went back to the house and Juma brought and opened our bottle. We were too wet, and too dirty with mud and blood to sit down to it, but stood up before a flaming fire in the dining room and drank our live, singing wine up quickly. We did not speak one word. In our hunt we had been a unity and we had nothing to say to one another.

# Mark Hudson

## *Our Grandmothers' Drums:*
## *A Portrait of Rural African Life and Culture*

In the middle of the afternoon, the Vice-President, Bakary Darbo, our local MP, came to the village to present the members of the committee who would be promoting the PPP in the forthcoming elections. The meeting was held under the mango trees outside the Community Centre. The elders of the village sat around the Vice-President and his party on wooden armchairs, or on the benches from the Supplement Centre, while in the middle sat the griots who would take it in turns to relay the words of the various speakers—bellowing over the heads of the assembled masses in ringing magisterial tones. It was an ancient tradition, designed equally to enhance the dignity of the great and to give voice to the shy and inarticulate.

There was no other amplification and this, combined with the heat of the afternoon sun and the gentle canopy of leaves overhead, gave the occasion a less formal atmosphere than other political meetings I had attended.

The women stood around the meeting place in a great circle, and from where I sat I could see every woman of the village with whom I'd ever had any dealings—some with faces strained in concentration at the words that were being said, others seemingly blank and indifferent. Again and again I found myself staring into the impassive eyes of the young woman in the bright red simiso. She had a small child tied on her back. Her face was round and very black. That morning I had met Sullu in the compound. He had told me that he would come with "the stranger" in the early evening. I decided that when all was said and done it was an intelligent face.

At six precisely, Sullu entered the living-room and sat down beside me. "She's coming," he said.

I had felt no apprehension about this event, as I couldn't believe that anything would actually happen; I was merely intrigued by the improbability of it all. But now events were upon me, and the intentness, the blunt purposefulness of Sullu's manner made me feel nervous.

What exactly was going to happen?

"After the talk I will go," he said, looking out over his shoulder towards the compound gates. "I only come the first time. The second, the third time and the fourth time I will not come." He started suddenly. "No one must come here," he said. "It doesn't matter about the tubabs, but no black must see her," he said.

"No one will come," I said.

Then she arrived, walking slowly along the frieze of mosquito-netted windows. She looked smaller and more vulnerable in a white petticoat.

"Mark," she said in greeting, slipping off her rubber flip-flop sandals as she entered.

"Come on," said Sullu, and led us into the office.

It was now evening, but a thick amber light still penetrated the curtains, filling the rather musty air of the room.

"Lock the door," said Sullu.

"It doesn't lock," I said.

We sat down on the office chairs. Behind us hung a curtain which obscured the two beds used by visitors.

Sullu began to talk, in even, measured tones, which helped to mask the extreme urgency, indeed the danger of the situation. Always using her first name, he spoke respectfully but authoritatively, like a grown-up brother advising a recalcitrant younger sister with whom he none the less wishes to remain on good terms. I could understand most of what he said, but my attention was so absorbed by the appearance of the woman that I scarcely heard it.

She sat on the edge of her seat, her hands folded on her lap, her feet tucked neatly beneath the chair. She lowered her head, her rather big eyes raised, expressionless, towards the door. She seemed remote inside her extreme blackness, as though she had withdrawn herself from the events that were taking place around her. Her hair, carefully plaited beneath the white tiko, the three tiny scars on each cheek, seemed marks of her differentness, her unapproachability. I suddenly saw her, not as an individual person, but as a "Mandinka woman"—the sort of tribal, primitive person one sees on a wildlife documentary—a fragile, exotic presence. It would be shameful to exploit such a person.

"Pass through," Sullu was saying, nodding towards the curtain.

The woman sat on the edge of her chair exactly as before, saying nothing, signalling nothing.

"She doesn't want to go," I said.

"She wants to," he said. "Pass through there. Go on."

I could only interpret the blankness of the woman as great unhappiness—though she had of course agreed to come. Then it occurred to me that perhaps Sullu had some hold over her that he had used to persuade her to come here.

"Let her go," I said. "She doesn't want to come."

"She wants to," he hissed.

"This man is an elder," he said to her in Mandinka. "Go there. You must not disappoint him."

There was a long pause. Then, without altering her expression, she got slowly to her feet and walked round to the other side of the curtain. I followed her.

She sat down on the end of my bed, staring straight ahead, a faint smile on her lips. I sat down beside her, and kissed her on the shoulder. Then I put my arm round her and kissed her mouth. Her lips did not yield. I prised my tongue effortfully between them, and felt the touch of something hard and slithery. She pulled her face away from me.

"You're sucking black mints," I said.

"Yes," she said.

Slowly and carefully I pushed against her shoulder. This was the action of seduction, the nominal forcing of the woman. She lay back at the touch, and then slid herself upwards so that she was lying fully on the bed. Then she pulled the folds of her faneau apart and lay there, with her arms by her sides, like a patient on an operating table, staring at the right-hand corner of the ceiling, a slight smile on her face. Between the silky blackness of her thighs, I could see the triangle of pubic hair, the jono . . .

I raised myself above her, and began mechanically unfastening my trousers. I smiled broadly at her in an attempt to introduce some sense of intimacy between us. She looked back uncomprehendingly. Her own slight smile vanished.

All the time, Sullu was sitting only a few feet away on the other side of the curtain.

I could have just entered her without ceremony, without even thinking about her feelings, as I knew I was meant to. But it would have seemed a callous, almost brutal act—for I could see no evidence from her behaviour that she even wanted to be there. I felt sure that she must have been forced in some way.

I hung over her, wondering what I should do next.

"Is this good?" I asked at length.

"It is not good," she said dryly.

"Why?"

"The sun is going down."

She slid past me, and went back around the curtain. I thought she must have been leaving, but then I heard her telling Sullu to leave the room. She came back and lay down on the bed, exactly as before.

By now I was completely confused. I just sat on the bed beside her for a few moments.

"Go," I said.

She got to her feet, and went to the door. Sullu came back into the room.

"She said you didn't do anything."

"She didn't want to."

"She wanted it."

I took out a ten-dalasis note and handed it to the woman. I felt she should have something for risking herself in this way, but she waved it away. I was astonished. That would have been a lot of money to her. She looked away, close to tears.

—

Sullu sat down on the sofa with a sigh when she had gone.

"He-e-eh, Mark," he said, shaking his head sadly. "You had the chance."

"I thought she didn't want to do it."

"What did you do?" he asked, curiously. "Did you do this?" He mimed the gestures of kissing and embracing.

"Yes."

He clicked his tongue. "They don't know that." He pointed to his groin. "They only know this."

—

I was in a state of utter misery as I walked along the red laterite road towards Karafa Kunda with Sharon. I'd told her everything that had happened. I had to tell someone. The burning of the bush had already begun, and the land at the side of the road was covered in indigo ash. But the flames had moved through the undergrowth with such speed that they hadn't had time to burn everything, and the leaves still hung brown and frazzled from the blackened branches. An orange moon hung low in the grey evening sky.

What a place! And what a landscape! It seemed to me as I reflected on the events of an hour before that the culture of the people was as harsh and as arid as the physical world in which they lived . . . Was that it? It somehow seemed so cruel, so lacking in human feeling . . . that a woman like her should know nothing else.

I had been told time and again that that was the way they did things, and I had not believed them. I had thought that when it happened to me it would be different. It hadn't been.

"Just forget it," said Sharon. "You can sort yourself out when you get back to England."

But I wasn't thinking about England. What distressed me most of all was the thought that I had disappointed the woman. She had gone there for me, and I had failed to appreciate the gesture. Well, if that was the way they did things, that was the way it would have to be.

—

I passed her in the compound two days later, and she greeted me with no trace of acrimony—simply speaking my name in the same toneless manner as before.

Then, two days after that, as Jojo and I were finishing work for the day, I caught sight of her sauntering slowly past the office window, a calabash balanced on her head. Where could she be going? I wondered. She was heading in the direction of Susan Lawrence's house, where Sullu was working.

How many hundreds of times had I seen Sullu at work in the compound, perched on his ladder by one of the houses or standing intent over his workbench, as through the seasons he attempted to keep the woodwork in a good state of repair. His was a presence that invited no questions—he was so much a part of the background that he had become almost invisible. And the women coming and going in the compound, always on some errand or other—bringing or taking this or that to the houses of the Europeans or to the Quarters—I had grown so used to seeing them that I no longer questioned their presence: they too had become part of the texture of the place. Now suddenly I saw in every passing figure a clandestine possibility. Any one of these people might be on their way to some secret assignation. It was extraordinary to think of the intrigues Sullu might have been arranging from his vantage point in the compound, of all the messages that were being exchanged as men and women passed each other only momentarily in the streets.

I was suddenly aware of a whole new dimension of life in the village—an under-layer: the secret world—and I saw how easily much of the real life of the place had passed me by, even while I was standing in the middle of it. One could have lived in that compound for years on end, one could have spent hours in the fields and even in the houses of the village itself, and still have had very little idea of what was going on around one. The scandals and the disasters of the village came and went, and unless they were medical in origin, they didn't impinge on the life of the camp at all. The sociability and the apparent informality of the Africans made it easy to live among them. The sense of goodwill between the village and the camp was entirely genuine, but only a certain amount was given out at the superficial level of courtesy. The word ku'lo—secret—was after all one of the most frequently used in their language, and unless one were part of their society, one would never know.

Those first months when I had sat each night at the Quarters, people coming and going all around me, communicating not only in languages that I could not understand but, unbeknownst to me, through the use of secret signs. It was hardly surprising that I felt not only not part of what was happening around me, but that I sometimes felt as though I were not even a solid part of the physical environment in which I sat.

———

One night, about a week later, I went to the village to look for Sullu. It was very dark. I could just make out the dense masses of the houses and the compound fences along the sides of the street in which Sullu lived. An even thicker area of darkness announced the overhanging eaves of his thatched house. A small figure was sitting in front of it, utterly motionless in an upright chair.

"Mark." It was Sullu. "Come inside."

The air was thick and hot inside the house. Sullu lit a lamp, which sent a feeble glow up into the thatched rafters. He sat back in an armchair with an air of exhausted satisfaction. We chatted for some time about nothing in particular, then I asked him if he would ask "my person" to come to my house the following day.

"In the evening?" he asked.

"In the early afternoon. About half-past two."

"She will come."

I was once again doubtful.

"Why does she want to do this?" I asked slowly.

"She likes it."

"What?"

"You."

The house had two doors—one onto the street, the other onto the yard which led through to the house of the women. His wife was breast feeding, so he had no sexual contact with her at the present time. If he was expecting company he would simply lock the back door and wait for a gentle knock at the front.

"I had someone here just now—immediately before you arrived."

"Who?"

"My girlfriend . . ." A smile of satisfaction spread over his face. "Munya!"

———

It was early afternoon; the hottest time of the day. The whole world had retreated from the harsh white glare of the sun. I sat on the Habitat sofa, peering out through the mosquito netting at the deserted compound forecourt. The watchman was hidden inside his pillbox, and only one figure sat on the bench beside it, slumped as though in sleep.

Then I saw her walking demurely out of the white heat of the afternoon. She was dressed largely in white—to the Christians the colour of purity, to the Muslims the colour of peace. My heart plunged into my stomach.

As she stepped lightly between the white walls that flanked the compound gates, I saw her bristle slightly as though, like a spy passing through an alien checkpoint, she expected a gun to be levelled at her head at any moment. But it was the attitude only of a split-second, unnoticeable to a casual observer. And then she had passed through, and walked on, inexorably, towards my house.

"I'm going to be sick," I thought.

———

I was so happy that evening. As I strode out along the old Karafa Kunda road towards the rice field of Sukoto, I sang at the top of my voice in Mandinka. I hope no one could hear me.

At the rice field, I found an old woman digging up some bulbous, crimson roots. She had a whole sackful of them. Here and there the women had burnt the ground in preparation for the coming season. The place looked like Regent's Park after some dreadful catastrophe.

In the middle distance, over towards the salt flats, I saw a great group of figures moving silently through the undergrowth. It was difficult at that distance to pick out the details of their features, but they seemed to walk almost upright. There must have been nearly a hundred of them, the biggest maybe two-thirds the size of a man. They went first, then the females, their young clinging to their chests. One of the largest of the males leapt onto a hanging branch, as the females passed, and bounced fiercely up and down, sending a hissing, rushing sound across the rice field.

"Baboons," said the old woman. "Go there. They will not hurt you."

I didn't think I would.

# Mirella Ricciardi

## *African Saga*

Every day at noon when the light was too strong for pictures, the tide was low, and the coral reef lay only inches below the surface of the water, I would spend long hours lying in the sun or bathing in the warm sea. One day I noticed two black specks in the distance standing out against the pale midday sky. They grew larger as they approached, until two men dressed only in diminutive striped *kikois* knotted around their hips stopped a few feet from me. Their tattered straw hats pulled low over their eyes, and with a worn coconut basket at the end of a stick hung over the shoulder of one of them. I greeted then in Kiswahili and asked them what they had in their basket. They squatted on their heels beside me.

"Shells," they said. "Do you want some?" and laid them around me.

"Where do you come from?"

"From the village over there," one of them said, and looked up at me from beneath his hat. I saw the most beautiful black face I had ever set eyes upon.

"What is your name?" I asked him.

"Shaibu," he answered. "What is yours?"

He invited me to tea at his house that evening to meet his family.

The coastal people of Kenya are a mixture of Arab and Bantu, and are not renowned for their height or beauty, but Shaibu was an exception. He was long and sinewy, and when he turned his head he arched his neck in a way which made him seem aloof and inaccessible. The skin of his face was smooth and silky and light brown. It rippled in the sunlight—I wanted to touch it. His long fine straight nose, delicate nostrils and soft, slightly slanted brown eyes were not typical of the tribe.

I spent six weeks at the coast and saw Shaibu every day. I went fishing and diving with him, and later sailed with him and his brothers in their dhow to the Arab town of Lamu and to the Bajun Islands.

*   *   *

When Shaibu crossed my life he was sixteen years younger than I. I was a colonial, deeply impregnated with colonial taboos. He was a Muslim whose code of religion and ethics was as refined as my own, if not more so.

One day I caught myself looking at him not as a black man but simply as a man. Something was happening to us, something that had never happened before and neither of us dared to admit this as we played and laughed and hid behind the false pretence of casual camaraderie. The pretence worked as long as we remained each on our own terrain, but when I left for the Bajun Islands with Shaibu and his three brothers on their dhow, I inadvertently trespassed onto his territory. Before leaving I spoke to an Italian friend of mine about the way I was beginning to feel for Shaibu.

"Be careful," he warned me. "You will upset the natural ecology of his life, while you yourself have nothing to lose."

The journey to Kisingitini lasted two and a half days. My new African friends treated me with respectful courtesy and Shaibu was full of tender attention. Each night he unrolled my mattress for me and built a shelter above my head with *kikois* knotted to the ropes. It seemed important to him that I should be comfortable and in need of nothing. His brothers slept some distance from me, but Shaibu curled up on a straw mat at my feet. We never touched, and kept our feelings secret.

A few days after we had settled on the island, I went to sea with Shaibu and his brothers in a canoe. When we were out of sight of land we were caught in heavy rain. The sky became dark and the wind was cold, so we dived into the warm tropical waters with our goggles and flippers.

The current was very strong and I drifted downstream. When Shaibu noticed how far from him I was he swam after me, put out a long, sinewy arm and grabbed hold of my wrist, pulling me to him. He slipped his arm around my waist, and pushed me gently under water beneath him. I looked up at him through my goggles and saw him hovering a few feet above, stretched out dark and powerful in a blaze of bright bubbles. He smiled down at me and I surfaced on the other side of him. With this gesture he had inadvertently taken the first step. He was the man, he took the decisions, and the wall that separated us began to crumble. Together we swam back to the boat.

That night in my tent beneath the palms we talked for the first time about the relationship between a man and a woman of different colours. I was very nervous but Shaibu remained calm. The glow from the hurricane lamp played on his face and naked chest and threw our shadows onto the canvas. We sat on the floor and listened to the sea. A pink crab scuttled from under the tarpaulin trailing white sand grains behind it. The jasmine blooms the women in the village had given us that evening lay scattered on the floor and filled the tent with their heady perfume.

I thought of Lorenzo and how I had been brainwashed for so long. I wondered if black men made love in the same way as white men do. I had never had these thoughts before. Excitement and confusion made me shake as if I had a fever.

That night I embarked on the most exciting love adventure of my life. It was to last for two years and was so natural that I wondered what all the fuss had been about. But Kimuyu sulked for days, he went listlessly about his chores and refused to talk to or cook for Shaibu. He glared at us disapprovingly and stared moodily at his fire. Kimuyu had been to school in a Protestant mission and read his Bible each night before retiring. In his view, black girls and white men were acceptable, but he had never yet had to deal with the converse. Whenever I spoke to him now he dropped his eyes in confusion.

When it was time for me to head back home, I tried to explain to Shaibu what it was like in the white man's world—the hostility, the resentment, the prejudice. I spelled it out ruthlessly to him, for it was important he should understand.

It was not possible for him to share my life as I had his. My world was not like his. But he did not listen; perhaps he did not understand; certainly he did not care. Young, impulsive and in love, he wanted only one thing—to be with me, regardless of the consequences. He looked at me imploringly, defiantly, his black eyes on fire and said, "Please take me with you." Aching to say yes, I said no and then capitulated and agreed.

When we reached Naivasha, he faced the first test when I went in by the front door and he went in by the back. I sat in the drawing-room with my parents, he sat in the servants' quarters with the house servants. The situation made me cringe, but there was nothing I could do about it. If we wanted to continue without upsetting the apple cart, these were the conditions, for if my father had found out he would have shot Shaibu, and probably me also and then himself. In Naples, crimes of passion are part of a code of life. Wives and daughters are treated like madonnas, to be revered but never touched—certainly not by a black man—and I had not forgotten how my father had chased Lorenzo out of the house brandishing his duelling sword because he caught him sitting on my bed reading a magazine at two in the afternoon in front of an open door. He was banished for a week from my life.

I had made all this clear to Shaibu before we left Watamu. Officially he was simply my assistant, all else had to remain a secret. He was given a hut in the servants' quarters and after everyone had gone to sleep he used to climb through the window of my bedroom to join me for the night.

I tried to find something for Shaibu to do on the farm, but I was not very successful and I noticed for the first time the class distinction that exists among Africans. Shaibu was half Arab and a Muslim, and there were certain things he just did not do. The privileged position he held as my personal assistant, the friendship that obviously existed between us, and the fact that he talked to me as an equal and called me by my Christian name antagonised the others.

When Lorenzo came to visit me in Naivasha, I told him I had a lover. I needed a reaction from him.

"Good," was all he said.

"But there is something else I don't know how to tell you."

"There is nothing you can't tell me," he smiled back, curiously.

"He is black."

"So what?" he retorted. "Invite him to dinner." Lorenzo did not have my inhibitions.

When I introduced them they struck up an immediate friendship and we all went to Kilifi for two months. They spent the days together, fishing, and Lorenzo did not seem to mind that Shaibu and I stayed together at night. But Shaibu found the situation difficult to accept—it was so entirely against his strict Muslim code of ethics.

At first, I was surprised by Lorenzo's reactions, but I knew it was not indifference. He had for many years tried to free himself from the conventions of his own society and had accepted that others should live as they wished. For him life was like a river where people flowed with the current. If I was happy with Shaibu, why should he interfere? "If I really love you I want you to be happy," he said. I understood then why my union with my husband, even if it was now only spiritual, would stretch into old age.

The time I spent with Shaibu taught me many things. From him I learned the fundamental truths and values of life. Like the lion, the giraffe, the fever tree and the ochre warrior, Shaibu belonged to Africa. At one with him, I was at one with Africa, an experience which has never repeated itself in sheer emotional and physical intensity.

Shaibu stayed with me until I had finished all the photographs for *Vanishing Africa*. When I told him I would be leaving Kenya for a year, while I saw the book through the press, he once more begged me to take him with me, but that, alas, was impossible.

"I can't take you with me," I tried to explain to him. "You are a man of the sea and I live on the land. I travel around and live in a tent and I am white, a *musungu*."

His parents also begged me to keep him with me. "He will die if you leave him here. He is your child now," they said. But it was painfully obvious that this was impossible. Our worlds were too far apart and there was no longer any place for him in mine. Kimuyu went back to my parents in Naivasha and Shaibu returned to his little village beneath the coconut trees.

When I returned to Kenya a year later I went to Watamu to find Shaibu again. His sister led me into his hut. He was lying asleep on a straw mat, a yellow and orange *kikoi* loosely thrown over his hips. His back was turned to the door. I knelt down beside him and put my hand on his shoulder. He turned in his sleep and then I saw his face. It was unrecognisable. I knew immediately he had begun to drink.

He looked as if he had been stung by bees. His eyes and cheeks were swollen, and flies crawled over a nasty cut on his forehead.

When he opened his eyes and saw me, he did not seem surprised. He smiled and yawned, and stretched like a lazy cat. He said nothing, and all that seemed to remain of his old self were the soft eyes and gentle smile.

After a little while we began to talk in the cool dark hut. He had been so totally uprooted by our encounter that he could not adapt to the simple life I had torn him from. He had grown fat and sloppy and shunned his life by the sea, and no longer cared about anything except money. He told me he was moving ivory from the bush to illicit buyers in Mombasa.

During the next few weeks I tried to reason with him but my words fell on deaf ears. I told him that I would never see him again if he did not stop drinking and pull himself together. He promised he would but he never did.

My Italian friend had been right when he had said: "You will upset the natural ecology of his life." My guilt over his condition was real, but the adventure had drawn me in, as it had him, and now it was too late. During the two years that we had been together I had found myself, but he had lost himself. Unwittingly I had torn him from his world and made him a victim of mine.

# ED HOOPER

## *Slim: A Reporter's Own Story of AIDS in East Africa*

Then, in late March 1986, I flew down to the Kenyan capital Nairobi, *en route* for Sudan, which was about to hold its first democratic elections for nearly twenty years. The feeling of release which arrival in Nairobi always imparts had put me in a particularly good mood that evening, and the mood improved further when I entered the bar next to my hotel, and bumped unexpectedly into Fiona, a former relief worker based in Sudan with whom I had enjoyed a romantic interlude the previous year. She was with a Kenyan friend, but we arranged a date for the following evening.

By then it was about ten o'clock, and the night still felt young; I decided to take a taxi up to "Buffalo Bill's Wild West Bar and Eating House." Buffalo Bill's, or BB's for short, is an establishment famous for its succulent and attractively-priced T-bone steaks, and for its *malayas*, or hookers, who are said by many of the male patrons to display similar characteristics. There is a choice of seating: one can perch outside in the open air, on a leather saddle; venture inside, to join a party in a covered wagon, or kick one's heels in the county gaol; or alternatively one can just join the happy throng fighting to get a drink at the horseshoe-shaped bar. With the promise of seeing Fiona the following evening, a pick-up was not on my mind, but I did feel like seeing a few friendly faces, and enjoying some beers and games of pinball.

Two women in their early twenties were already playing the machine when I arrived. They let me join them on the table, and we talked a bit, but not much, in between plays. Their names were Sue and Maria, and they were cousins. I identified them both as Batutsi, which they confirmed, and they told me that their parents, like so many others in the tribe, had been forced to flee Rwanda for Uganda in the early 1960s. They had that beauty which is peculiar to the Tutsi, being slender and elegant, with high foreheads and cheek-bones, and something almost oriental about the eyes. They were also pleasant company, although neither spoke English very well. After a while I bought them each a drink. And when I ran out of change for the machine, they paid for my games; they had 30 shillings or more spread out territorially on the glass top.

And so it continued to the end of the evening. We played pinball, we talked and we drank, but I never entirely forgot the date with Fiona the following night. I really didn't want to complicate my life by going home with somebody else.

"It is a very nice game," Maria was saying. "You are too good."

"What about yourself?" I enthused. "I just love your double flip." I mimed the move in question, a strike by both flippers in quick succession, which retrieves the ball when it appears to be heading out of play, by flicking it from the tip of one flipper across to the meat of the other, and then back up the table. "And you keep getting us free games. Where did you learn to play so well?"

"Oh yes," said Maria, grinning a little shyly now. "You are right."

Maria and I were drinking beers whereas Sue, after accepting one bottle of beer, had reverted to sodas. She now explained my question to her cousin.

"I just know," explained Maria, eventually.

"You see," I carried on, "I have been a pinball fan ever since I was very small." I held my palm out, horizontally, 3 feet above the floor, and began enunciating very clearly, separating the words. "And the beauty of the game is that it is very simple. You press the button—like this—and the flipper moves. You keep cool..." with a jerk of the neck, I took up a solid stance with legs apart and arms outstretched, and then shot my cuffs a couple of times, a pinball wizard for all to see, "... and you watch the silver ball. Except sometimes you have to give Lady Luck a helping hand, and then you have to *push and shove just a little bit.*" At this point, I grabbed hold of the table, moved back until my eyes were almost level with the glass, and then, with much swivelling of the bottom, and exaggerated slapping of the machine with the palms, I mimed a particularly spectacular escape shot. Then I turned around, flicking imaginary sweat from the brow, to take my applause. Maria was laughing noisily; Sue, by contrast, was looking at me quite directly, with a slight smile. Then she turned to say something to Maria, who rummaged in her handbag, and finally produced a 10-shilling note.

"I think you are drinking White Cap, isn't it?" And before I could answer, Sue had disappeared into the mêlée around the bar.

It wasn't just that she was so beautiful, for that fact, and her small face, were largely concealed by the braided and becowried hair style that she had at the time, which was not one of my favourites. It wasn't just that she spoke the better English of the two. It was something else—probably something in the eyes—a quality of straightforwardness and intelligence which I missed in her cousin. It was also, I concede, not entirely unrelated to the impact on a tired constitution of several beers and some attentive female company. But it struck me quite suddenly that I wanted to take Sue back to my hotel. This realisation was not accompanied by a surge of lust, but it did feel important—and sufficiently so for me to be nervous about the outcome. But it was past midnight, the bar was closing up, and I reverted to self-protective adolescent habit by laying down some false trails.

"Now which of you two girls am I going to take home with me?" I demanded. A few hurried words passed between the two of them, and then Maria started tutting and wagging her finger at me. Sue, by contrast, held back and watched. Eventually the three of us walked off together to the car park, to find a taxi. I felt excited; I really wasn't sure how things were going to end up. But then I got in the back with Maria, and told Sue to direct the driver back to their home.

Home turned out to be Dorothy's Place, a collection of single-room apartments built on a nearby plot of waste land, near several of Nairobi's major tourist hotels. The redoubtable Dorothy was still living there. She was a former prostitute, by then in her mid-forties, who had just recently, in an infamous and spectacular row, thrown out the *balokoli,* or born-again Christians, who had held sway over her heart—and purse-strings—for the previous ten years. The tenants had derived great amusement from watching Dorothy burn her religious tracts and pictures of saints, but only later did they appreciate the benefits to be derived from a saved Dorothy, when the unsaved version suddenly announced a sizeable rise in the rents. The *malayas* who occupied most of the apartments responded by sharing four to a room instead of three.

By the time the taxi had stopped, I knew what I was going to do. I leant across to Maria, on the other side of the back seat, and gave her a kiss on the cheek. "Goodnight," I said. "We'll see you in the morning." Maria duly got out, and said a few words through the window to Sue in a language I didn't recognise.

As we set off again, Sue turned around from the front seat, and gave my hand a squeeze. "You," she said, in the African way that betokens affection combined with a light slap on the wrist. "You give Maria a big surprise."

There were three long flights of stairs up to my hotel room, and we raced each other. I got there first, but I was so out of breath that it took an eternity to get the key into the lock. As soon as we entered the room, I flopped on to the bed. The alcohol had taken its toll, and I could feel the mental and physical tiredness accumulated from several weeks of working without a break. Suddenly, cool sheets seemed preferable to warm arms.

So this, I thought, is the man who was so excited just half an hour ago. Feeling rather less than gallant, I struggled to open my eyes. Sue was just slipping out of her T-shirt. Then she stood there naked, with hands on hips, smiling down at me. I can still remember being shocked by that first sight of her body, illuminated only by the neon lights outside—I had not realised before how slight and graceful she was, how proud the tilt of her breasts.

"You want to take off your clothes?" she asked. "Or you want me to do it?"

\* \* \*

"And Jonathan as well," she said, almost as an afterthought, from where she sat over on the other bed.

"You're kidding. But you always told me that you hadn't done anything with him."

"I know," she sighed; then all was silence. "I don't think you can ever trust me again, can you?" she said, finally. It was more a statement than a question.

For the previous hour, Sue had been telling me about the other men she had slept with since she had first met me nearly a year before. Jonathan was the last on the list. And somehow he was the hardest of all to accept, possibly because I had felt it in my bones all along. In fact, my constantly anticipating it had in all probability helped it to happen. In the end it had all been rather prosaic, with Jonathan returning to Dorothy's

Place late one January night, after a party, while I was still busy kicking nicotine and licking my imagined wounds down on the coast. Sue was alone in the flat, they drank some whisky together and ended up making love. In the morning she regretted it, knowing that even though Maria and Jonathan had split up, her cousin would never forgive her if she found out. "And I am not feeling very nice afterwards. It is like I am going to bed with my brother," she added. I still felt jealous. Brothers, after all, are sacrosanct.

There were ten men altogether, although Sue had previously mentioned only two of them. In Nairobi, apart from Jonathan and the diminutive Frenchman Jean-Michel, there was Rolf, the tall blond German with whom I had seen her ten days before, and a couple of Kenyans—one black and one white. There had also been two or three one-night stands in Kampala, as well as Patrick, the French diplomat whom Catherine had tipped me off about on Christmas Eve. Sue had seen him a number of times when I was out of town, as well as on the night of the "Rwandese dinner party." In addition, she had slept with Nigel Beale, who had treated her cheaply, giving her a *malaya*'s tip when she left in the morning. Knowing Beale's nature, I could imagine how he must have enjoyed taking his revenge on my own philanderings with his girlfriend Helen—and, of course, it was a fair cop. Sue had also, during my absences, been having a quiet affair with the kid brother of one of her Ugandan friends; it didn't help very much when she explained in mitigation that "he is very good-looking you know; very nice for girls."

After she had finished telling me, it was three in the morning, and I sat on the other bed with my head in my hands. The room was in darkness. Periodically, I would come up with the name of another mutual friend, and ask "What about him? Did you sleep with him too?" And she would answer quietly, "No Eddie, I think I am telling you, everybody." But even as I finished the last of the bottles of Tusker, and felt the room swaying, I knew what courage it had taken for her to come clean.

"Come on," I said finally, my mouth thick with the taste of beer. "It's time we went to bed."

In the narrow single bed we held each other tightly and said nothing, though each knew that the other was awake. I was thinking how long ago it seemed that I had got the thumbs-up from Dr. Carswell, although in reality it was just twelve hours before. And then I thought back to touching down in Nairobi, and taking the taxi straight to Dorothy's Place, sitting down with Sue and telling her the good news about the test. Then asking her angry questions about the blond man I had seen her with, and getting sullen, non-committal replies. Later, telling her that I wanted her to come back to Kampala with me, to be with me and no one else, and her refusing, again and again. In the end, taking out the air ticket I had bought her, and throwing it down on the bed as I walked out. "You might as well have it, since it's in your name. Throw it in the bin if you want, it's up to you." And walking off down the hill, that same walk I had taken so many times in the preceding weeks, down to Buffalo Bill's to drown my sorrows.

Then some time later, shortly before closing time, Sue's friend Rosemary coming over to my table to tell me that Sue was waiting outside. Feeling quietly elated, but saying I didn't want to see her; demanding, in fact, that she go away. Rosemary asking me again, pleading over and over. And going outside to find Sue waiting in the shadow of a tree, away from the lights, dressed hurriedly in a T-shirt, a *khanga* and a pair of flip-flops, and my asking her what she wanted, and she crying and saying she wanted to be with me, and the long silence which continued for the taxi ride back to the hotel. It was only when we were up in my room that I told her my terms: that she tell me about all her other sexual contacts, making sure that none were missed out.

And so, afterwards, I lay there holding her, our bodies both slightly chilled despite the crush in the small bed. I could feel her ribs pressing hard against her skin, and remembered how whenever I came back from abroad, and we went to bed that first time, she was always so thin, and when I asked her she would say, as if it was not important, "Oh, I am not eating so much these days." How after a week with me, she was always that little bit plumper, more filled-out. Yes, I thought, whatever she does do when I'm away, she doesn't get to eat very much *matooke*.

There was, of course, another potential explanation for her slenderness. But had we not been tested together, only two months before in December, and both found negative? But of course that test had been meaningless, given the fact that she had certainly had other partners in the weeks preceding it. And then all that talk of Amboseli, all that "I don't care, we can have AIDS together" nonsense, when, in fact, she had been taking more risks than I during the month we had been apart. And that, really, was the crux of it. Sue was not a *malaya*, but she did like to have a good time, and she still hadn't realised how dangerous it was to sleep around, even with a relatively small number of men. All my explanations to her, and the photographs I had shown her of people dying horribly because of Slim, had failed to get through. Or rather she had been shocked, but only on an emotional level; she still didn't associate having different boyfriends with what she saw in those pictures. I cursed the fact that our limited mutual vocabulary made some subjects so difficult to discuss. And yet I knew that, over the last six years, I had been a lot more promiscuous than Sue. The problem was that I had finally seen the error of my ways, whereas Sue had not. At the beginning of 1986, of course, it had taken me several weeks before I really got the message; perhaps, therefore, I should not be quite so hard on her.

And so, at first light started to seep under the curtain, and the throb of the Hollywood disco near by was replaced by the early morning sounds of the wakening city, I began, slowly, to explain to Sue what I was feeling, that over and above the jealousy and possessiveness, I was really worried that one of us was going to get the virus, and give it to the other, and then that would be the end of the story. "I know that," she told me. "And if I sleep with someone else, I make him wear a Durex. I tell him that I go for a test with you, and I am OK. I don't want anyone to spoil my test." I began to put her on the spot, asking her about this time, and that; and soon she was telling me she "didn't remember." I realised that whatever the good intentions, the question of whether or not a condom was used on a particular occasion was finally a matter of chance, dependent on a myriad of random factors.

And then I remembered the day with Emma, and the time at Amboseli when I threw away the Durex, and I realised how easy it was to be irresponsible, and that if she had the virus then I probably had it too by now, that it would have been too early for any antibodies to show on the blood test which I'd just had, and then I shouted "Oh God" and held her to me, and finally we made love.

# ASIA

# Robyn Davidson

## *Desert Places: A Woman's Odyssey with the Wanderers of the Indian Desert*

Narendra was the centrifugal point in the middle of my whirling. He was the interpreter of where I was. He had, in a way, *become* India to me. But to truly understand someone you have to understand his inner dialogue—that perpetual discussion with what formed him—his culture. When I had to accept that in this person I loved there were areas of foreignness which could never be mapped, and that this was mutual, I felt as if I had set myself adrift in this baffling place and would never find my way home. Once he had begged me not to ride a bicycle because it was "the easiest way for someone to murder you."

"But no one's trying to murder me," I had said, aghast.

"How do you know?" he had countered and I had searched the horizon for something familiar on which to rest my eyes. Usually there was no sense of strangeness between us and the unlikeliness of our friendship was obscured by its strength. But so remote did he sometimes seem from anything I could comprehend, it was as if I had lost my footing and was falling. It was not that our thoughts were different, that was to be expected, but that the ways in which we thought were different. But inevitably a gear would shift and I would be back with my friend in the warmth of a deeper, human understanding.

When I said goodbye to him, it was a little like setting off from an island on which one has been entirely happy and safe but, once through the reef (the farm gates), turning to face an uncharted sea.

# J. R. ACKERLEY

## *Hindoo Holiday: An Indian Journey*

*January 5th*

His Highness has told his "valet" that I thought him more beautiful than the Gods. This morning, after breakfast, the young clerk whom I saw with the valet yesterday followed me to the house and asked if he might come in. He told me at once that he knew I had seen the Gods dance.

"How do you know?" I asked.

"My friend," he murmured, "he tell me . . . my friend you say 'like Krishna.'"

"Better than Krishna," I said. "So the Maharajah Sahib told him?"

"Yes," he answered; then added, after a moment, "But do not say to Maharajah Sahib, or he will be angry with me."

I promised.

"Do you like Europeans?" I asked.

"Yes."

"Why?"

"Because he is so wisdom."

*January 6th*

. . . Sharma paid me a call in the late afternoon. I had not seen him for four days, and asked in Hindi why I had been neglected; but I did not understand his reply. He did not seem in the least nervous of me now, made no attempt to hang the curtain over the door so as to have his friend Narayan in view, and even came and sat by me on the sofa while I traced for him my intended journey on the map.

I looked at him sitting there, all bunched up, his bony hands on his knee, his toes turned in. He had not removed his shoes on entering, I noticed, which I have been told is a very grave discourtesy. They were ordinary black laced shoes, but the laces had been taken out, and since he was not wearing socks or stockings I asked whether he would like me to give him some; but he said he had plenty at home.

"Who is more beautiful than the Gods?" I asked, looking at his wild eyes and childish mouth, and he was pleased and smiled, exposing small, undeveloped teeth discoloured with betel-juice. I had never seen him without his turban, and asked him to take it off, which he did; but the result was disappointing and a little shocking, for he showed very large ears and a skull as undeveloped as his teeth, with a low narrow brow towards which his short coarse hairs pointed. I told him to put it on again.

"You are not frightened of me now?" I asked, when he was once more beautiful.

"No."

"Then we are friends?" He nodded, smiling.

"Then give me a kiss." Still smiling, he shook his head. Then, after idly turning over the pages of a book on Indian architecture, and pointing, without comment, to some of the illustrations, he got up and, taking another cigarette from the table, shambled off.

"Good . . . bye," he said in childish English as he left.

*January 18th*

. . . It appears that Sharma has been very naughty. The Maharajah gave him a small gift of ten rupees last night, and since this was received in silence, asked:

"Are you not pleased?"

"No," said Sharma sullenly. "It spoils me."

"Then why do you not give it back?"

"I do. Here—take it!"

"Very well. Then, since presents spoil you, why do you not give me back all the other things I have given you—the money, clothes, and ornaments?"

"I do. I give them all back. I will bring them now."

"Bring them to-morrow morning," said His Highness, exerting what little dignity and authority remained to him; "and meanwhile go, and do not return until I send for you."

"He is a very bad boy," concluded the King morosely when he had recounted this deplorable incident.

"Oh, no," I smiled; "he's a good boy really; he's only a child!"

"He is a very bad boy," repeated His Highness, gazing straight before him. "He says that when he came up to see you the other day, you tried to—to—to cling him, that you threw him down and tried to cling him."

"What!" I exclaimed, considerably startled.

"That is what he told me," said His Highness.

"It's an absolute lie," I said.

"That is what I told him," he replied, turning upon me wide eyes that politely reflected my indignation; "and I said that if he repeated the lie to anyone else I would send him to hell. He is a very bad boy!"

"A *very* bad boy!" I warmly agreed.

He did not appear to have anything more to say, and for some moments we rolled slowly along the empty road in silence. Then it seemed to me that in justice to Sharma I should explain what had actually taken place.

"I asked for a kiss," I said, "and he refused. That's all that happened. I didn't lay a finger on him."

"But you must not do such things, Mr. Ackerley," remarked His Highness, without the smallest change of tone.

"But good Lord!" I exclaimed. "I must kiss *somebody*."

His small body began to shake, and he hid his face in his sleeve.

"I suppose this explains why he didn't come for a ride with me this morning?" I asked, after a pause.

"Did he say he *would* come?" he enquired huskily, looking very grave.

"Yes, he did. However, if he comes to-morrow I will forget that he didn't come to-day."

"I will tell him he *must* come."

"Tell him he *may* come," I said.


*January 20th*

...When I returned to the encampment in the dusk, Narayan came down the path to meet me. I thought how graceful he looked in his white muslin clothes, the sleeves of his loose vest widening out at the wrist, the long streamers of his turban floating behind him. The breeze puffed at his *dhoti* as he approached, moulding the soft stuff to the shape of his thigh; then as he turned a bend in the path another gentle gust took the garment from behind and blew it aside, momentarily baring a slim brown leg. I took his hand and led him into my tent, and he told me that His Highness had invited him to return to the New *Bakhri,* but that he feared to do so lest he should be treated with disrespect, and anyway it did not matter much because he liked being with me.

"I want to love you very much," he said.

"You mean you do love me very much."

"I want to."

"Then why not?"

"You will go to England and I shall be sorry. But you will not be sorry. I am only a boy and I shall be sorry."

When he got up to go, he asked me not to accompany him as usual to the fair-ground where he meets Sharma, but to let him go back alone this evening; then before I had time to reply, he suddenly laughed softly and drew me after him. And in the dark roadway, overshadowed by trees, he put up his face and kissed me on the cheek. I returned his kiss; but he at once drew back, crying out:

"Not the mouth! You eat meat! You eat meat!"

"Yes, and I will eat you in a minute," I said, and kissed him on the lips again, and this time he did not draw away.

*April 25th*

Narayan has intercourse with his wife once every two or three nights. She is fourteen years old and he twenty, and they have been married and together for three years. During the first two years he went with her too much; frequently they had intercourse two or three times a day and he found this bad for his health. She was then nearing twelve and he was seventeen. He had had many affairs with other girls before her, during his sixteenth year, and has had many since. She is not beautiful and he does not love her much.

He was sitting with me in my room in the late morning when he told me these things.

A dim green light filtered through the grass door-screen against which, from the outside, water was flung at short intervals, and the sweet smell of the grass pervaded the air. I said I should have thought it injurious for a girl to begin sexual practices at the age of eleven, but he disagreed. Girls were ripe for the marriage bed, he said, when they grew their breasts.

"But has a child of eleven breasts?" I asked.

"Yes. Little, little. So big. Like a lemon."

"How old is Sharma's wife?"

"Twelve years."

"And she has her breasts?"

"Yes. Like a lemon."

"Does he lie down with her?"

"I do not know."

"Do you not know?"

"I have not ask. If I ask, he get much shame."

"Why should he get much shame?"

"I do not know."

"How would he show his shame?"

"He would turn away his face."

"Ah, Sharma!" I said, smiling. "He is certainly a shameful boy."

"He Maharajah Sahib's lover-boy," Narayan said.

"Does he like that?" I asked.

"No, he does not like."

"Then why does he do it?"

"I do not know. He is half-made."

"You don't approve either, do you?"

"No, I do not like. It is bad, wrong. But what can I do?"

Swish went the water against the screen, swish, swish. I closed my eyes drowsily.

"*You* get much love Sharma one time," said Narayan, after a pause, smiling at me.

"What did he tell you?" I asked.

"He tell me 'The sahib try to kiss me.'"

"And what did you say?"

"I say he must kiss you if you want."

* * *

In the evening I walked with Sharma down to the caravanserai outside the city gate, where Narayan had arranged to meet us, and there we came upon the largest bullock we had either of us ever seen, harnessed to a wagon. It came from Deogarh, we learnt, and was worth one hundred and sixty rupees as against the normal price of fifty or sixty; and yet it was not a perfect specimen, its owner said; it was over-fat and stood too high on its legs. But how magnificent it was!

I gazed in wonder and admiration at the huge white marble form and calm, majestic face. How peaceful were the long drooping ears! How beautiful the line of the heavy dewlap and the gentle jowls! Above the wide rounded forehead two short black incurving horns rose; and the large dark glowing eyes set far apart were finely marked with black as though their heavy lids were rimmed with soot. Over each a double wrinkle lent to the great white face a grave wisdom and benignity of expression. A cord ran through the dark nostrils. No wonder, I thought, these beasts are venerated, and the females thought to be the seat of the Generator. I glanced at Sharma. His attention also was absorbed in the brute, and I noticed the expression of awe in his great silly eyes, and beneath his vest and *dhoti* the fugitive lines of his animal body.

"Ah, my fine young bullocks!" I thought.

# Sarah Lloyd

## *An Indian Attachment: True Story of an Englishwoman's Love of a Sikh*

For three days I had been in an Indian train, crossing the country from its western extremity in Gujerat to Calcutta in the east. The company had been as unexciting as the landscape; I'd been stuck in a carriage full of tedious people all grumbling about how tedious everyone else was. One little girl had found me so tedious (sitting reading a history of the Sikhs all the way) that she'd given me a sharp slap to wake me up. I gave her one back and her father laughed, whereupon we all fell back into collective boredom until the lush watery landscape of Bengal announced the proximity of Calcutta.

It was wonderful to be out of the train and back in the familiar chaos and electric energy of the bazaar street life. It was nice to be welcomed by big smiles from people who knew me at the gurdwara. And in the corner of the sleeping hall a man was sitting cross-legged on a blanket, with the long black beard of the tenth Sikh Guru, and the eyes of Buddha, sweeping up at the corners.

He had a powerful face that instantly compelled me: high forehead, long nose, and skin the colour of almonds; but the eyes suggested sadness, a past full of grief. On his head he wore a dome of blue turbans. A length of orange fabric was tied around the waist of his aquamarine tunic, and a second piece hung over his shoulder, loose. In front of him lay a sword.

Jungli was a Nihang, a self-elected member of an informal religious army maintained by the Sikhs for the defence of their faith. The clothes he wore, the code he followed and the ideals he lived by had survived un-altered the three hundred years of their existence.

At that time I was going through a being-charitable-to-Nihangs phase. Many were poor and some were homeless; as far as I could tell they were dependent on the generosity of others. I had been told they were pre-pared to forfeit their lives in defending their faith, yet few ordinary Sikhs showed them either kindness or respect. Returning from the bazaar later on in the evening I bought Jungli milk sweets and fruit.

———

At the end of a week it was time to leave; I had already stayed too long. Jungli, Inderjit and Bir were returning, defeated, to Amritsar, and I was catching a train to Bangladesh. We went down into the street and headed for the hotel to make a final assault on Bir's recalcitrant brother. Inderjit and Bir walked ahead. In the middle of the crowded Howrah Bridge, trams squealing, structure creaking, cartmasters cursing, rickshaw wal-lahs shouting, engines stalling, beggars wailing, horns hooting, wheels rat-tling, feet thundering, Jungli said, "I love you."

I looked at him. I didn't know he knew any English. The words sounded unreal. Then he was swallowed up in the crowd.

He came with me next morning to Sealdah Station.

"When are you coming to Amritsar?" he asked again and again as we waited for my train. He had plenty of time in which to do so as we were on the wrong platform.

"In about a month," I hazarded. I don't follow an itinerary when I'm traveling, and I find that sort of question hard to answer. I told him to love God and forget about me, for just as I was leaving Calcutta I would also leave Amritsar. God, on the other hand, wasn't going anywhere.

When my train eventually left, we didn't even touch hands. I watched him standing on the disappearing platform, a lone figure in blue holding a sword, diminished by the great Victorian canopy of Sealdah Station.

* * *

India had me trapped. Part of me remained there—not at the dehra or anywhere in particular, but in the abstract idea of India. It took six months and a small and beautiful island of green hills and deep blue sea in the West Indies to shatter the spell.

Jungli and I still wrote. I found it increasingly difficult, for less and less of what I was doing had any meaning or relevance to him. He wrote more often—sad, sad letters that reawakened my feelings of self-reproach for leaving a man who had been unable to accompany me. The letters told me nothing, for they were always about me. He believed I would come back and lived in that hope.

I cannot go back: I can only ever go on. It seemed to me that Jungli and I were no longer being vitalized by each other. His lack of reasoning power made it hard to communicate. His lack of enthusiasm disturbed me, as did his negative filling of days with sleep. And I was afraid of him. We could never have made each other happy, but my guilt still gnawed at my stomach. I knew with absolute certainty that Jungli would love me until his death.

# Hugo Williams

## *All the Time in the World*

I was at the Station Hotel, Haadyai, in the south of Thailand and no one spoke a word of English. I was longing to sleep, but there were mosquitoes all over the place, just waiting for the new blood to turn in. They had two legs at the back they didn't use, which arched back and up. "Flit," I said to the manager, but he wasn't even insulted. I might as well have said "Lyle's Golden Syrup."

That night I went out. I was with an English corporal and we went into a sort of café which was a brothel. It was terrible. Tons of hopeful chairs everywhere and strip lighting and a row of girls by the wall. They sat there like wallflowers, waiting to be asked to dance. But there was no one to ask them. All that waiting. That must be the worst part. Waiting and waiting about for your youth to fall. We sat down and joined all the eyes vacantly fastened on a meaningless television, sneaking glances round for a sympathetic face, but finding none. Then we got out.

The night-club was rather smart. Spots revolved on the floor and up the walls and there was a small band. Near the bar were about ten girls. We ordered drinks and two of them brought them over and sat down with us. We offered them drinks, but they didn't want any—or cigarettes. So we danced. Mine was called Lily. She looked rather like Sophia Loren, about 20 and taller than most Thai girls. She was also very inquisitive—not about why I was there, or how I'd got there, but about my family, how many brothers, sisters, rooms I had, what my father was. Anything about myself she merely found amusing. She wanted to know how old I was and when I told her she threw back her head and laughed and laughed and said I was her brother and I could come and stay with her if I liked. I gulped. I couldn't believe it. I thought she must be joking. But she soon said her flat-mate was with some Americans at another night-club and we could go there if I liked. They had a better band or something. But if I wanted to go I would have to buy her out for the evening. I think I would have given all the money I had to do so, but it was only 25s.

"The Rainbow" was open air and Lily's friend Pia was there with some other girls and half a dozen American Military Advisers. We stayed there till it closed, then Pia and the other girls went off in jeeps with the Americans. Lily said Pia wouldn't be coming back that night so I could stay with her if I wanted. She just seemed to think it was the simplest thing to do in the circumstances. But I was nervous and pretended to be worried about money. Money didn't matter, she said. I'd bought her out of the club, hadn't I? So we began to walk through the dark streets to her house. Even then I couldn't believe it. I had the idea she was keeping me occupied while my room was being sacked, or else she was leading me into an ambush. The streets of Haadyai look very like those of a Wild West town and I knew they had gunfights there. We seemed to be walking so slowly and to be going round in circles. Who were we waiting for? I must have been mad. Life just isn't like that, I would have said a few days later. But for some reason I can never take for granted the singularity of people. I must have learnt too young at school that people hunt in groups and think collectively. I am always being surprised to find them individuals, sometimes lonely.

And I suppose Lily was lonely. As soon as I saw her room with its old radio and pin-ups, I knew she was human.

———

Before I left the corporal in the night club he had said: "You watch these Thai girls. All they're after is your money. You can buy anyone's friendship in this place." But either he'd been unlucky or Lily was an exception. If anything it was my friendship she bought with hers. As for money, it lay about the flat like telephone messages. The first morning she asked for some to buy food with and I gave her all the Thai money I had, about 30s. She took it and promptly leant out the window and threw it down to a boy to go and get some chicken and rice and Coke. Later she told him to take me to my hotel to pick up my suitcase and when I came back she unpacked my things and hung them in her wardrobe. I was to stay, she said and I was beginning to believe it. There was something so whole-hearted about her decisions. She didn't seem to suspect, as we do, the easy way out, the obvious solution. She merely took them in her stride. It was the kind of trust which begs deception and I supposed that was why she was a tart—to protect herself. She seemed to lack the subtle gift of antagonism and part-playing which are the weapons of the sex war in the West. There was something defenceless and rather sad about her using "happiness" for "pleasure" and "sleep" for "make love." If she had been in the sex war she would have been defeated and lovingly subsidized for the rest of her life.

Her room too was sort of undefended. In daylight, the luxury disappeared, leaving the dressing table, the mosquito net over the bed, the radio, the pin-ups, as islands in the bare boards which reached half-way up the walls to where wire netting separated her room from the next. At night we could hear the breathing of a family next door. And during the day her friends wandered in to speak a few words of English to me, try on one of her dresses, or dance a bit to the radio. How our privacy would have frightened them.

All day the lilting, minor-keyed Thai songs warbled from the radio, the wistful, childlike voices ending always on the same note of helplessness. Lily knew all the singers and all the songs. The sound was like her and part of the room for me.

One morning, after I had been there about three days, Lily suddenly gave me a medallion. She stood on a chair and took it down from a little shrine she had on top of her wardrobe. The shrine was of Buddha under a glass dome with dried flowers, fragments of gold leaf and medallions cast in temples, laid round it as offerings. The medallion she gave me was of To-wat, Buddha's disciple in this part of the world. It was shield-shaped and Lily said it would protect me in battle. She mimed machine-gun fire and clearly believed it. Then she yelled out of the window to her trishaw boy and he came running up straight into her room with a smile like a melon on his face. He had on a new hat and Lily immediately had to get it off because he'd just had his head shaved. He was going to be a monk, she said. We all laughed, but it turned out to be true. Then she gave him the medallion and some money and he ran off. Ten minutes later he was back with the medallion sealed in a little perspex container and hung on a chain. Lily took it and hung it round my neck. I was knocked out, but that was the kind of thing she did. With an uncertain look on her face she would do something utterly memorable and touching like that.

I supposed this was what Maugham meant when he talked about East-ern girls knowing how to make men happy. Europeans, he said, were sometimes psychologically unable to leave the East on account of them and I believe if I'd been thirty years older I'd have stayed and been will-ingly milked to death of my past. As it was I knew all the time that I was getting the best of it, because all my means of returning the compliment were at home. In fact that's what being foreign meant to me: a kind of im-potence. The best I could do was accept and thank. I could never really prove anything. Even our few common words were not enough to amuse with stories of my trip. So the happiness was only the passive one of en-joyment. I could only let the place happen to me, like a holiday. That is why I didn't fall in love with Lily.

———

We used to tell the time by the sun. Every few hours a woman came out on to her balcony opposite to move a bird-cage out of the shade. All day I sat about the sunny flat in a shirt and sarong, reading, or watching Lily stitching something. There was a pregnant cat living with her and when it lay in the sun you could see the little forms snuggling under its skin. Haadyai was preparing for a holiday and every now and then a jazz band went past in a lorry and Lily and Pia would run to the window to watch it. At 9:30 every day they had to go to English classes, so after lunch I had to help them with their homework: "Pat is good *because* she works hard." "Pat works hard, *therefore* she shall be rewarded." Perhaps that was why Lily always insisted on referring to herself in the third person: "Lily doesn't like working at the club, *therefore* she shall not be rewarded," she said.

Once when I was helping them I made some habitually un-American remark about an American spelling, which didn't go down at all. "We like Americans here," they said, speaking a lot for Thai humanity rather than their hospitality, for they didn't seem to think strangers any different from themselves and certainly not strange.

Sometimes Pia didn't feel like going to school—she had caught her American—but Lily always took off her make-up, put her hair up, got into a black and white dress and bicycled uncertainly off, usually into a light storm.

———

I had lived there ten days. Twice I tried to go, but Lily made me stay and that was all I wanted to hear. I don't think she loved me, but she did hug me very hard occasionally, for no particular reason, rather as she hugged the cat, and I was very fond of her. I think she just wanted me around and above all to do as I wanted. Everything she did had to have my blessing: "Hugo want us to go dancing?" "Hugo want Lily to wash her hair?" She wanted me to stay with her, whether as a status symbol or a pet I don't know, but the ironical thing was she wanted more than anything that I stay because *I* wanted to—though probably not forever. I don't think she cared about forever. It was always by giving in to each other that we pretended to come to our own decisions.

I soon discovered what it was all about. She had to go back to the club "just as a waitress" and she couldn't expect me to stay just because she said I must after that. It had to be my own idea, and of course that is what it became. I realized I would stay anyway and as soon as Lily realized it she decided not to go to the club and we went out to the pictures instead. It was an Italian film with little high-pitched Thai voices bubbling higgledy-piggledy from the lips of a giant Romulus and Remus. Lily adored it and wanted to see it round again, but I refused. So we bought some beer and talked about our favourite subject, our families.

Perhaps we shouldn't have. Next morning the trishaw boy came running upstairs very worried, saying that Lily's brother-in-law was waiting for her downstairs. Lily was frantic. She said he'd come all the way from Bangkok to take her back to her family and she wasn't going. She hated it there and she hated her brother-in-law. But she put on her black and white dress and went down to talk to him. She was away about an hour and when she came back she was livid, not with him, but with me, for jumping about on the floor like that. I had only walked up and down, but he had looked up at the ceiling and she'd had to make up some story. What would he have said if he'd known? I apologized, but she seemed more worried than angry and couldn't remember her English. I suppose that was the end of it there and then. Her home came between us like a wall. I felt utterly superfluous, like a walk-on actor or a ponce. What was I doing there? I had a sudden horror at my pigmy ways. I should have taken her to the seaside, or Bangkok, or married her. But I realized I still felt selfish, and that I was not only unable but unwilling to go further. Lily must have known I wasn't worth waiting for, because that night she went back to work. She came home early with two bottles of beer, but she was talking forcedly, already distant. I remember wishing her brother-in-law hadn't turned up and that perhaps I loved her. But it was too late.

Next day I left Haadyai. The trishaw boy was sent off to buy me a ticket for Bangkok. At the station Lily waved me goodbye with tears in her eyes and her eyes wandering over the other people on the train and platform. I think she was crying at her own restlessness. As the train drew away, I felt my face setting in new lines as the expression of sympathy and regret was wrenched from it into the distance.

# JON SWAIN

## *River of Time: A Memoir of Vietnam*

The eternal Mekong, gliding by the city on its way to the sea, provided some of the more bizarre distractions. On Sundays after Mass at Phnom Penh's Roman Catholic cathedral—later dynamited by the Khmer Rouge—some French people went water-skiing on its safer stretches, while Cambodian gunboats provided them with protection. This led to its own kind of tragedy when a French girl was cut to ribbons by a boat's propeller. Wartime is the time to do wild things; another form of relaxation could be found in the company of the girls at the *maisons flottantes,* bordering the river a few miles outside Phnom Penh or with the cyclo-girls who congregated outside the Café de Paris. There were opium parlours and Madame Nam's, a brothel specialising in *caresses délicieuses.* The journalist Donald Wise said he once spotted a sign on a doorway saying "Cunnilingus is spoken here." One establishment whose location was a jealously guarded secret of the French *colons* refined this art by training its girls first on bananas. Sex and opium played important parts in our lives in Cambodia; these diversions were an essential ingredient of survival.

The wartime capital encouraged all kinds of indiscretions. It had its own resident French lady of pleasure, like a small town in Provence: Madame Cha-Cha, red-bonneted, face caked with coarse make-up, was a grotesque figure compared to the graceful Asian girls who almost floated down the streets. She had had a chequered history, beginning as a *pute* in the rue Saint-Denis, graduating to Marseilles, then to Algeria and finally serving the French Corps Expéditionnaire in Indo-China. Who knows why she stayed? Perhaps out of sentiment. In any case, she was a favourite with Cambodian army officers who regarded her as a stalwart specimen of French womanhood.

Venereal disease was rife, and one or two clinics treated it to the exclusion of almost every other disease. Obsolete treatments, dating back to the French army days and involving courses of mercury, were still in use. "Be prudent," Doctor Grauwin advised. "Always take precautions. Remember the old saying we had in the Corps Expéditionnaire. 'Three minutes with Venus is three years with mercury.'" Even so, the press corps went down like flies; one unfortunate colleague was afflicted eleven times.

Jean-Pierre Martini was a young French mathematics professor who taught at Phnom Penh university as a *coopérant,* an alternative to Service Militaire. An habitué of Studio Six, he was a Maoist at heart, believing in permanent revolution. He had a wonderfully warped view of life. His Paris 1968 background had convinced him of the righteousness of the communist cause in Cambodia. However Jean-Pierre's number one passion was not politics but voyeurism. He used to regale me with stories of his sexual exploits and experiments with Cambodian girls, and seemed to be in a state of perpetual adolescence. It was he who made the interesting observation that the borderline between Cambodia and Vietnam is also the boundary of the female *labia majora;* on the Cambodian side women's genitalia are more often fully developed as a result of their Indian heritage, but in Vietnam and further eastwards they are small and shell-like in the Mongoloid tradition.

Once, he returned from a visit to Phnom Penh Central Market with the perfectly formed rim of the eye of a deer he had spotted at a stall of Cambodian folk medicine where they also sold tigers' teeth and the bile of cobras. He explained, with a flourish, that Cambodian men liked to stick it on the end of their penis like a "tickler" to excite their partner better during intercourse. No woman, regardless of her looks, was spared his advances. There was a secretary at the New Zealand embassy whom we called Pinched Lips because of her pursed unsmiling mouth. One of Jean-Pierre's maxims was that it was not a woman's looks that mattered when making love, it was her "technique"; if that was good, she gave plea-sure even if she was plug-ugly. One afternoon, he arrived in the studio, a little out of breath, eyes sparkling with mischief, to announce. "Je l'ai baisé." What was it like, I asked. "C'était formidable!" he cried. "C'était la Technique Commonwealth!"

# Graham Greene

## *Ways of Escape: An Autobiography*

My experience of opium began in October 1951 when I was in Haiphong on the way to the Baie d'Along. A French official took me after dinner to a small apartment in a back street—I could smell the opium as I came up the stairs. It was like the first sight of a beautiful woman with whom one realises that a relationship is possible: somebody whose memory will not be dimmed by a night's sleep.

The madame decided that as I was a *débutant* I must have only four pipes, and so I am grateful to her that my first experience was delightful and not spoiled by the nausea of over-smoking. The *ambiance* won my heart at once—the hard couch, the leather pillow like a brick—these stand for a certain austerity, the athleticism of pleasure, while the small lamp glowing on the face of the pipe-maker, as he kneads his little ball of brown gum over the flame until it bubbles and alters shape like a dream, the dimmed lights, the little chaste cups of unsweetened green tea, these stand for the *"luxe et volupté."*

Each pipe from the moment the needle plunges the little ball home and the bowl is reversed over the flame lasts no more than a quarter of a minute—the true inhaler can draw a whole pipeful into his lungs in one long inhalation. After two pipes I felt a certain drowsiness, after four my mind felt alert and calm—unhappiness and fear of the future became like something dimly remembered which I had thought important once. I, who feel shy at exhibiting the grossness of my French, found myself reciting a poem of Baudelaire to my companion, that beautiful poem of escape, *Invitation au Voyage*. When I got home that night I experienced for the first time the white night of opium. One lies relaxed and wakeful, not wanting sleep. We dread wakefulness when our thoughts are disturbed, but in this state one is calm—it would be wrong even to say that one is happy—happiness disturbs the pulse. And then suddenly without warning one sleeps. Never has one slept so deeply a whole night-long sleep, and then the waking and the luminous dial of the clock showing that twenty minutes of so-called real time have gone by. Again the calm lying awake, again the deep brief all-night sleep. Once in Saigon after smoking I went to bed at 1:30 and had to rise again at 4:00 to catch a bomber to Hanoi, but in those less-than-three hours I slept all tiredness away.

Not that night, but many nights later, I had a curiously vivid dream. One does not dream as a rule after smoking, though sometimes one wakes with panic terror; one dreams, they say, during disintoxication, like de Quincey, when the mind and the body are at war. I dreamed that in some intellectual discussion I made the remark, "It would have been interesting if at the birth of Our Lord there had been present someone who saw nothing at all," and then, in the way that dreams have, I was that man. The shepherds were kneeling in prayer, the Wise Men were offering their gifts (I can still see in memory the shoulder and red-brown robe of one of them—the Ethiopian), but they were praying to, offering gifts to, nothing—a blank wall. I was puzzled and disturbed. I thought, "If they are offering to nothing, they know what they are about, so I will offer to nothing too," and putting my hand in my pocket I found a gold piece with which I had intended to buy myself a woman in Bethlehem. Years later I was reading one of the gospels and recognised the scene at which I had been an onlooker. "So they were offering their gifts to the mother of God," I thought. "Well, I brought that gold piece to Bethlehem to give to a woman, and it seems I gave it to a woman after all."

\* \* \*

*January 18, 1954*

After drinking with M and D of the Sûreté and a dinner with a number of people from the Legation, I returned early to the hotel in order to meet a police commissioner (half-caste) and two Vietnamese plain-clothes men who were going to take me on a tour of Saigon's night side. Our first *fumerie* was in the *paillote* district—a district of thatched houses in a bad state of repair. In a small yard off the main street one found a complete village life—there was a café, a restaurant, a brothel, a *fumerie*. We climbed up a wooden ladder to an attic immediately under the thatch. The sloping roof was too low to stand upright, so that one could only crawl from the ladder on to one of the two big double mattresses spread on the floor covered with a clean white sheet. A cook was fetched and a girl, an attractive, dirty, slightly squint-eyed girl, who had obviously been summoned for my private pleasure. The police commissioner said, "There is a saying that a pipe prepared by a woman is more sweet." In fact the girl only went through the motions of warming the opium bead for a moment before handing it over to the expert cook. Not knowing how many *fumeries* the night would produce I smoked only two pipes, and after the first pipe the Vietnamese police scrambled discreetly down the ladder so that I could make use of the double bed. This I had no wish to do. If there had been no other reason it would still have been difficult to concentrate on pleasure, with the three Vietnamese police officers at the bottom of the ladder, a few feet away, listening and drinking cups of tea. My only word of Vietnamese was "No," and the girl's only word of English was "OK," and it became a polite struggle between the two phrases.

At the bottom of the ladder I had a cup of tea with the police officers and the very beautiful madame who had the calm face of a young nun. I tried to explain to the Vietnamese commissioner that my interest tonight was in *ambiance* only. This dampened the spirits of the party.

I asked them whether they could show me a more elegant brothel and they drove at once towards the outskirts of the city. It was now about one o'clock in the morning. We stopped by a small wayside café and entered. Immediately inside the door there was a large bed with a tumble of girls on it and one man emerging from the flurry. I caught sight of a face, a sleeve, a foot. We went through to the café and drank orangeade. The madame reminded me of the old Javanese bawd in *South Pacific*. When we left the man on the bed had gone and a couple of Americans sat among the girls, waiting for their pipes. One was bearded and gold-spectacled and looked like a professor and the other was wearing shorts. The night was very mosquitoey and he must have been bitten almost beyond endurance. Perhaps this made his temper short. He seemed to think we had come in to close the place and resented me.

After the loud angry voices of the Americans, the bearded face and the fat knees, it was a change to enter a Chinese *fumerie* in Cholon. Here in this place of bare wooden shelves were quiet and courtesy. The price of pipes—one price for small pipes and one price for large pipes—hung on the wall. I had never seen this before in a *fumerie*. I smoked two pipes only and the Chinese proprietor refused to allow me to pay. He said I was the first European to smoke there and that he would not take my money. It was 2:30 and I went home to bed. I had disappointed my Vietnamese companions. In the night I woke dispirited by the faults of the play I was writing, *The Potting Shed*, and tried unsuccessfully to revise it in my mind.

# John David Morley

## Pictures from the Water Trade:
## An Englishman in Japan

In Kanazawa it was raining steadily. Neither of them was in the mood for sightseeing so they drove out to a hotel on the outskirts of the town. Once in the privacy of the car Mariko began to relax. On the train she had sat tight and unapproachable, hardly listening to Boon; he spoke softly, aware of the other passengers sitting there silently. Their silence had about it a quality that seemed to isolate himself and Mariko. Perhaps she had felt it too.

They reached a large white house on the spur of a hill. In the valley below them, grey with wind and rain, lay the washed-out roofs of Kanazawa. Mariko ducked her head and stumbled across the wet gravel while he was paying off the driver. A man in a black suit and bow tie waited under the awning at the entrance to usher him inside, apologising for the rain as if it were his personal responsibility. Boon followed him into the dining hall. The weak afternoon light was already beginning to fade. He joined Mariko at a table with a window overlooking the valley. Apart from themselves the place was deserted.

They ordered coffee.

"What made you choose this particular place?" he asked.

"Oh, well. I've been coming here for years. Don't you like it?"

"It's a bit gloomy."

"Gloomy? D'you think so?"

"Rain, nobody here, waiter in black. It's like a very private funeral. Who do you usually come here with?"

"Oh, various friends."

She rearranged the cutlery on the table and looked out of the window. He could feel her slipping away.

"How do you usually spend Sundays?"

"At home, usually. Sometimes I go out. Sometimes I visit my brother. He's my only family, so he feels responsible for me."

"When did your parents die?"

"My father when I was still very small. I hardly remember him. My mother died when I was twelve."

"D'you miss them?"

She sighed.

"Not my father. My mother, yes. At least I used to miss her; perhaps not any more. I suppose what I still miss is not having any family. There's my brother, of course, but . . . life in Japan isn't easy without family. I mean, not to live with, but just . . . in the background."

"I can understand that. So who brought you up?"

"My grandfather. When my mother died I went to live with my grandfather. Until then the three of us had lived together—my brother, myself and my mother. It was a happy time; at least in my memory it is. My mother was very gentle, very gentle . . . I used to sleep in one bed with her and I can still remember clearly the scent of her body. A beautiful scent, not something she used, just the natural scent of her body. When she died and I moved to grandfather's everything changed. My brother was also there for the first couple of years, but still. It was, I don't know . . . a dark house, somehow. He was a stern old man. I never played much as a child. I was glad to get out."

Boon tried to imagine to himself Mariko's mother and the scent of her body. She spoke matter-of-factly, but in the subtle texture of her voice there were resonances conveying something different from what her actual words were saying.

"How old were you then?"

"Nineteen."

"And what did you do? Did you get a job right away?"

"No. I had a little money from my grandfather. My brother helped too. I went to college for three years. I was taught the usual things suitable for young women: the tea ceremony, *ikebana*, dressmaking and design. That was fun. What I enjoyed most of all was being with people my own age. I missed that at grandfather's. I started working part-time in a ladies' fashion shop, and after I left college I worked there for several months. That was before I took up my present job."

"How old were you when you started at the bar?"

"Twenty-two."

"So you've been there six years."

"Seven. I was twenty-nine in February."

"What made you switch there from the shop?"

Mariko glanced at her hands and then back to the window.

"I suppose it was money."

*Okane desho.* Her voice left soft, questioning echoes in the air.

Boon touched her hands and she placed them in his. On the inside of the index and middle fingers he noticed sores where she must have scratched the skin with the corners of her fingernails. Unexpectedly she laughed and leaning forward over the table kissed him lightly on the lips.

"It's still raining," she said.

He turned to look out, but it was already dark. The valley had disappeared and he could see nothing but their own reflection against a tracery of raindrops on the far side of the window. Somebody must have come into the room to turn on the lights. He had not noticed it at the time.

The rain continued throughout the night and for most of the next three days. It was still raining in Kanazawa when they arrived there for the second time. Mariko bought a pink umbrella in a souvenir shop outside the castle. She was wearing the same trouser-suit, but had exchanged the pink necktie for a yellow blouse. She also carried a black bag. Boon didn't like the bag; it was out of place. But they wandered round the castle, peering at restored walls and illegible stone tablets, and he was happy in the knowledge that she was walking there beside him.

They left the castle and after a while found themselves in a wide green-bordered street with the scent of flowers and damp leaves. Crowds of flower-viewers, leisurely with children and umbrellas, picked their way under the dripping trees. From time to time they stopped, slanted their umbrellas and looked up, pointed, talked, passed on. Plum blossoms were bursting from pale green sheaths, here and there a spray of white. Mariko and Boon were drawn into the flocking holiday crowds and drifted separately to an exit on the far side of the park. There were too many people. They took a cab and drove up into the hills beyond the town.

In the hills it was just as crowded; lines of cars on the roadside with closed windows, hot-dog stands, immaculate hikers. Mariko wanted to sit down. There wasn't a bench in sight. They set off hopefully down a grass track leading away from the town into the valley. There were still no benches. Finally the track petered out on a knoll sheltered by a huge pine tree, with a view for miles over the tops of steeply-raked conifers into the smoky hills beyond.

"We're standing on somebody's grave."

Mariko crouched down by a stone under the pine tree and tried to make out the inscription. The stone faced the distant hills, exposed to wind and rain and listing badly; whatever memorial it once bore had long since been obliterated. Boon leaned against the tree with his hands in his pockets, looking for the waterfall he could hear faintly in the distance. The knoll on which they were standing reminded him of the magical hanging scenery in Hokusai's picture of the waterfall of Amida; the same quiet lay over the landscape in front of him like a glaze.

"Aren't you getting wet?"

"I'm all right."

Mariko stood up and drew him to her under the shelter of her umbrella. He folded his arms round her waist and kissed her cheek, resting against the tree. They stood together for a long time, their bodies gradually warming until they seemed to have softened into one mould. He closed his eyes. From the movement of her cheek against his lips he knew when she turned her head. The corner of her mouth, dryness first and then moisture, a slight shock: her lips were cooler than her cheek. A flurry of raindrops overhead caused him to open his eyes. A little beyond her eyelashes and the darker webbing of her hair the pink haze of her umbrella spanned his vision like a tent; almost, it seemed for a moment, like the interior of his own eyelids. Her mouth softened against his and he sank deep into her. He shut his eyes again. There was almost no change. This was how it might look from inside her, in a warm light filtered through the transparency of her skin. He was peaceful there, free of all desire.

He squatted in front of her and ran his fingertips up her spine. She shivered.

"Are you cold?"

"No. I'm not cold."

"It'll be dark soon."

"Soon. There's still time."

The bones under the skin of her back felt fragile. He could almost span her waist with his hands. There was a little slackness in her belly. He drew aside a corner of her blouse and kissed the smooth white fold of skin. The fleshed roundedness of her belly was unexpected; the skin so soft, fuller than elsewhere on her body, and somehow more vulnerable. He uncovered her hips and belly and stroked her with the palms of his hands, palming the flesh of her belly outwards and wringing it at her hips. The whiteness of her body started out against the dark encircling trees, banked green, the rusty bark of pines. The cool air pricked her skin, bared from the breasts to the pit of her belly. Excited by his hands, aware of her white naked belly, not resisting her pleasure, she shuddered and moaned. He laid his head against her and waited until she was quiet.

Later, with flushed cheeks and dancing eyes, Mariko sat in the lounge of the hotel where they had spent a wet afternoon the week before. Boon was astonished at the change in her. When her face shed its tiredness she became truly beautiful. In her manner towards him there was at times something tender. He had never yet seen her tender. For the first time in her company he had the feeling she wanted to be closer to him than to anyone else who happened to be around them. He had embraced her under the pine tree in the valley; they shared a secret now.

# J. R. ACKERLEY

## *The Letters of J. R. Ackerley*

To E. M. FORSTER (1879–1970)

Dearest Morgan

Kyoto was hotter even than Tokyo, but is cooler now. Francis met my
train with his car, whipped me off to his large comfortable office-house (4
dogs, 2 cats, 3 Japanese servants, sliding doors, wire and net windows,
shoes off on the threshold), then on to a party, most of his "gay" English
and American friends and their "gay" Jap. boys—high-balls until 1 a.m. I
was dropping with fatigue after no sleep and the air and train journeys,
but I never say no. Where have we not been since (Francis is the kindest
and most assiduous host) . . . the Kokedera or Moss Temple, the Silver
Pavilion, Nijo Castle, the Pure Water Temple, the Heian Shrine, Mount
Higashiyama and Mount Rocco for the views, not to mention a judo
demonstration by students of the university, a conversazione with High
School boys and girls, including a tea-ceremony and, yesterday, a drive (2
hours) to Kobe (squalid landscape), where he had to teach and where we
dined with a friend. Jap. students pop into the house to chat all the time.
My impressions? Oh confusion, confusion, will clarity ever emerge? The
size, the distance, the ant-heap—all so daunting. Though in Kyoto, I suppose we are five miles from the centre, if there is one: endless innumerable streets, crammed with shops and cafés, crammed with people, all
gaily glittering with coloured lights at night, I never know where I am—

could never get there again. We go from "gay" bar to "gay" bar of an evening, tiny bar-rooms containing "gay" boys, sometimes in kimonos. 1 small bedroom at the back to which you can take one if you fancy him. 25/- about the lowest tariff. Not really my cup of saké, not to mention my pocket. Bad breath, I am told, no circumcision. Good torsos, no legs. One sees an occasional handsome face, the Simian look predominates. There is so much Westernisation I hardly feel myself to be in the East, as I did in India. . . .

It was my birthday two days later and I was given the nicest present in the world. At 9:30 p.m. The time mattered because it brought it all about. I was sitting in my bedroom concocting an article for *The Listener* (they've asked me)—Impressions of Japan—and you may be surprised to hear,— giving it and the Japanese the highest praise—, when I found my watch had stopped. There was a clock in the passage near the communal wash-house and I went to look. And a young man came out of the wash-house at that moment and gave me a backward look as he went to his room. The whole thing came out of the blue and took place in a trice. He left his door ajar for me to follow. He is a Japanese. His name is Saito. Since then he has been to my room. Once again from the wash-house (one has to wait and hang about, anything but embarrass) "I will come to your room in a few minutes." He was going to have a bath after his day's work. He is a business-man, somewhere between 25 and 30, a salesman in a brewery (how romantic!), to me very beautiful. He came in fresh and spotless linen, smelling of scent. So affectionate. So kind. He has been in America for a bit and can speak English. Of course I knew it would happen. The question was where. I thought it might happen in Sendai, but it didn't. It is a country where it must happen; age does not matter and the Japanese are so charming and uninhibited and curious, and so affectionate.

*   *   *

All Japanese are taught English, and perhaps because they are taught mainly by Japanese or Americans they can seldom speak it and scarcely ever understand it. "Queerness" here is called "gayness," there are "gay" bars to which the "gay" go, and there are brothels in which they can be bought (1000 yen, an English pound), and there are slave markets, where, for the same sum, the normal, in return for board and lodging while they search about for work, have to consent to "gaiety." You describe your personal tastes to the proprietor, samples are paraded, and you take your choice or go elsewhere. This delight is obtainable in only one city that I know of, Osaka, about an hour's train journey from Kyoto. The "gay" set off thither in the evening, for organised "gaiety" begins nowhere until 9:00–10:00 p.m.; it is like going from London to Brighton after dinner for half-an-hour's pleasure.

*　*　*

The last letter I wrote to you was over-confident. My romance came to a quick death and I am off to Kyoto tomorrow morning early, for the last lap of my stay here. I wrote unguardedly to William too: perhaps you could tell him that my letter to him, instead of anticipating a future, marked a full-stop. The chap never came near me again, and only with the utmost trouble and difficulty did I manage to have even a word with him. The answer to it all I can't supply. Francis, to whom I wrote, supplies one, which may be right. He generalises all the time about the Japanese, their sexual feelings and so on, and I think it may be true that they are a race about whom one may generalise. Well, never mind. I have been two weeks here today, and the first week was wonderful, the second wretched. Fortunately however, when I was at my lowest, a kind providence put compensation in my way—again in the useful wash-house. Nothing like so glamorous, but it served me well, it comforted. The compensation also vanished afterwards for ever: it may indeed be best to live in a fairy-tale world (as Jim seems to think) in which good fairies are not desired to do more than wave their wands over one once and then disappear. The trouble with Saito was that I had started to fall in love with him—if gradualness can happen in that sorry business—and how difficult it is to behave sensibly in such a situation. I fear I may have tangled matters, but shall never know the truth. He left today with a formal bow to some apartment he had found, I don't know where, I don't even know his full name. But I comfort myself with the reflection that if it *had* progressed as I once hoped, I should have been in an awful fix, for what is the good of having a lover in Tokyo, unless one can stay on for ever. I hope I may manage to forget about it in Kyoto in the brothels of Osaka.

# JANWILLEM VAN DE WETERING

## The Empty Mirror:
### Experiences in a Japanese Zen Monastery

Every morning the master made the rounds of the temple and we, the monks and I, followed him through the long corridors of the monastery. At every niche he stopped, and we stopped too, of course, and recited a prayer, mumbling and slurring the words, for our own benefit or whoever was represented in the niche. Sometimes there were statues of Bodhisatvas, sometimes a Buddha was shown, in meditation, or while lecturing, but there were also Chinese or Japanese gods who had no relation to Buddhism at all. There was even a fat little God of physical well-being. Flowers were placed in vases and the master lit incense sticks. During one of these performances I remembered that my passport had to be renewed. This meant I would have to go to Kobe. Have to, because the authority of worldly power, in this case that of the queen of the Netherlands, could not be ignored by the monks.

The head monk, for this reason, allowed me to break my promised eight months' continuous stay in the monastery and gave me an entire day off, and I took the tram to the station. I had put on a new nylon shirt which wouldn't let perspiration through and it was a warm day. I looked at freedom through the open windows of the bumping and shaking tram and realised that I had lived for almost five months in seclusion. I had been through the gate every now and then but never further than, at the most, half a mile. I saw crowds of people, enormous advertisements for films, showing half-naked women and aggressive men handling firearms, show-windows full of puppets dressed in new clothes, and grey heavy buildings housing banks and trading companies. I felt relieved but also irritated. I hadn't chosen the monastic life but rather had accepted it, as a means to an end, but now that I was free of the pressure of the monastery, I longed for the silence of the garden with its lovely grey and green shades and the monotonous robes of the monks. Here there was too much bustle; it was too full, too exaggerated. The screaming colours of the advertisements weren't necessary, the shouting and laughing were annoying. Perhaps it would be a good idea to force everybody to meditate regularly, in halls which would be built in all the cities of the world. Every evening from seven to nine, compulsory silence, and every morning at 3:30, an unavoidable visit to a master. A master to every street.

And nature would have to be restored so that all cities would be surrounded by vast forests, and in the forests huts could be built for hermits who didn't feel the need to work under a master. A public soup-kitchen in every forest. And as a means of transport we could use the horse again, or the camel, perhaps elephants as well so that we would all learn to live with animals again, with beings of another order. And meanwhile technology could continue, with efficient factories holding monopolies and producing the best quality which scientists could develop, and fast noiseless trains and ships and aeroplanes and rockets so that everybody could have his food and drink and clothes and other necessities with a minimum outlay of energy. The tram bounced along and I reached the station. There were a lot of people about and because I didn't want to push my way through them I almost missed my train. There was plenty of room to move about but Japanese always seem to push each other on platforms; at first they wait calmly and behave in a civilised manner, but when the train appears they are suddenly caught up in a fierce panic and everyone has to get through the door at the same time. That I didn't want to push with the others seemed, to my mind, proof of having gained a little by the monastic discipline. I had, obviously, become calm and selfless. But I had to admit that I had never pushed, not in Rotterdam either when the trams were full. I had preferred, in those days, to walk to school or to wait for the next tram. The need to find out whether the training was having any effect had long been an obsession, as if *satori*, enlightenment, reaching the holy goal, were bound to a certain place and I should be getting closer and closer to that particular spot. "Have I got anywhere or not? Am I getting more detached from whatever is happening around me? Am I understanding more? Am I getting lighter, more loose?" I kept on asking myself, although the master often warned me against the folly of such measuring. "You'll find out anyway," he would say, "you shouldn't worry like that. Your achievements are quite unimportant; rather try to solve your *koan*. What is the answer to your *koan*? What do you have to tell me? Say it!"

But I said nothing and continued counting non-existent milestones.

In the train I found myself pressed against several people, one of them a woman, some twenty years old perhaps. I had already looked at her and noticed that she was beautiful, with rather a sensuous body, large slanting eyes and thick black hair. Attracting the attention of women I don't know has always been below my sense of dignity, or perhaps I am too shy for that sort of thing; anyway I didn't try it that time either, although I was enjoying the contact with her body. I thought of the concentration exercise I had been doing for months. It could be tried. Before I knew it I began to breathe deeply and very slowly and fixed the image of the woman, as I remembered it from one short glance, in my thoughts. I tried to think of nothing else and when I knew that I had gained a certain measure of concentration I ordered her to press herself against me. And miracle of miracles, she obeyed. I felt how she rubbed herself, softly and furtively at first, but gradually more firmly, against me and I heard her breathing becoming deep and heavy. And while she rubbed herself against the side of my body she trembled.

"What now?" I thought, for the contact made my blood surge. "Shall I talk to her? Shall I ask her to get off at the next station? We can go to a hotel room—I have enough money on me. And I can go to Kobe this afternoon. The consul has time to spare."

But my excitement broke my concentration, the woman was released and moved away a little. She looked up at me and I saw a troubled look in her eyes. The train happened to pull up at a station and she got out. My skin was prickly under the nylon shirt and sweat was running down my face. "Black magic isn't all it's cracked up to be," I thought. "A lot of trouble and waste of energy. Suppose she had gone with me, so what? An adventure, a step into a vacuum, a memory to disturb future meditation. One shouldn't shy away from it, Gerald said. Maybe he went in for tricks in trains as well?" I asked him later, but he pretended not to know what I was talking about.

I didn't tell the master. The experiment seemed clear enough and I could do without his sarcastic wit. That someone who has trained his will can influence others, without saying anything, without doing anything observable, had now been proved. The monks told me that there are witches in Japan who, for a certain fee, are prepared to perform tricks. A troublesome competitor or a rival in love can be forced to break his leg or catch a nasty cold, depending on the price and on the concentration of the witch. "But," the monks said "you have to be very careful; the power which is caused by concentration continues to exist and will in the end turn itself against whoever created it. Witches punish themselves, and their clients pay a heavy price in the end."

I comforted myself by the idea that I hadn't wanted anything evil, just some sexual pleasure, shared cosiness with a climax and no harm done.

# PICO IYER

## *The Lady and the Monk: Four Seasons in Kyoto*

One delicate autumn day a few days later—the sky now gray, now blue, always like a woman's uncertain heart, a light drizzle falling, and then subsiding, and falling once more—I met Sachiko outside an Indonesian store, for a trip to Kurama. She was, as ever, girlishly dressed, her hair falling thickly over one side of her face, held back on the other by a black comb with red-stone heart in its middle; the tongues of her black sneakers hanging out from under lime-green leg-warmers.

As we traveled towards the hillside village, she set down her backpack beside her on the train and began telling me excitedly about her friend Sandy, and how it was Sandy who had first introduced her to Zen, Sandy who had first taken her to a temple, Sandy who had first encouraged her to try *zazen* meditation. "I Japanese," she said softly. "But I not know my country before. Sandy my teacher." More than that, she said, it was Sandy who had shown her another way of life and given her the confidence to try new things. Sandy, supporting two children alone in a foreign country and at the same time embarked on a full-length course of Zen studies, had shown her that it was possible, even for a woman, to have a strong heart.

Now, she went on, Sandy was planning to send her children back to America for high school. "I dream maybe Hiroshi go your country, Sandy's son together. You see this movie *Stand by Me*?" I nodded. "Very beautiful movie. I want give my son this life. I dream he little *Stand by Me* world feeling." And what about her husband's view on all this? An embarrassed giggle. "I don't know. Little difficult. But I much dream children go other country." She paused, deep in thought. "But I also want children have Zen spirit inside, Japanese feeling." I asked her to explain. "Example—you and Sandy, *zazen* very difficult. Japanese people, *zazen* very easy. I want my children have this spirit."

"But if your children go away, they may grow distant. Maybe never talk to you. Maybe forget all Japanese things. Wouldn't that make you sad?"

"*Tabun.* Maybe."

"It's very difficult, I think."

And so we get off the train, and climb from shrine to shrine, scattered across the steep hills of Kurama, and the rain now drizzles down, now stops again, and the two of us huddle under her umbrella, sweaters brushing, her hair almost falling on my arm. "*Ai to ai gasa,*" I say, thinking of the phrase I had read in a Yosano Akiko poem, describing two people sharing a single umbrella. "Maybe," she says, with a lilting laugh, and we climb some more, the hills before us resplendent now, and then still higher, in the gentle rain, till we are sitting on a log.

In front of us, the trees are blazing. "I like color now," she says, pensive. "Later, I not so like. More sad. Leaves die. Many things change." And then, carried away by the view, perhaps, she recalls the only other time she has come to this hill. Kurama is only a few miles north of Kyoto, a thirty-minute train ride. But Sachiko has not been here for fifteen years, and all that time, she says, she has longed to return. "I so happy," she whispers, as if in the presence of the sacred. "I so excited. Thank you. Thank you very much. I very happy. Very fun. Before I coming here, little teenage size, together three best friend. We climbing mountain, I very afraid, because I thinking snake. Much laughing, many joke. Very fun. My friends' names, Junko, Sumiko, and Michiko. But Osaka now. Very busy, marry ladies."

We walk down again, through the drizzle and the mist, then up slippery paths, between the trees. "I much love Kurama," she says quietly, as if in thought. "Sometimes I ask husband come here; he say, 'You always want play. I very busy. I cannot.' And come here together children, very difficult. Soon tired. Thank you very much, come here this place with me."

This is all rather sad. She tells me of her adventures and the smallness of it all makes me sad again: how when she was a little girl, she went with her cousin and brother and aunt to a cinema, and her aunt allowed her to go and see *The Sound of Music* alone. "I very scared. All dark. Many person there. But then film begin, I soon forget. I much love. I dream I Julie Andrews." She also describes reading about Genghis Khan. "I dream I trip together Genghis Khan. I many trip in my heart, many adventure. But only in my heart." She tells me how once, last year, for the first time ever, she went alone to Osaka, forty minutes away, to see the Norwegian teenybopper group a-ha in concert, and then, exhilarated by this event, went again that same week to another of their concerts, in Kobe, with her son and her cousin, all three of them sharing a room in a luxury hotel. The night she spent in the hotel, the trip to the coffee shop after the concert, the way she had chanced to see the lead singer's parents in the coffee shop and then to meet the star himself in an elevator—all live on in her as what seems almost the brightest moment in her life. "I very lucky. I very excited. I dream, maybe next summer, I go this hotel again. See other a-ha concert."

And when she says, more than once, "I live in Kyoto all life; you come here only one month, but you know more place, very well," I feel again, with a pang, a sense of the tightly drawn limits of a Japanese woman's life, like the autumn paths vanishing in mist around us. For I could see that she was saying something more than the usual "Tourists know more of towns than their residents ever do," and I could catch a glimpse of the astonishing circumscription of her life. Even while her brother had been to Kansas City to study for three years and was now in his third year of pursuing Jung in Switzerland, she had never really been outside Kyoto. She now worked two mornings a week in a doctor's office, but it was the same place where she had worked during junior high school and high school, in vacations, just around the corner from her parents' house. Her cousin, a kind of surrogate sister, sometimes worked in the same place. Her own house was in the next neighborhood down, within walking distance of her parents-in-law's house. And her mother still called her every night, to see how she was doing.

Every year, she said, her husband got three or four days of holiday, and the trips the family took together on these breaks—to the sea once, and once to Tokyo Disneyland—still lived within them as peak experiences. Even a trip such as the one today, for a few hours to a suburb, seemed a rare and unforgettable adventure.

"Please tell me your adventure," she begins to say. "Please tell me other country. I want imagine all place," but I don't know where to begin, or how to convey them to someone who has never been in a plane, and what cloak-and-dagger episodes in Cuba, or nights in the Thai jungle, will mean to one who has scarcely left Kyoto.

"I dream you life-style," she goes on, as if sensing my unease. "You are bird, you go everywhere in world, very easy. I all life living only Kyoto. So I dream I go together you. I have many, many dream in my heart. But I not have strong heart. You very different."

"Maybe. I was lucky that I got used to going to school by plane when I was nine."

"You very lucky. I afraid other country. Because thinking, maybe I go away, my mother ill, maybe die. If I come back, maybe no mother here." Her mother, she explains, developed very serious allergies—because, it seemed, of the new atmospheric conditions in Japan. (All this I found increasingly hard to follow in part because Sachiko used "allergy" to mean "age"—she regularly referred to the "Heian allergy," and when she was talking about "war allergy," I honestly didn't know if it was a medical or a historical point she was making. I, of course, was no better, confusing *sabishii* with *subarashii*, and so, in trying to say, "Your husband must be lonely," invariably coming out with "Your husband is wonderful. Just fantastic," which left her frowning in confusion more than ever.)

"When I little children size, my mother many times in hospital. And Grandma too. And when my brother in Kansas City, my grandma die. He never say good-bye. She see my husband, she think he my brother. Very sad time. So I always dream in heart, because many sad thing happen. But dream stay in heart." This seemed a sorrowful way to approach the universe, though eminently pragmatic. Yet she held to it staunchly. "Maybe tomorrow I have accident. I die. So I always keep dream." That was lovely, elegant, Sachiko: Sachiko, in her teenager's high-tops, keeping a picture of Sting in her wallet and sometimes losing sleep over him—a thirty-year-old girl with daydreams.

All this gets us on to what is fast becoming a recurrent theme in our talks, the competing merits of the Japanese and the American family systems. I, of course, argue heartily for the Japanese.

"It makes me so happy to see mothers and children playing together here, or going to temples together, and movies, and coffee shops. In America, mothers and daughters are often strangers. People do not know their parents, let alone their grandparents. Sometimes, in California, parents just fly around, with very young girlfriends or boyfriends, and leave their children with lots of money but no love." (My sense of America, in Japan, was getting as simplistic and stereotyped as my sense of Japan had been in America.) "So fifteen-year-old girls have babies and drive cars, and have money, many boyfriends, and lots of drugs."

"Maybe. But in your country, I think, children have strong heart. Do anything, very easy. Here in Japan, no strong heart. Even grown-up person, very weak!" I think she means that they lack adventure, recklessness, and freedom, and in all that I suppose she is right, and not only because twelve Japanese CEOs have literally collapsed this year under the pressures of a strong yen. And she, of course, as a foreigner, sees only the pro ledger in America, while I, over here, stress only the con—though when I am in America, I find myself bringing back to American friends an outsider's sense of their country's evergreen hopefulness.

And as we continue walking, a few other people trudge past us up the hill, elders most of them, with sticks, the men in berets and raincoats, the women in print dresses, occasionally looking back through the curtain of fine drizzle at the strange sight of a pretty young Japanese girl with a shifty Indian male. Sachiko, however, seems lost in another world.

"What is your blood type?" she suddenly asks, eyes flashing into mine.

"I don't know."

"True?"

"True."

"Whyyy?" she squeals, in the tone of a high school girl seeking a rock star's autograph.

"I don't know. In my country, people aren't concerned about blood types."

"But maybe you have accident. Go hospital."

"I don't know."

"Really? True??"

"Really. Foreigners think it's strange that the Japanese are so interested in blood types."

"Really? *Hontō ni?*"

"Yes." I am beginning to feel I am letting her down in some way, so I quickly ask if she is interested in the Chinese calendar, or astrology. All this, though, is frightful to try to translate, and when Sachiko says that she is the sign of the "ship" and I say, "Ah yes, you mean the waves," she looks very agitated. "No, no waves! Ship!" Now it's my turn to look startled.

What is going on here? "The Water Bearer?" "No." "The Fish?" "No. Ship!" She is sounding adamant. Then, suddenly, I recall that Aries is the ram. (Thank God, I think, for all those years in California!) "Oh—sheep! You are the sheep sign." "Yes, Ship."

And then, of a sudden, she plops down on a bench, and draws out from her backpack a Japanese edition of Hesse, and shows me the stories she likes, and repeats how he had struck a chord in her when young. "When I little high school size, I much much like. But Goldmund, not so like. When I twenty, it not so touch my heart, not same feeling. Now thirty, maybe different feeling. Which you like?"

"I don't know. That's why I'm reading it again now. When I was young, I liked Goldmund. Then, later, I understood Narziss a little better. For a long time, I spent one month living like Goldmund, traveling around the world, and one month like Narziss, leading a monk's life at home. Now I'm trying both at the same time, to see which one is better."

Somehow the world has misted over as we talk, and time and space are gone: the world, I think, begins and ends on this small bench. And as we sit there, sometimes with her dainty pink umbrella unfurled, sometimes not, I pointing to the yellow trees, or the blue in the sky, and saying, *"Onna-no kokoro, Kurama-no tenki"* (The weather in Kurama is like a woman's heart), I can see her perfect white teeth when she laughs, the mole above her lips, a wisp of hair across her forehead, another fine strand that slips into her ear. She bends over to look at the magazine in my hands, and her hair falls all about me.

"You tell parent about girlfriend?" she says, looking up.

"Well, for many years, I haven't had—or wanted—a girlfriend."

"So what am I?" A long silence. "I man?" She giggles girlishly, and I don't know where that puts us: our discourse is soft and blurred as autumn rain.

"I think you're a very beautiful lady," I say, looking down at my outstretched legs like a bashful schoolboy. "Your husband is a very lucky man."

"I not so think. I bad wife."

And then, seizing the closeness in the air, she tries to formulate more complex thoughts. "I very happy. Today, time stop. Thank you very much, coming here this place together me. I only know you short time, but you best friend feeling. I think I know you long time. I no afraid, no weak heart. You foreigner man, but I alone together you, very easy. I think

maybe you very busy man. But talking very easy. I very fun, thank you."
All of this is a little heartbreaking, I think, together on a bench on a misty
autumn day, and she so excited to see me after only two weeks of acquaintance.

Standing up, we start walking slowly down the hill, through faint drizzle, talking of her closeness to her mother, and the poems of Yosano
Akiko. And as we leave the hill of temples behind us, she turns and bows
towards the shrine, pressing her palms together and closing her eyes very
tight.

———

That evening, I read Yosano Akiko late into the night and try to recall the
short *tanka* Sachiko had recited to me on the hill. But I know only that it
begins with *kimi,* the intimate form of "you," as so many of Akiko's poems
do. Falling asleep over the book, I awaken with a start in the dead of night,
imagining that I am holding her by the hand and saying, "Sachiko-san,
I'm sorry to disturb you. I know you have a husband, and I'm very sorry,
but..."

And later in the night, I think of the two of us under her pink umbrella, and flip hurriedly through the book in search of the phrase *"ai to ai
gasa."* When I find it, my heart seems almost to stop: it is, it seems, a classic image of intimacy, and one of the most famous figures in Japan for
lovers.

# AIMÉE CROCKER

## *And I'd Do It Again*

There is, or was, a famous tea-house in Shanghai which is perhaps better known than any other in the world because it is the model of the Willow Pattern China that every one knows so well. I met two Englishwomen there whom I knew slightly. Now Englishwomen often give the impression that they are very proper and very reserved. But my experience with these two, and a great many after them, has led me to believe that the calm exterior of the British woman conceals something really more adventurous than one ever suspects.

The story begins when I got into conversation with Miss B. and Lady D. Miss B. was telling the story of the Willow Tearoom plate, and it was very sweet and just what I would have expected from the trim, boyish-looking young woman. It is even worth while to repeat it here before going into my adventures, because it contrasts with them so much.

In that very house where the tearoom was, there lived a man with a beautiful daughter whom he wanted to marry to a rich mandarin. But the girl, whose name was Koong Shee, loved Chang, a retainer of her father's. She refused to marry the mandarin, and had to see her lover banished and herself a prisoner on the little lake in the tiny house where the weeping willow can still be seen.

Chang hid in a house the other side of the lake, and sent half a co-coanut shell with a little sail in it to carry her a message of his constant love and to invite her to elope with him. She sent the message back that she would, and they did.

Father was angry but the mandarin was more so, and he came and burned the boy's little house where the two had hidden, and their two souls, like doves, floated over the pond for many a day.

Very pretty and very Chinese, but very much unlike what I have got to say now.

Our conversation covered many things, and it came out somehow that I was interested in adventures. Suddenly Lady D. looked steadily through her lorgnette at her friend and said:

"You know, we have just time to take her to the most wonderful of all adventures. Do you think she would care to come?"

Miss B. thought I would, and I protested that I would try anything once. The upshot was that we all hired a chair and away we went to an address that I did not hear. I speak of the fact that we hired a chair, because it was evident that the two English ladies did not want their own bearers to know where they were going.

However, I was not nervous.

After threading through the amazing streets of the old city, we came to a courtyard which was hidden away as if to keep the world from knowing about it, but where there was a very decent looking house, clean, and seemingly newer than the century-old buildings about it.

My guides got out and went to the door and after pressing on a panel, engaged themselves in conversation with an old woman.

We went in.

I was amazed to see the luxury inside, for the outside of this house, though clean and decent, would never lead one to suspect the richness that it concealed.

The walls were paneled. The paneling was composed of strips of carved ivory, worked into lace-like ornamentation, and bound, every panel, in polished teakwood, likewise carved to frame the beauties of the ivory.

This room was an anteroom, and we sat on two long comfortable benches indicated by the old woman. She in turn left through heavy curtains at the room's further end and left us alone.

I had courage enough to ask my friends what kind of experience was in store for us. I learned little.

"Even if we could tell you," said Lady D., "it would be useless. But you may believe that it is an experience which you will never forget and which, in your turn, you will never be able to describe."

She was right.

She was so right that I hesitate to go further with this feeble attempt at making you understand it. But it has left such an impression on me, and it is so utterly unheard of, in so far as I know, that, after all these years, I am going to try.

The aged attendant returned after a few anxious minutes, and she made my companions understand that all was ready. Lady D. looked at her watch, and insisted that there would not be time for us all to "have the experience" (she constantly used that expression) but that she would withdraw this time so that her friend and I could do so. There was nothing very tense about the place. There was apparently nobody in the house but ourselves, for it was not large and their presence would have been felt or heard. To say that I was bewildered and excitedly curious is putting the case mildly. I was fairly twitching with nervousness.

The two of us were led into another room, also richly furnished, and then up a staircase to one of the most charmingly feminine boudoirs imaginable. Then three young girls in black satin costumes and tight little caps on their heads came in, bringing loose robes. They made us understand that we were to undress and put on the wraps. We did so, I still more nervously, and even Miss B. growing silent and tense.

Then the old woman appeared and beckoned to us.

I insisted that Miss B. go first, and I remember almost better than any other moment in my life the next twenty minutes or so while I sat alone in that strange place, wondering.

I heard almost nothing through the thick curtains that concealed the door through which she had passed, but there was a vague whining sound, like music. It reminded me of a violin, playing far away. Sometimes, when the sound was more distinct, I would feel a slight perspiration and a shiver. It is hard to explain.

After a while, there was dead silence.

Finally I heard the shuffling of slippers, and the curtain was drawn back. It was Miss B. returning.

She was staring straight ahead of her. She did not see me. Her eyes were dilated, her face was flushed. She seemed in a trance. It was as though she had taken a powerful drug. What was it? I almost decided to run away, but the old woman was motioning to me, and I felt obliged to follow her through the door into darkness.

I say darkness. That is not exact. There was the soft glow of a lamp . . .

a single flame, burning like a soul. It made shadows on the carved ivory panels of the walls. The shadows flickered over a large Chinese bed in the room's center. There was a grass mat on the floor, and absolutely nothing else in the place. The one window back of the bed was covered by an impenetrable curtain. There was not a sound.

The old woman's hands were held out for my robe. Frightened to refuse, I gave it to her, but I was terrified to give it. It seemed as though my last defense . . . against a mysterious, imagined something . . . were being taken away.

She softly pushed me to the bed and motioned me to lie down. I did, as if I were hypnotized. Naked I lay out straight on my back, across the bed. I could see nothing but the flickering shadows of the lamp, and the old woman departing.

Then suddenly there was some one in the room. I had not seen him come in. It was an old man, a very old man, with a thin, wax-like face.

Almost without a sound, he shuffled in silken slippers over towards me, stopped about two yards from the bed, and peered at me in silence. His hands were folded under his large sleeves. His eyes glowed and picked up the light of the lamp from in back of me.

Then, still looking fixedly at me, he unfolded his arms and brought out from somewhere a small stringed instrument with an abnormally long neck. He sat down cross-legged on the floor, turned his back on me, and began to play.

That first note . . . it was as though it were drawn from my heartstrings. It was as though something in me were being played with a bow. It drew from the vitals of my life and being and plunged me into a voluptuousness that cannot be described.

It was as though invisible hands were touching me and pouring a rich current of electricity through me and into me. My eyes closed, my body relaxed. Like a million hands pressing my body, torturing me with a delicious torture, that sound . . . or was it music? . . . enwrapped me and carried me out of myself into an orgy of physical hysteria.

No, I cannot explain it. I cannot make myself clear. It was not alone sexual, not alone sensual. It transcended every and all physical pleasure I have ever known. All my body, all my soul and mind and conceptions were thrown into a maelstromic wave of incomparable joy, of supreme pleasure that was not unlike pain. For ages or minutes I was not capable of thought or action, only of the exquisite drinking of sensation. I felt my-

self going mad. Then I writhed on the bed, a prisoner of senses and pleasure. Faster and faster and more rich the sound came from the little man's
hands, rhythm after rhythm consumed me and lighted fires of passion and
madness in me that are unspeakable, unfathomable. . . .

Then it stopped.

I was left panting and in pain at the contrast. I was hardly conscious.
Every nerve in my body was torn and strained, every muscle exhausted,
every fiber of me trembling. I did not see the old man go nor the old
woman come in with my robe, and I hardly regained complete understanding of actual life again until I was being led downstairs by Miss B.,
whose firm arm was tightly around me, guiding me and bracing me for
fear that I fall. I tried to speak, to ask questions, but I found no voice. I felt
myself being led out to the waiting chair and carried off by our coolies.

Then I fainted completely from exhaustion, and knew nothing until I
found myself in the ladies' dressing-room of one of the foreign Clubs of
Shanghai with an Irish attendant holding smelling-salts under my nose.

I asked after Lady D. and her friend, when I could talk.

"Lady D.?" queried the girl. "But it was a gentleman brought you here.
He said you had a fainting spell and to look after you, Lady. But there was
nobody else."

A man? Who? Where had he found me? Where were my English
friends? What did it all mean?

I never found out. I have never been able to find the house of the
strange Chinese violin. I could not find my two friends in Shanghai again,
either to thank them or to learn more of the extraordinary "experience."
And before I could ever trace them or the wonderful house of the ivory
panels that turns pleasure into madness, I left Shanghai . . . quite suddenly
and precipitately.

Explanation? None in so far as I know. I have read of strange experiences with vibrations. It is a fact that the Medieval Chinese could kill by
breaking the nerve cells of the body with the vibrations of a gong. It is
true that at a certain Tabernacle in America, so-called "religious" fanati-
cism which was really sensual or even sexual, has been produced by a hidden organ pipe which vibrated at a certain pitch which the ear could not
detect. But I have never had an explanation for what I shall always remember as my "experience of the Chinese violin."

# AUSTRALASIA

# RUPERT BROOKE

## *The Letters of Rupert Brooke*

To Cathleen Nesbitt          *Mataia, Tahiti and Papeete 7 February [1914]*

The boat's ready to start. The brown lovely people in their bright clothes are gathered on the old wharf to wave her away. Everyone has a white flower behind their ear—Tuatamata had given me one. Do you know the significance of a white flower worn over the ear? A white flower over the *right* ear means

> I am looking for a sweetheart

A white flower over the left ear means

> I have found a sweetheart

and a white flower over each ear means

> I have one sweetheart and am looking for another.

A white flower over each ear, my dear, is dreadfully the most fashionable way of adorning yourself in Tahiti.

# Paul Gauguin

## Noa Noa: The Tahitian Journal

Every day gets better for me, in the end I understand the language quite
well, my neighbours (three close by, the others at various distances) regard me almost as one of themselves; my naked feet, from daily contact
with the rock, have got used to the ground; my body, almost always naked,
no longer fears the sun; civilization leaves me bit by bit and I begin to
think simply, to have only a little hatred for my neighbour, and I function
in an animal way, freely—with the certainty of the morrow [being] like
today; every morning the sun rises serene for me as for everyone, I become carefree and calm and loving. I have a natural friend, who has come
to see me every day naturally, without any interested motive. My paintings in colour [and] my wood-carvings astonished him and my answers to
his questions taught him something. Not a day when I work but he comes
to watch me. One day when, handing him my tools, I asked him to try a
sculpture, he gazed at me in amazement and said to me simply, with sincerity, that I was not like other men; and he was perhaps the first of my
fellows to tell me that I was useful to others. A child. . . . One has to be, to
think that an artist is something useful.

The young man was faultlessly handsome and we were great friends.
Sometimes in the evening, when I was resting from my day's work, he
would ask me the questions of a young savage who wants to know a lot of
things about love in Europe, questions which often embarrassed me.

One day I wished to have for sculpture a tree of rosewood, a piece of considerable size and not hollow. "For that," he told me, "you must go up the mountain to a certain place where I know several fine trees that might satisfy you. If you like, I'll take you there and we'll carry it back, the two of us."

We left in the early morning.

The Indian paths in Tahiti are quite difficult for a European: between two unscalable mountains there is a cleft where the water purifies itself by twisting between detached boulders, rolled down, left at rest, then caught up again on a torrent day to be rolled down further, and so on to the sea. On either side of the stream there cascades a semblance of a path: trees pell-mell, monster ferns, all sorts of vegetation growing wilder, more and more impenetrable as you climb towards the centre of the island.

We went naked, both of us, except for the loincloth, and axe in hand, crossing the river many a time to take advantage of a bit of track which my companion seemed to smell out, so little visible [it was], so deeply shaded.—Complete silence,—only the noise of water crying against rock, monotonous as the silence. And two we certainly were, two friends, he a quite young man and I almost an old man in body and soul, in civilized vices: in lost illusions. His lithe animal body had graceful contours, he walked in front of me sexless. . . .

From all this youth, from this perfect harmony with the nature which surrounded us, there emanated a beauty, a fragrance *(noa noa)* that enchanted my artist soul. From this friendship so well cemented by the mutual attraction between simple and composite, love took power to blossom in me.

And we were only . . . the two of us——

I had a sort of presentiment of crime, the desire for the unknown, the awakening of evil—Then weariness of the male role, having always to be strong, protective; shoulders that are a heavy load. To be for a minute the weak being who loves and obeys.

I drew close, without fear of laws, my temples throbbing.

The path had come to an end . . . we had to cross the river; my companion turned at that moment, so that his chest was towards me. The hermaphrodite had vanished; it was a young man, after all; his innocent eyes resembled the limpidity of the water. Calm suddenly came back into my soul, and this time I enjoyed the coolness of the stream deliciously, plunging into it with delight—*"Toe toe,"* he said to me ("it's cold"). "Oh no," I answered, and this denial, answering my previous desire, drove in among the cliffs like an echo. Fiercely I thrust my way with energy into the thicket, [which had] become more and more wild; the boy went on his way, still limpid-eyed. He had not understood. I alone carried the burden of an evil thought, a whole civilization had been before me in evil and had educated me.

We were reaching our destination.—At that point the crags of the mountain drew apart, and behind a curtain of tangled trees a semblance of a plateau [lay] hidden but not unknown. There several trees (rosewood) extended their huge branches. Savages both of us, we attacked with the axe a magnificent tree which had to be destroyed to get a branch suitable to my desires. I struck furiously and, my hands covered with blood, hacked away with the pleasure of sating one's brutality and of destroying something. In time with the noise of the axe I sang:

> "Cut down by the foot the whole forest (of desires)
> Cut down in yourself the love of yourself, as a man
> would cut down with his hand in autumn the Lotus."

Well and truly destroyed indeed, all the old remnant of civilized man in me. I returned at peace, feeling myself thenceforward a different man, a Maori. The two of us carried our heavy load cheerfully, and I could again admire, in front of me, the graceful curves of my young friend—and calmly: curves robust like the tree we were carrying. The tree smelt of roses, *Noa Noa.* We got back in the afternoon, tired. He said to me: "Are you pleased?" "Yes"—and inside myself I repeated: "Yes."

I was definitely at peace from then on.

I gave not a single blow of the chisel to that piece of wood without having memories of a sweet quietude, a fragrance, a victory and a rejuvenation.

* * *

I move on. Arrived at Taravao (far end of the island) the gendarme lends me his horse, I ride along the East coast, not much frequented by Europeans. Arrived at Faone, the small district that comes before that of Itia, a native hails me. "Hey! man who makes men" (he knows that I am a painter), "come and eat with us *(Haere mai ta maha)*"—the phrase of welcome. I do not need to be asked twice, his face is so gentle. I dismount from the horse, he takes it and ties it to a branch, without any servility, simply and efficiently. I go into a house where several men, women and children are gathered, sitting on the ground chatting and smoking—"Where are you going?" says a fine Maori woman of about forty. "I'm going to Itia." "What for?" An idea passed through my brain. I answered: "To look for a wife. Itia has plenty, and pretty ones." "Do you want one?" "Yes." "If you like I'll give you one. She's my daughter."

"Is she young?" "AE"——

"Is she pretty?" "AE"——

"Is she in good health?" "AE"——

"Good, go and fetch her for me."

She went away for a quarter of an hour; and as they brought the Maori meal of wild bananas and some crayfish, the old woman returned, followed by a tall young girl carrying a small parcel. Through her excessively transparent dress of pink muslin the golden skin of her shoulders and arms could be seen. Two nipples thrust out firmly from her chest. Her charming face appeared to me different from the others I had seen on the island up to the present, and her bushy hair was slightly crinkled. In the sunshine an orgy of chrome yellows. I found out that she was of Tongan origin.

When she had sat down beside me I asked her some questions:
"You aren't afraid of me?" *"Aita* (no)."
"Would you like to live always in my hut?" *"Eha."*
"You've never been ill?" *"Aita."*

That was all. And my heart throbbed as, impassively, she laid out on the ground before me, on a large banana-leaf, the food that was offered me. Though hungry, I ate timidly. That girl—a child of about 13—enchanted me and scared me: what was going on in her soul? and at this contract so hastily thought of and signed I felt a shy hesitation about the signing—I, nearly an old man. Perhaps the mother had ordered it, with her mind on money. And yet in that tall child the independent pride of all that race ... the serenity of a thing deserving praise. The mocking, though tender, lip showed clearly that the danger was for me, not for her. I left the hut, I will not say without fear, took my horse and mounted. The girl followed behind; the mother, a man and two young women—her aunts, she said—followed also. We took the road back to Taravao, 9 kilometres from Faone—After a kilometre I was told: *"Parahi teie* (Stop here)." I dismounted and entered a large hut, well kept and smelling almost opulent. The opulence of the wealth of the earth. Pretty mats on the ground, on top of straw. . . . A family, quite young and as gracious as could be, lived there, and the girl sat down next to her mother, whom she introduced to me. A silence. Cool water, which we drank in turn like a libation. And the young mother said to me, with tears in her eyes: "Are you kind?" . . .

When I had examined my conscience I answered uneasily: "Yes."

"Will you make my daughter happy?" "Yes."

"In 8 days let her come back. If she is not happy she will leave you."

A long silence—We emerged and again I moved off on horseback. They followed behind. On the road we met several people. "Well, well, you're the *vahine* of a Frenchman now, are you? Be happy. Good luck."

That matter of two mothers worried me. I asked the old woman who had offered me her daughter: "Why did you tell me a lie?" Tehamana's mother (that was my wife's name) answered: "The other is also her mother, her nursing mother."

We reached Taravao. I gave the gendarme back his horse.

His wife (a Frenchwoman) said to me (not indeed maliciously, but tactlessly): "What! have you brought back a trollop with you?" And her eyes undressed the impassive girl, now grown haughty: decrepitude was staring at the new flowering, the virtue of the law was breathing impurely upon the native but pure unashamedness of trust, faith. And against that so blue sky I saw with grief this dirty cloud of smoke. I felt ashamed of my race, and my eyes turned away from that mud—quickly I forgot it—to gaze upon this gold which already I loved—I remember that. The family farewells took place at Taravao, at the house of the Chinese who there deals in everything—men and beasts. My fiancée and I took the public carriage, which brought us to Mataiea, 25 kilometres from there,—my home.

———

My new wife was not very talkative, [she was] melancholy and ironic. We observed each other: she was impenetrable, I was quickly beaten in that struggle—in spite of all my inward resolutions my nerves rapidly got the upper hand and I was soon, for her, an open book——

Maori character (yields itself only in time)

French character

A week went by, during which I was childish to a point that surprised me. I loved her and I told her so, which made her smile. (She knew it perfectly well!) She seemed to love me and never told me so. Sometimes, at night, *flashes of light . . . played across Tehamana's golden skin.* That was all. It was a great deal. That week, swift as a day, as an hour, was over: she asked me to let her go and see her mother at Faone. I had promised——

She left and sadly I put her in the public carriage with a few piastres in her handkerchief to pay the fare and give her father some rum.... To me it seemed a good-bye. Would she come back?

Several days later she came back.

I set to work again and happiness succeeded to happiness. Every day at the first ray of sun the light was radiant in my room. The gold of Tehamana's face flooded all about it, and the two of us would go naturally, simply, as in Paradise, to refresh ourselves in a near-by stream.

The life of every day—Tehamana yields herself daily more and more, docile and loving; the Tahitian *noa noa* pervades the whole of me; I am no longer conscious of the days and the hours, of Evil and of Good—all is beautiful—all is well. Instinctively, when I am working, when I am meditating, Tehamana keeps silence, she always knows when to speak to me without disturbing me.

Conversations about what happens in Europe, about God, about the Gods. She learns from me, I learn from her. ...

In bed, at nightfall, conversations.

The stars interest her greatly: she asks me what the morning star and the evening star are called in French. She finds it hard to understand that the earth goes round the sun. She, in turn, tells me the names of the stars in her language.

# CHARLES WARREN STODDARD

## *Cruising the South Seas*

Fate, or the Doctor, or something else, brought me first to this loveliest of valleys, so shut out from everything but itself that there were no temptations which might not be satisfied. Well! here, as I was looking about at the singular loveliness of the place—you know this was my first glimpse of its abrupt walls, hung with tapestries of fern and clambering convolvulus; at one end two exquisite waterfalls, rivalling one another in whiteness and airiness, at the other the sea, the real South Sea, breaking and foaming over a genuine reef, and even rippling the placid current of the river that slipped quietly down to its embracing tide from the deep basins at these waterfalls—right in the midst of all this, before I had been ten minutes in the valley, I saw a straw hat, bound with wreaths of fern and *maile;* under it a snow-white garment, rather short all around, low in the neck, and with no sleeves whatever.

There was no sex to that garment; it was the spontaneous offspring of a scant material and a large necessity. I'd seen plenty of that sort of thing, but never upon a model like this, so entirely tropical—almost Oriental. As this singular phenomenon made directly for me, and, having come within reach, there stopped and stayed, I asked its name, using one of my seven stock phrases for the purpose; I found it was called Kána-aná. Down it went into my note-book; for I knew I was to have an experience with this young scion of a race of chiefs. Sure enough, I have had it. He continued to regard me steadily, without embarrassment. He seated himself before me; I felt myself at the mercy of one whose calm analysis was questioning every motive of my soul. This sage inquirer was, perhaps, sixteen years of age. His eye was so earnest and so honest, I could return his look. I saw a round, full, rather girlish face; lips ripe and expressive, not quite so sensual as those of most of his race; not a bad nose, by any means; eyes perfectly glorious—regular almonds—with the mythical lashes "that sweep," etc., etc. The smile which presently transfigured his face was of the nature that flatters you into submission against your will.

Having weighed me in his balance—and you may be sure his instincts didn't cheat him; they don't do that sort of thing—he placed his two hands on my two knees, and declared, "I was his best friend, as he was mine; I must come at once to his house, and there live always with him." What could I do but go? He pointed me to his lodge across the river, saying, "There was his home and mine." By this time, my *native* without a master was quite exhausted. I wonder what would have happened if some one hadn't come to my rescue, just at that moment of trial, with a fresh vocabulary? As it was, we settled the matter at once. This was our little plan—an entirely private arrangement between Kána-aná and myself: I was to leave with the Doctor in an hour; but, at the expiration of a week we should both return hither; then I would stop with him, and the Doctor could go his way.

There was an immense amount of secrecy, and many vows, and I was almost crying, when the Doctor hurried me up that terrible precipice, and we lost sight of the beautiful valley. Kána-aná swore he would watch continually for my return, and I vowed I'd hurry back; and so we parted. Looking down from the heights, I thought I could distinguish his white garment; at any rate, I knew the little fellow was somewhere about, feeling as miserably as I felt—and nobody has any business to feel worse. How many times I thought of him through the week! I was always wondering if he still thought of me. I had found those natives to be impulsive, demonstrative, and, I feared, inconstant. Yet why should he forget me, having so little to remember in his idle life, while I could still think of him, and put aside a hundred pleasant memories for his sake? The whole island was a delight to me. I often wondered if I should ever again behold such a series of valleys, hills, and highlands in so small a compass. That land is a world in miniature, the dearest spot of which, to me, was that secluded valley; for there was a young soul watching for my return.

That was rather a slow week for me, but it ended finally; and just at sunset, on the day appointed, the Doctor and I found ourselves back on the edge of the valley. I looked all up and down its green expanse, regarding every living creature, in the hope of discovering Kána-aná in the attitude of the watcher. I let the Doctor ride ahead of me on the trail to Bolabola's hut, and it was quite in the twilight when I heard the approach of a swift horseman. I turned, and at that moment there was a collision of two constitutions that were just fitted for one another; and all the doubts and apprehensions of the week just over were indignantly dismissed, for Kána-aná and I were one and inseparable, which was perfectly satisfactory to both parties!

The plot, which had been thickening all the week, culminated then, much to the disgust of the Doctor, who had kept his watchful eye upon me all these days—to my advantage, as he supposed. There was no disguising our project any longer, so I out with it as mildly as possible. "There was a dear fellow here," I said, "who loved me, and wanted me to live with him; all his people wanted me to stop, also; his mother and his grandmother had specially desired it. They didn't care for money; they had much love for me, and therefore implored me to stay a little. Then the valley was most beautiful; I was tired; after our hard riding, I needed rest; his mother and his grandmother assured me that I needed rest. Now, why not let me rest here awhile?"

The Doctor looked very grave. I knew that he misunderstood—placed a wrong interpretation upon my motives; the worse for him, I say. He tried to talk me over to the paths of virtue and propriety; but I wouldn't be talked over. Then the final blast was blown; war was declared at once. The Doctor never spoke again, but to abuse me; and off he rode in high dudgeon, and the sun kept going down on his wrath. Thereupon I renounced all the follies of this world, actually hating civilization, and feeling entirely above the formalities of society. I resolved on the spot to be a barbarian, and, perhaps, dwell forever and ever in this secluded spot. And here I am back to the beginning of this story, just after the shower at Bolabola's hut, as the Doctor rode off alone and in anger.

That resolution was considerable for me to make. I found, by the time the Doctor was out of sight and I was quite alone, with the natives regarding me so curiously, that I was very tired indeed. So Kána-aná brought up his horse, got me on to it some way or other, and mounted behind me to pilot the animal and sustain me in my first bare-back act. Over the sand we went, and through the river to his hut, where I was taken in, fed, and petted in every possible way, and finally put to bed, where Kána-aná monopolized me, growling in true savage fashion if any one came near me. I didn't sleep much, after all. I think I must have been excited. I thought how strangely I was situated: alone in a wilderness, among barbarians; my bosom friend, who was hugging me like a young bear, not able to speak one syllable of English, and I very shaky on a few bad phrases in his tongue. We two lay upon an enormous old-fashioned bed with high posts—very high they seemed to me in the dim rushlight. The natives always burn a small light after dark; some superstition or other prompts it. The bed, well stocked with pillows or cushions of various sizes, covered with bright-colored chintz, was hung about with numerous shawls, so that I might be dreadfully modest behind them. It was quite a grand affair, gotten up expressly for my benefit. The rest of the house—all in one room, as usual—was covered with mats, on which various recumbent forms and several individual snores betrayed the proximity of Kána-aná's relatives. How queer the whole atmosphere of the place was! The heavy beams of the house were of some rare wood, which, being polished, looked like colossal sticks of peanut candy. Slender canes were bound across this framework, and the soft, dried grass of the meadows was braided over it— all completing our tenement, and making it as fresh and sweet as new-mown hay.

The natives have a passion for perfumes. Little bunches of sweet-smelling herbs hung in the peak of the roof, and wreaths of fragrant berries were strung in various parts of the house. I found our bedposts festooned with them in the morning. O, that bed! It might have come from England in the Elizabethan era and been wrecked off the coast; hence the mystery of its presence. It was big enough for a Mormon. There was a little opening in the room opposite our bed; you might call it a window, I suppose. The sun, shining through it made our tent of shawls perfectly gorgeous in crimson light, barred and starred with gold. I lifted our bed-curtain, and watched the rocks through this window—the shining rocks, with the sea leaping above them in the sun. There were cocoa-palms so slender they seemed to cast no shadow, while their fringed leaves glistened like frost-work as the sun glanced over them. A bit of cliff, also, remote and misty, running far into the sea, was just visible from my pyramid of pillows. I wondered what more I could ask for to delight the eye. Kána-aná was still asleep, but he never let loose his hold on me, as though he feared his pale-faced friend would fade away from him. He lay close by me. His sleek figure, supple and graceful in repose, was the embodiment of free, untrammelled youth. You who are brought up under cover know nothing of its luxuriousness. How I longed to take him over the sea with me, and show him something of life as we find it. Thinking upon it, I dropped off into one of those delicious morning naps. I awoke again presently; my companion-in-arms was the occasion this time. He had awakened, stolen softly away, resumed his single garment—said garment and all others he considered superfluous after dark—and had prepared for me, with his own hands, a breakfast which he now declared to me, in violent and suggestive pantomime, was all ready to be eaten. It was not a bad bill of fare—fresh fish, taro, poe, and goat's milk. I ate as well as I could, under the circumstances. I found that Robinson Crusoe must have had some tedious rehearsals before he acquired that perfect resignation to Providence which delights us in book form. There was a veritable and most unexpected tablecloth for me alone. I do not presume to question the nature of its miraculous appearance. Dishes there were—dishes, if you're not particular as to shape or completeness; forks with a prong or two—a bent and abbreviated prong or two; knives that had survived their handles; and one solitary spoon. All these were tributes of the too generous people, who, for the first time in their lives, were at the inconvenience of entertaining a distinguished stranger. Hence this reckless display of tableware. I ate as well as I could, but surely not enough to satisfy my crony; for, when I had finished eating, he sat about two hours in deep and depressing silence, at the expiration of which time he suddenly darted off on his bareback steed and was gone till dark, when he returned with a fat mutton slung over his animal. Now, mutton doesn't grow wild thereabout, neither were his relatives shepherds; consequently, in eating, I asked no questions for conscience' sake.

The series of entertainments offered me were such as the little valley had not known for years: canoe-rides up and down the winding stream; bathings in the sea and in the river, and in every possible bit of water, at all possible hours; expeditions into the recesses of the mountains, to the waterfalls that plunged into cool basins of fern and cresses, and to the orange-grove through acres and acres of guava orchards; some climbings up the precipices; goat hunting, once or twice, as far as a solitary cavern, said to be haunted—these tramps always by daylight; then a new course of bathings and sailings, interspersed with monotonous singing and occasional smokes under the eaves of the hut at evening.

If it is a question how long a man may withstand the seductions of nature, and the consolations and conveniences of the state of nature, I have solved it in one case; for I was as natural as possible in about three days.

I wonder if I was growing to feel more at home, or more hungry, that I found an appetite at last equal to any table that was offered me! Chicken was added to my already bountiful rations, nicely cooked by being swathed in a broad, succulent leaf, and roasted or steeped in hot ashes. I ate it with my fingers, using the leaf for a platter.

Almost every day something new was offered at the door for my edification. Now, a net full of large guavas or mangoes, or a sack of leaves crammed with most delicious oranges from the mountains, that seemed to have absorbed the very dew of heaven, they were so fresh and sweet. Immense lemons perfumed the house, waiting to make me a capital drink. Those superb citrons, with their rough, golden crusts, refreshed me. Cocoanuts were heaped at the door; and yams, grown miles away, were sent for, so that I might be satisfied. All these additions to my table were the result of long and vigorous arguments between the respective heads of the house. I detected trouble and anxiety in their expressive faces. I picked out a word, here and there, which betrayed their secret sorrow. No assertions, no remonstrances on my part, had the slightest effect upon the poor souls, who believed I was starving. Eat I must, at all hours and in all places; and eat, moreover, before they would touch a mouthful. So Nature teaches her children a hospitality which all the arts of the capital cannot affect.

I wonder what it was that finally made me restless and eager to see new faces! Perhaps my unhappy disposition, that urged me thither, and then lured me back to the pride of life and the glory of the world. Certain I am that Kána-aná never wearied me with his attentions, though they were incessant. Day and night he was by me. When he was silent, I knew he was conceiving some surprise in the shape of a new fruit, or a new view to beguile me. I was, indeed, beguiled; I was growing to like the little heathen altogether too well. What should I do when I was at last compelled to return out of my seclusion, and find no soul so faithful and loving in all the earth beside? Day by day this thought grew upon me, and with it I realized the necessity of a speedy departure.

There were those in the world I could still remember with that exquisitely painful pleasure that is the secret of true love. Those still voices seemed incessantly calling me, and something in my heart answered them of its own accord. How strangely idle the days had grown! We used to lie by the hour—Kána-aná and I—watching a strip of sand on which a wild poppy was nodding in the wind. This poppy seemed to me typical of their life in the quiet valley. Living only to occupy so much space in the universe, it buds, blossoms, goes to seed, dies, and is forgotten.

These natives do not even distinguish the memory of their great dead, if they ever had any. It was the legend of some mythical god that Kána-aná told me, and of which I could not understand a twentieth part; a god whose triumphs were achieved in an age beyond the comprehension of the very people who are delivering its story, by word of mouth, from generation to generation. Watching the sea was a great source of amusement with us. I discovered in our long watches that there is a very complicated and magnificent rhythm in its solemn song. This wave that breaks upon the shore is the heaviest of a series that preceded it; and these are greater and less, alternately, every fifteen or twenty minutes. Over this dual impulse the tides prevail, while through the year there is a variation in their rise and fall. What an intricate and wonderful mechanism regulates and repairs all this!

There was an entertainment in watching a particular cliff, in a peculiar light, at a certain hour, and finding soon enough that change visited even that hidden quarter of the globe. The exquisite perfection of this moment, for instance, is not again repeated on to-morrow, or the day after, but in its stead appears some new tint or picture, which, perhaps, does not satisfy like this. That was the most distressing disappointment that came upon us there. I used to spend half an hour in idly observing the splendid curtains of our bed swing in the light air from the sea; and I have speculated for days upon the probable destiny awaiting one of those superb spiders, with a tremendous stomach and a striped waistcoat, looking a century old, as he clung tenaciously to the fringes of our canopy.

We had fitful spells of conversation upon some trivial theme, after long intervals of intense silence. We began to develop symptoms of imbecility. There was laughter at the least occurrence, though quite barren of humor; also, eating and drinking to pass the time; bathing to make one's self cool, after the heat and drowsiness of the day. So life flowed out in an unruffled current, and so the prodigal lived riotously and wasted his substance. There came a day when we promised ourselves an actual occurrence in our Crusoe life. Some one had seen a floating object far out at sea. It might be a boat adrift; and, in truth, it looked very like a boat. Two or three canoes darted off through the surf to the rescue, while we gathered on the rocks, watching and ruminating. It was long before the rescuers returned, and then they came empty-handed. It was only a log after all, drifted, probably, from America. We talked it all over, there by the shore, and went home to renew the subject; it lasted us a week or more, and we kept harping upon it till that log—drifting slowly, O how slowly! from the far mainland to our island—seemed almost to overpower me with a sense of the unutterable loneliness of its voyage. I used to lie and think about it, and get very solemn, indeed; then Kána-aná would think of some fresh appetizer or other, and try to make me merry with good feeling. Again and again he would come with a delicious banana to the bed where I was lying, and insist upon my gorging myself, when I had but barely recovered from a late orgie of fruit, flesh, or fowl. He would mesmerize me into a most refreshing sleep with a prolonged and pleasing manipulation. It was a reminiscence of the baths of Stamboul not to be withstood. From this sleep I would presently be awakened by Kána-aná's performance upon a rude sort of harp, that gave out a weird and eccentric music. The mouth being applied to the instrument, words were pronounced in a guttural voice, while the fingers twanged the strings in measure. It was a flow of monotones, shaped into legends and lyrics. I liked it amazingly; all the better, perhaps, that it was as good as Greek to me, for I understood it as little as I understood the strange and persuasive silence of that beloved place, which seemed slowly but surely weaving a spell of enchantment about me. I resolved to desert peremptorily, and managed to hire a canoe and a couple of natives to cross the channel with me. There were other reasons for this prompt action.

Hour by hour I was beginning to realize one of the inevitable results of time. My boots were giving out; their best sides were the uppers, and their soles had about left them. As I walked, I could no longer disguise this pitiful fact. It was getting hard on me, especially in the gravel. Yet, regularly each morning, my pieces of boot were carefully oiled, then rubbed, or petted, or coaxed into some sort of a polish, which was a labor of love. O Kána-aná! how could you wring my soul with those touching offices of friendship!—those kindnesses unfailing, unsurpassed!

Having resolved to sail early in the morning, before the drowsy citizens of the valley had fairly shaken the dew out of their forelocks, all that day—my last with Kána-aná—I breathed about me silent benedictions and farewells. I could not begin to do enough for Kána-aná, who was more than ever devoted to me. He almost seemed to suspect our sudden separation, for he clung to me with a sort of subdued desperation. That was the day he took from his head his hat—a very neat one, plaited by his mother—insisting that I should wear it (mine was quite in tatters), while he went bareheaded in the sun. That hat hangs in my room now, the only tangible relic of my prodigal days. My plan was to steal off at dawn, while he slept; to awaken my native crew, and escape to sea before my absence was detected. I dared not trust a parting with him before the eyes of the valley. Well, I managed to wake and rouse my sailor boys. To tell the truth, I didn't sleep a wink that night. We launched the canoe, entered, put off, and had safely mounted the second big roller just as it broke under us with terrific power, when I heard a shrill cry above the roar of the waters. I knew the voice and its import. There was Kána-aná rushing madly toward us; he had discovered all, and couldn't even wait for that white garment, but ran after us like one gone daft, and plunged into the cold sea, calling my name over and over as he fought the breakers. I urged the natives forward. I knew if he overtook us I should never be able to escape again. We fairly flew over the water. I saw him rise and fall with the swell, looking like a seal; for it was his second nature, this surf-swimming. I believe in my heart I wished the paddles would break or the canoe split on the reef, though all the time I was urging the rascals forward; and they, like stupids, took me at my word. They couldn't break a paddle, or get on the reef, or have any sort of an accident. Presently we rounded the headland—the same hazy point I used to watch from the grass house, through the little window, of a sunshiny morning. There we lost sight of the valley and the grass house, and everything that was associated with the past—but that was nothing. We lost sight of the little sea-god, Kána-aná, shaking the spray from his forehead like a porpoise; and this was all in all. I didn't care for anything else after that, or anybody else, either. I went straight home, and got civilized again, or partly so, at least. I've never seen the Doctor since, and never want to. He had no business to take me there or leave me there. I couldn't make up my mind to stay; yet I'm always dying to go back again.

So I grew tired over my husks. I arose and went unto my father. I wanted to finish up the Prodigal business. I ran and fell upon his neck and kissed him, and said unto him, "Father, *if* I have sinned against Heaven and in thy sight, I'm afraid I don't care much. Don't kill anything. I don't want any calf. Take back the ring, I don't deserve it; for I'd give more this minute to see that dear little velvet-skinned, coffee-colored Kána-aná than anything else in the wide world—because he hates business, and so do I. He's a regular brick, father, molded of the purest clay, and baked in God's sunshine. He's about half sunshine himself; and, above all others, and more than any one else ever can, he loved your Prodigal."

# LUCY IRVINE

## *Castaway*

My body has become an instrument of the sun. I am its acolyte, cup-bearer to the Gods of white fire. The giant hand of the sun plucks me from my refuge in the sea and flings me upon a flat rock spreadeagled and wanton as a flame. The heat from the baked surface of the rock flares throughout my limbs, thrusts deep into the bone at the points where it touches first, elbows, shoulder blades, coccyx, heels. Far up the beach there is a quivering heat mirage melting the sand. If I were standing there, looking this way, the mirage would be here. I am lying within the mirage.

Words. Jetsam of memory. Toasting to "Lepanto." After the third verse I will lie upside down and the sun will come right up underneath my breasts and between my toes. It has burnished the ends of my pubic hairs and bleached my fringe and the short down at the back of my neck. The top of my coiled plait is going fair. I am a golden gazelle with the head of a striped tiger. I am going to commit adultery with a sunbeam. Whoops, I am not going to read this aloud to G. You have to have a concave navel to make love to a sunbeam. I have the most beautiful navel on Tuin. They enter directly from above when the sun is perpendicular to the earth. If caught on a rock alone at this hour of the day you are almost certain to be ravished. You cannot deny the sun. His seduction is absolute: invasion, conquest, occupation.

G reckons I have sex with goannas. It is not true. The sun is my beloved.

\* \* \*

An aura of body warmth emanated from Titom, although we were not touching. He was looking down at his hands which were making little men in boats out of the stiff pink-tasselled cups that held the mangrove pods, with twigs and wongai pits to represent the figures.

"Kids make like this on island," he said.

Then with one impatient movement he swept them all aside, saying: "You tink this kind play stupid."

"No," I said. "No."

I was dying for a pee and, unaccustomed to having to wait, wriggled away several yards and let it go, just remembering to lower my pants which still felt strange to wear. When the rain stopped and we headed back to camp via Long Beach and the interior, Titom said:

"You been make me want give you one."

Gormlessly I said: "Give me one what?"

He made an unequivocal gesture with an upward thrust bent arm. This time there was an element of proposition. He seemed to be waiting for an answer of some kind. I would love to be able to say that I deflected a potentially awkward situation with a poised and sensible response, but all I said, rather feebly, was:

"No, I don't think we had better do that."

As an afterthought I added: "You told me you have plenty of girl-friends."

"Yes, plenty," he said with relish. "We do them things everytime. If woman got 'usband we don't say nothing, that way no got trouble. She like all right."

He seemed to accept without offence that I was not game and as we passed through Coconut Alley he climbed a tree and cut down a few peepas for me. But he did not come all the way into camp, turning off instead as soon as we came to the beach and swimming out to his dinghy without greeting or saying goodbye to G.

The anger and bitter recriminations that followed stirred up all the ugly resentment in both of us which had first let fly after the exit of the catamaran boys. G accused me of having "fucked" Titom and I accused him of being obsessed and sordid. When he carried on talking as though it were an undisputed fact that I had spent the entire morning in premeditated lascivious activities, I became so incensed that I could no longer reply. Instead I grabbed the axe and vented my fury on a solid branch of tee-tree which was lying beside the woodpile awaiting just such a burst of activity. Between blows I heard G say:

"It's not just sour grapes on my part, Lu. I just think you're being stupid, throwing yourself at young bucks. You'll get yourself into trouble one day."

As there was no response other than the crashing thumps of the axe as it bit into the branch in half a dozen different places, he started on a new tack:

"How would you like it if a pretty girl came to the island and I went off for all-morning walks with her?"

Pausing in my onslaught with the axe I stabbed cruelly at him with words:

"I would not mind at all. I wish one would come, and I wouldn't mind what you did with her. Release your tension and get it off me!"

"And what place do you think you'd have with me if I got something to fuck?"

"I don't need a place with you. I get along fine with Tuin."

This was not strictly true, and was perhaps the worst way of expressing what on other occasions I had already failed to put into words. I never did manage to explain adequately to G the peculiar and, to me, beautiful relationship I had with Tuin. Since the visitors had started coming and it was obvious that G was sick and tired of the rock-bottom survival business, I had given up all hope of his ever really giving himself to the island as I had done. But to be honest, I must admit that I had reached a stage where I so cherished my times alone in the depths of Tuin that had G suddenly wanted to accompany me his presence would have felt like an intrusion. I was more possessive of Tuin than I had ever been of any man.

We wrangled and snarled on and off for a couple of days and then abandoned the subject and reverted to treating one another as the companions we had by now become, despite the unsolved problem of our non-existent sex life.

# WILLIAM DIAPEA

## Cannibal Jack: The True Autobiography of a White Man in the South Seas

After all this, all that I remember is, that the main part of the canoe—the big one of the two—parted from the decking completely, and drifted clear away, but the decks still held together, but were reduced to an angle of about thirty degrees of inclination, in consequence of the other and smaller canoe being still intact, causing my body to droop forward in its fast, strong rope-lashings, so that I was now suspended by the middle, still, however, retaining my seat, somewhat after the fashion of a public-house sign, which I had in my youth frequently seen in London, and called the "Golden Fleece."

How long I remained in this position—whether a week, a day, an hour or two, or even a month—if possible for the human body to retain its vital spark for this last conjectured long period—it is impossible for me to say, as I had no means of ascertaining, even approximately, because I did not know even the name of the month, to say nothing of its date, when that little amusing episode took place. All that I know is, that *sometime* after this, in my incipient state of regaining consciousness, I just unclosed my eyes for about two seconds—no more—and was then fain to close them again from languid weakness; but still they were unclosed long enough for me to get a glimpse that I was not alone, but in the company of an angel, I thought—not a white one, but a black one—and that there was something superlatively pleasant as well as wonderfully mysterious about it, because it is said that they "neither marry nor are given in marriage" in the angelic regions, which, of course, implies that they are of the neuter gender, whereas this one was of the feminine gender! It was like a vision of a heavenly aspect, and so I lay, at least, twelve days longer, before I thoroughly recovered full consciousness, and which I did, however, by degrees, at the expiration of that long period; but should I live for a thousand years longer, I shall never forget the soothing, placid happiness which I experienced the whole of that twelve days, whilst hovering between the two worlds! To make a long story short, I was in the bush on a Fiji island, under a large banyan tree, with a Fiji girl watching me; but before I regained full consciousness I felt that I was in heaven—and if heaven proves to be half as blissful a state as those days were to me, then it is, indeed, worth trying to gain at whatever sacrifice!

I felt that I was in my mother's company, and who, by the by, died a thorough saint, albeit I had never known her in this grosser world, but I did there in that heavenly one, also my sister, Marianne, who also died a most exemplary Christian. I was given to understand that I was there partly through their prayers—the latter reminding me of that solemn warning she had given me ten minutes previous to her death, when she called me closer to her dying bed, and repeated my Christian name three distinct times—"William, William, William, *Remember your dying sister!*"

I thought that we were all mixed in one rapturous joy, in the company of innumerable angels—black and white. The Virgin Mary, also her blessed Son, were there also, and they were all receiving me with unfeigned delight!

When I found that I was really and truly back to this sublunary state, I felt, for the moment, horribly disappointed!

This girl, when I opened my eyes for the first time for those few seconds only, and whom I took to be an angel, and which appeared to me to be enacted in another world, or a mere vision only, and not at all a reality, was then plying me with sustenance, consisting of the nice, white, delicate, soft, custard-like meat, mixed with the heated milk or water of the delicious young coco-nuts, by gently parting my lips with her tender fingers for the reception of the same, and which act, together with its reviving influence, no doubt caused me to partially (but exceedingly evanescently) recover; but, as I said above, I immediately afterwards relapsed into that languid weakness, and continued in that state, she said, for twelve consecutive days,—she continuing all that long period to ply me with that and other nutritious sops at regular stated intervals, day and night, without for one moment relaxing this exceedingly kind and more than human vigilance, excepting for the purpose of rest, and now and then returning to the village for the sake of allaying suspicion, should her absence become too prolonged, and thereby become suspicious.

She told me that during all that time I occasionally opened my eyes as at first, merely looking at her, and then closed them again as before; but during the last four or five days of this "long sleep," as she called it, this opening of the eyes happened oftener and continued longer, till, at last, I recovered entirely, that is, in regard to consciousness and strength too.

"I looked about me" she said "with apparent great wonderment," and at last answered all her incessant questionings.

She now told me that I was on the small island of "Komo" in the "lau" or windward group of Fiji, subject to Lekeba, the residence of Tuniau, the king, "and that she herself was the daughter of the chief of this island, residing in the only village or township on the island, and that it was situated just round the point"—the distance being about a mile off, I afterwards learned—"and that, whilst searching for shell-fish along the shore at a distance from the village, and quite out of sight of it, she had been the first to discover the small part of a large sailing canoe, stranded on the shingly beach hard by, with myself lashed so securely to the back rail or banister of the canoe house, and that she had great difficulty in getting me clear when she first essayed to cast off the rope with her fingers; but perceiving my large, and, as it proved to be sharp knife, she quickly drew it from its sheath and severed the different parts of the rope, and then conveyed me on her back up to the spot where we were now sitting upon for interment, as she thought I was dead, and that she would not take me to the village, even had she been able, because the people there were not like herself 'lotu' (religious) and would be sure to cut up some capers with my body, and even perhaps eat it, when they found that it did not yet stink, and that all her entreaties would be of no avail, because she was not like one of Tuniau's daughters of Lekeba, he being a great king, whereas her father was only a chief of a small island, consequently the people cared very little about him, and, of course, much less for herself—she being a mere girl! But as she had learned to read in God's book, whilst at Mrs. Calvert's school at Lekeba, where her father had left her when he went in to pay his yearly tribute to Tuniau, and that book had told her to be good to everybody, and more especially to the unfortunate and afflicted, and when she found I was alive and not dead as she at first thought, she had constantly prayed to God for my perfect recovery, and that He had answered her prayers by making me well again!"

And now I asked her how it would be with me if I ventured into the village in her company, whether her father would receive me and not kill me? She said that *he* himself would not hurt me for her sake, she being his only daughter, and that her mother was dead. I then said, but perhaps the people will insist upon "knocking the salt water from my eyes"—as it is termed—fearing the god of the sea more than your father? She said that she would have to consider this well over, asking God's help, before she could venture to give me an answer to this most difficult question: "taro dredre."

I now inquired for my knife and also for my belt, which she produced from a hollow of a rotten knot of the tree, where she had deposited them for safe keeping. I found the 100 sovereigns quite correct, which it will be remembered by the reader that I had received as a reward for my perseverance, when I acted in the capacity of detective in recovering the whole of the missing 1,000*l.* which had been purloined from the "Sailor Boy"— the pugilistic hero—by a native. She said she had discovered this inner belt when she stripped me for the purpose of rinsing my clothes as well as my body with fresh water, so as to cleanse them of the remains of the salt water. The part of this remark which alluded particularly to the rinsing of my body, although it is generally thought that dark people's blushes are never visible, but that is a wrong conclusion, because this most delicate as well as religious girl, more than I ever witnessed before with either black or white, blushed so palpably, and, more than that, could never afterwards be induced by any means to make the most distant allusion to that particular part of the subject, but always so adroitly turned the conversation on to some other subject!

One day, on her regular return to me, from her father's at the village, which she never omitted to visit, on the pretence of carrying home a basket of shell-fish, for the very requisite purpose of throwing dust into the eyes of all the rest of these very acute savages as well as his own, and thereby to account for her frequent and sometimes longish absences, in order to secure ample time for her self-imposed work of mercy, in regard to seeing to the well-being of her now convalescent protégé.

And now, I suspect, if to judge by my own feelings, she viewed me in the shape of her truly affianced partner, sent to her by the hand and will of that all-providing Providence, and in whom she so implicitly believed and so fully trusted, in her simple but strong faith. I say, on this particular day she seemed unusually sad, when I, of course, wished to know, at any rate, *something* of its cause; but the only answer I got, and that after long waiting for, from this more than woman in regard to sentiment, was a most ungovernable burst of grief and uncontrollable torrent of tears and sobs, ejaculating and bemoaning her hard fate, declaring in a most heartrending paroxysm of grief that she was utterly undone—*"Au saca!" "Au saca sara!!"*

After this violent grief (this violent paroxysm almost annihilating her) had somewhat subsided, and something like reason began to assume its wonted sway, I managed to elicit—piecemeal as it were—from her, that the people of the town had been collecting property, preparatory to presenting it to her father, according to the immemorial heathen custom, so as to celebrate the shortly forthcoming marriage between herself and the lad to whom she had been ceremoniously betrothed in her infancy, and this first ceremony had been confirmed by stated periodical instalments of property-gifts ever since, up till now that she had arrived at the full age of puberty, between sixteen and seventeen—the girls of the tropics being precocious in body as well as mind. And now the dreaded climax was at hand!

I asked her "if she did not like the lad?" When this hitherto more than lamb in gentleness, turned, for the nonce, more than tigress, in the vehemence of the two passions which had, for the time being, taken complete possession of her, said, "I liked him well enough till I saw you, you little, blind, white fool! but not in the way I like you, and I insist upon you liking me in the same manner!" when she clasped me with such a passionate embrace, that I really thought that she would squeeze the very life out of me! and then as suddenly desisted, forcing me on to my knees, herself assuming the same posture, and poured out her whole soul in the most eloquent supplications, asking forgiveness for her waywardness, and help and strength from above to guide her in the right path for the future!

She got up, now transformed into an angel of light and meekness!

This girl's form was of that sylph-like symmetry so common to the nymphs of the South Sea Islands, and especially at that time—before degeneracy had begun to set in—and her features of such exquisite regularity, while her eyes were liquid with love and adoration! Her skin, though dark, not black, was as soft, smooth, and glossy as the most beautiful of silk-velvet, and the long tapering fingers of her beautiful aristocratic hands, capable of being bent as far backwards, almost, as they were forwards, in their exceeding pliability, besides the beauty of her neatly turned ankles and her exquisitely formed feet. Her teeth were perfectly regular and as white as snow, and the *tout ensemble* of this lovely creature, and which I do not know what to compare it to, unless perhaps the human gazelle, fairly ravished me, and her name was "Ande Litia"—Miss Litia!

About this time a trading schooner from the second biggest island of Fiji—Vanua Levu—and from the district called Soleau situated on that large island, and which the whites, since their expulsion from Levuka by Cakobau, had made their permanent residence, came along on a trading expedition, and when night came on soon after her arrival, this girl put into the water with her own hands, unperceived by a single soul but herself, a small paddling canoe, and paddled it up to the shingly beach, and hastened up to the banyan tree, and forthwith proceeded to hurry me down to the canoe, and then paddled me off to the schooner, saying that God had answered her many prayers, and that she now saw her way clear of all danger of the salt-water being knocked out of my eyes, and securing me for her own and only husband, besides; because she would put me on board the schooner that night and the next day I could land with her in the regular way, as she would carry on board some presents in the shape of a fowl or two, some fruit, etc., the next morning, and select me for her friend—a thing always allowed even in the wildest times; and then I could land as one of the crew, and go up in the ordinary way to her father's house with her as his daughter's friend, without being in the slightest danger from the people of the village, "magaiti-nada!"—a curse, which will not here bear a literal interpretation, especially as it comes from the pretty lips of the religious and moral Litia herself! Suffice it to say, that it has reference to their mothers, and is, after all, only a little harmless expletive, used by this sorely tried poor girl in her excitement. When we were within hearing distance and almost or quite within sight, it not being very dark, I hailed the schooner in English, and as the man who had anchor watch could perceive at a glance, as it were, that no treachery was intended, he allowed me to come on board, and this brave girl paddled me up alongside, not really sure that she would not be fired at, it being night, as the whole of the whites at Fiji, at that time, most religiously guarded against all communication with the natives during the hours of darkness—and which fact most of the natives were aware of—whilst on a trading expedition, lest treachery might supervene—a thing they were shockingly prone to throughout the whole length and breadth of this proverbially treacherous country!

I now told her to hasten back to the shore, haul the canoe up in its place, go to bed, and come on board with her presents the next morning, as arranged—myself remaining on board the schooner.

The next morning, bright and early, she was on board with her fowls, fruit, a couple of fancy mats, etc., her little brother paddling the canoe this time for her. She jumped on board, when I immediately made up to her, bidding her good morning ("Saiadra!"), as though I had never seen her before, asking her in the purest Fiji if she had come to trade these things off for property, or if she preferred forming a connection in the shape of friendship, which in Fiji is called "veitau"? This completely blinded the brother—a lad of some twelve years old—as to our former acquaintance. She made answer that she would prefer making the things a present to myself, seeing that I was so very fluent in her own language, she said.

———

I accordingly accepted this present, took a couple of sovereigns from my belt, retired into the cabin, expended it principally in print, together with other accessories—such as needles, cotton, thimble, tape, buttons, etc., etc., in fact, all and sundry which go to the making up a lady's toilet, and which, by the by, is no very great deal when the recipient is a *Fiji* lady. I also bought a large fourteen-inch knife for her father, when we betook ourselves to the canoe, the boy paddling for the shore as highly rejoiced as if his sister had suddenly come into a large fortune—and it was a fortune to her, poor girl!

We landed, and as I passed up towards the chief's house, the girl leading the way, I saw under a shed—a mere sun-break—the part of the canoe which had been my salvation, and so very nearly, alas! my destruction too.

As I looked at it, the girl gave me a very significant glance, which meant, as plainly as words could have said, "There's your old friend!" It was now converted into a very nice single canoe, called a "cama kau," and which name conveys its own meaning—a canoe with a single, wooden spar outrigger. It was even now capable of carrying quite a score of people, with perfect safety, in ordinary weather. I saw also a largish sail, spread out on the nice little grass plot beside the shed, very near completion, made from the new, narrow, sail-matting. She also gave me another

significant look, confirming what I was then thinking, that this latter was
for my "old friend."

We entered her father's house without molestation, and, in fact, excepting for their notorious cannibalism—and which horrid practice, by
the by, they have inherited from their forefathers—these simple people,
and especially those of almost all the small islands, one would take, on his
first entrance among them, to be quite civilized, so civil, orderly, and domestic, apparently, are all their almost patriarchal bearings, and their
countenances wear a contented and even benevolent expression; and
were it not for the rites of their horrid, false, and heathen religion, they
would be all they ordinarily appeared. As it is, they but seldom have an
opportunity of exercising these horrid rites, unless some foolish unfortu-
nates like myself happen to drop into their clutches, sent by the sea god,
and they always drop into their capacious maws, unless thwarted by the
wily stratagems of such prodigies as Litia, as in my own, so far, lucky case!

Litia presented her father with the long knife, and which would prove
an exceedingly useful article to him for numberless purposes—such as
clearing away bush when cutting new gardens, or weeding old ones; cutting off the branches of bananas from the trees of the dozen—more or
less—different species, when mature, ready for hanging up to ripen, this
plan being generally adopted, instead of the more natural one of being
left to become so on the trees, because the birds in this country are especially troublesome—parrots principally—and there the flying-fox or
vampire bat—whether bird or beast or a little of both—can go his share
of ripe bananas as well as all other kinds of fruit. And then the knife is exceedingly useful for cutting the tree itself down, and cutting it into pieces
to scatter over the ground to become manure, instead of uselessly en-
cumbering the earth after it has borne the one and only bunch it ever
bears, and giving its suckers a chance of sun, light, and air, so as to enable
them to bear in their turn the same as their mothers.

She told him that she had secured this useful article especially for
himself, from her good "friend," pointing to me, asking in a very playful
manner, if she was not an excellent judge of human nature in respect to
generosity, in the selection of her friend? She also exhibited all her own
riches, prattling away all the time with the greatest glee, and then tore off
from her print three or four fathoms, and straightway proceeded to equip
her brother in the accustomed style which they use the native tappa or
"masi" for, and he being a chief's son it formed a train which commoner

youths dare not adopt, and with which he aired his consequence, by immediately dragging it all through the dirt, throughout the whole village, as pleased as a dog with two tails!

They then proceeded to make a small feast for me, as it was through my means that he had been first breeched, and consequently—rather prematurely—made a man of, his hitherto state being perfectly nude, whereas it was now only partially so, and as this metamorphosis is always accompanied by a rejoicing ceremonial feast, exchanging of gifts, a dance, etc., etc., and so, not two, but, in this case, three birds were killed by the one stone—to wit, the making me welcome, and actually adopting me, as it were, into this very interesting family, besides consecrating this, always considered momentous change.

The whole of the simple inhabitants of this village were rendered extremely happy at the celebration of this little episode, and the father of Litia was at the height of his glory at having his boy turned into a man so suddenly, and all through the good offices of his more than idolized daughter; and seeing that he was a widower of not more than forty years of age, the whole of his hitherto concentrated conjugal affections had been transferred to this living type of his never to be forgotten, but for ever lost, faithful partner! Seeing that these small isolated places are so monotonously cut off from all the rest of the outside world, no wonder that the least excitement out of the ordinary humdrum routine tends to elate these poor people to a degree scarcely credible—in fact, it is something comparable to being brought from *death* itself to *life* itself!

They were so prodigiously rejoiced that they were never tired of telling me "that whenever I called again—and which they sincerely hoped would be often—that I knew where to make straight for my real home"!

But it soon began to appear that this kind of merely tacit adoption, which seemed to satisfy everybody else, would not by any means satisfy Litia, whose expectations were decidedly of a more tangible form, and me being adopted into the family so that I should always have a home whenever I occasionally called—if ever, by the by!—on my return trips, as these simple blockheads thought, would not, of course, suit this self-willed beauty. She knew her power and acted accordingly. She aimed at nothing short of adoption, and absorption too, of my whole being, body and soul, into her very essence! No half-measures for Litia! for when the time came for me to repair on board the schooner for the purpose of proceeding on to Lekeba, and at the arrival of the boat on the beach to convey me on board, the hand-shaking business was prolonged with that lingering procrastination, easier imagined, under the circumstances, than described! but when it came that I *must* go or be left for good, in essaying to embark, I was held on to with that desperate tenaciousness, and even franticness, which is almost impossible to describe!

The whole of the people of the village were down at the beach, and they tried to console her by saying that, as soon as the vessel had gone, the ceremony of marriage with her betrothed would be performed, and that it had only been postponed for a more leisurely time, as all the property had some time previous been collected in readiness to convey to her father, and his brother, her uncle, called in Fiji little father—"tamana lailai"; but instead of consoling, this irritated her to the last degree, and when her affianced, at the suggestion of all the bystanders, offered to lead her away, she spurned and spit at him, declaring, that even if she loved him instead of hating him as she implacably did, she said, she wished to know how or by whose means this ceremony could be performed?—marrying a heathen to a Christian, most absurd and preposterous! she said. And now her uncle attempted to drag her forcibly away, but in dragging her he was dragging me also, for it was next to impossible to unclasp her hands from around my body, which she had so firmly clasped in her almost frantic despair, as well as her determination to carry her point! She declared that she would strangle herself (a thing there was not much doubt about, as they were always terribly prone to suicide) unless she was allowed to have the husband, whom God in His goodness had sent to her, in answer to her many prayers!

And now the father stepped up to me and whispered in my ear, that although it was not for him, an ignorant black man, to dictate to a white gentleman from the wise land ("vanna vuka"), yet he thought as she had in the first place saved my life the least I could do was now to save hers! And so it appeared that this real good fellow was in the secret as well as his daughter how I had first arrived on the island; this intelligence, of course, had been communicated to him by his loving and confiding offspring.

The boat's crew, thinking that this girl was and had been, some time previous to this, my *bona fide* wife, as they knew next to nothing of my previous history, and that she was merely objecting, albeit with extreme vehemence, to me going to Lekeba, got tired of this somewhat prolonged and not very amusing drama, shoved off, when her father said aloud to me, "Take her into Lekeba and get married by Mr. Calvert," but I re-marked "that if that was his real intention I could find a much handier shop than Lekeba to accomplish that little matter," when he said that that was, of course, his real intention, because he had not the slightest desire to run the risk of losing his daughter by strangulation, or even for her to live unhappy. As all the people looked greatly surprised, if not exactly shocked, at this declaration, I asked, "What about the betrothed lad?" and this young man hearing me, said, *"Au sa cata, Au sa cata vakadua sara!"* which was equivalent to forswearing this very perverse affianced of his for ever! I then hailed the boat again, when she returned and took us both on board—she being nothing loth—and we repaired to the schooner, where I bought an assortment of goods, among the rest ten muskets, a pig of lead, and a keg of powder, besides several large boxes of military percus-sion caps, ball moulds, etc., expending some twenty-five or thirty sover-eigns from my belt. We were both put on shore again with the goods, when the boat returned to the schooner, and she was immediately got under way, set sail, and proceeded on her voyage, and that was the last I ever saw of her. The things were all carried to the chief's house, where all three of us followed, and then I sent over to the betrothed lad a quantity of stuff—a new American axe, a couple of tomahawks, some knives, etc.,—and which would greatly assist him in procuring another wife. The chief's brother received also an American axe, which I had sent across the way for him, and I did all this for the sake of keeping peace and quietness, and prevent all dissatisfaction, consequently all chance of an irruption would thereby be avoided as far as it was possible for human foresight to guard against.

# THE AMERICAS

# TOBIAS SCHNEEBAUM

## *Keep the River on Your Right*

There came another hunting trip with many men, and me among them freshly painted, going farther and farther into the forest, carrying in my hand my bow and arrows, while they carried theirs, too, and axes of stone as well. The rains of the season had already begun and sheets of water drenched the jungle and flooded the rivers. Streams turned into raging torrents, and we would cross them slowly, leaning against the current, the water rushing violently over our legs; quickly it reached our waists and we strained to make headway, holding our weapons above our heads. Michii grabbed my hand and ran at an angle with the current until there was no bottom and we were suddenly being swept downstream and finally jolted into a far bank. Thick mud was everywhere and we sank deep into marshes and struggled in slime, pulling ourselves out by grasping vines. It was any day and any time of my life, the rain a little heavier. The scarlet of our faces was streaked with water and dropped in stains that paled upon our bodies. A silence came over the whole of us and we stood in a small open area on wet leaves and formed a circle around our propped-up arrows and axes, our arms on each other's shoulders, so close our hips were touching, and we swayed back and forth, heads leaning to one side. "Ooooo-ooooo," we whispered in a low growl. "Ooooo-ooooo," the sound came out from deep inside, sending a shiver along the line of arms. Michii broke from the circle and stepped inside, the gap closing in a smack of flesh. He held up his penis and began to rub it hard. He walked to the man beside me who was himself then half erect, and touched the ends of their penises together, then moved in a counter-clockwise fashion from one to another, pressing slightly on each penis with his own, ending up with mine, and re-entering the circle at my side. We growled once again in whispers and I wondered at this ceremony, performed so far from home, thinking not where it might end or why no one had shot the nutria we had startled in its sleep, but only thinking in the present and allowing all to enter in.

# EDMUND WHITE

## States of Desire: Travels in Gay America

The great baths—and they are as great for the beauty of the clientele as for that of the setting—are the 8709 Club Baths. To get in you need I.D. (a driver's license or a passport) and the name and membership number of someone who has referred you. The first visit costs six dollars for a locker, four dollars afterward. The place is huge and seems still larger because it is mined with mirrors. L.A. has the most beautiful men in the world, and it is only appropriate that it should celebrate them with their multiplied images. I can still see one young man combing his hair under a blower and then shaking his head minutely from side to side so that the duck feathers might lie flat and overlap as *L'Uomo*—if not nature intended. In his eyes were pinpoints of anxiety and across his brow one furrow of concentration, the fold in the taut silk.

These bodies are silken, tan, hairless. In each city we might say there is one body type, the Platonic form for that locality. In New York the body might be burly, Neapolitan hairy, bulbously muscular and less interesting from behind than in front. In San Francisco the body is trim, five-foot-ten, and the face wears a dark beard and mustache below warm brown eyes radiating good will. In L.A. the body is slender, the buttocks pneumatic with youth, a trail of gold dust shading the hollow just above the coccyx and between the pecs. Something fragile about the clavicle and tender about the nape causes the figure to oscillate between boyhood and maturity. The eyes are blue.

In one dark cul-de-sac I encountered someone who applied to my body hands and lips of such curious alertness that I led him by the hand back into the light and asked him why he was so feeling, so sensitive.

My question found a ready response. He told me about himself. "I'm from Genoa," he said, "by way of Buffalo. Now I'm out here, where I'm not very happy. You meet someone, you exchange numbers, but he never calls. And there are such distances here and no friendly little squares where people bump into their friends. I lived for a year just three blocks away from an old buddy I didn't know was out here—and I never saw him once. You don't bump into people in L.A. very easily."

So he's an Italian, I thought. That's why he's lonely for a piazza. Yet wasn't there something else about him he wasn't mentioning?

At last he explained. "I'm Catholic. See that man over there? He's a friend, a Dominican. I was very religious; I still am, but I can't stomach the Church as it is. So I just wander around. I'm a member of Dignity, the Catholic gay group. You'll think this is weird, but my way of worshiping God (I know this sounds heavy) is to come here and make love to as many men as possible. You see, I think God is in people."

# Jonathan Raban

## *Old Glory: A Voyage Down the Mississippi*

Somewhere in the deranged alphabet of local radio stations I met a woman who asked me what I was doing for dinner that evening.

Her first word when she arrived was "Plus—" Sally lived in the middle of sentences to which she was making constant additions. She began with afterthoughts.

"Plus I had to stop for gas, which is why I'm late. Plus, I was late anyway."

Her long fur coat looked as if she made a habit of going swimming in it. Her pale hair was making a successful jailbreak from the pins that she had jammed into it. She hadn't yet removed the price tag from the neck of her scarlet cocktail dress.

"Plus . . . I don't know. Oh, hell, just give me what you're drinking, huh? What *are* you drinking?"

"Martini."

"I *hate* Martinis. Yeah. Okay. No, that's what I want. I'd like a Martini."

She brought with her a buzz of static electricity. Tense, slender, she was all sparks and crackling filaments. Thinking, she scrunched up her narrow face as thoughts escaped from her in dozens like her unruly hair. Most of what I got was just the spin-offs and industrial waste of this complicated process. Scrunching, she said, "God! . . . like . . . because . . ." and her hand slapped at the air as if she'd seen a blow-fly overhead. ". . . kind of . . . well, *you* know . . . right?" Somewhere in the dots between the words lay a whole succession of rejected ideas. It was hard to tell whether they were of the order of grocery lists or of Einstein's relativity theory.

We ate at Anthony's. The big, half-empty restaurant was unnaturally dark; its napery, by fitful candlelight, was unnaturally white. The waiter, insofar as I could clearly see his face, was Henry Kissinger.

"You're not into *cars*—" Sally said, turning on me in a sudden bristle of angry boredom.

"No, not at all." I felt stung.

"God."

"Why?"

"What? Oh . . . I dunno. Yeah. I remembered. Sorry. No, the last guy I dated here, he was into cars. You know what the conversation was? He was going on about *car washes*. I was pretty well switched off, not listening; then he leans over the table and says in this, like, *intimate* voice, 'Which part do you like best? The washing or the waxing?' That was our conversation, for godsake. I went into hiding in the powder room. God, he was a drag."

"Which part *do* you like best—the washing or the waxing?"

"Have you seen my car? I don't wash it. I hate car washes, period." She gave a dismissive, ponylike shake of her head. Pins tinkled on the plates below.

Sally's voice had kept the dry, sandy tone of the Midwest, but it was a voice that had been places. She'd gone to college first in Philadelphia, then on the West Coast. She spent weekends in New York. Her $220-a-week job in her hometown was a stopover between planes, and she was fizzing with impatience at St. Louis. Technically speaking, she was twenty-seven, but she managed to slip, at almost every sentence end, from being seventeen to thirty-four and back again. She liked to keep things fluid. The rush and scatter of her talk left me limping behind, feeling elderly and slow.

"*God*, no—that wasn't on the kib*butz;* this was in the Chinese restaurant in San Fran*cisco* . . ."

In leaps and swoops, we covered the world. I learned how she'd broken with her last "guy" six months before, how she'd rowed with her Catholic boss that morning, how she'd backpacked through France and Italy, how she hated going into bars alone, how she got "dizzy" on wine, how her mother was having difficulty selling luncheon tickets for the forthcoming visit of Isaac Bashevis Singer to the local Hadassah. Just occasionally, I found a couple of bits of the scrambled jigsaw that did fit together.

When I lit her cigarette for her over the cheese board, she cupped her hand around mine to steady the flame. Two days later, following the tracks of several hundred thousand St. Louisans before me, I moved west, into Sally's apartment in Clayton.

———

It was a magical transformation. Seen from this new angle, from out "in the county," St. Louis was changed as effectively as if a wand had been waved over it. I, too. Repatriated to domestic life, I took to it with the gratitude of a shipwrecked man rescued from a desert island.

In Clayton, estates of half-timbered Tudor houses, gloomy with conifers, stood behind tall wrought-iron gates. As streets in Clayton went, our own street was mean and ordinary; a long avenue of rippling leaves and gabled villas. Women in our neighborhood went shopping in little British sports cars. The neighborhood laundry sold spray cans of Mace for blinding rapists and muggers—the one reminder that another, nastier world lay just a few miles off beyond the trees, that our own safe green exile might come under attack one day. Our country lanes, broad lawns and leaded windows had the special preciousness of things we'd won against the odds from the ugly city at the wrong end of the highway.

Sally's three-room apartment was a little out of phase with Clayton. It didn't feel precious. It had the temporary air of a motel cabin from which she was about to move out at any moment. Nothing in the place looked as if she had deliberately chosen it. Her possessions seemed to have happened to her by accident. There were a foot-high replica of Rodin's *Thinker,* a Buddha, an African girl in fake ebony, a mildly repulsive wall clock made of petrified wood from Arizona, some tired potted plants with candy-striped bows tied around their necks, a glass cylinder of heart-shaped candies. She had papered the walls of her kitchen with a design, terrifying in the early mornings, of black feet on a blood-colored ground. She said that she'd thought "it looked kind of cute," but the emphasis was on the past tense. I wondered whether she had been given the other objects in her life, or whether, like the wallpaper, they were all the results of some long-ago passing impulse, tolerated now because Sally had ceased to notice them. I wondered, with a premonitory spasm of disquiet, where I fitted in. Was I kin to the Buddha, the wall clock and the potted plants? I half-suspected so, and rather warmed to them.

The bookshelf in her living room didn't give much away, either. *The Amy Vanderbilt Complete Book of Etiquette* stood at one end; Joseph Heller's

*Good as Gold* at the other. In the middle, *The World According to Garp* had *The Shikse's Guide to Jewish Men* as its next-door neighbor.

"You want to put a record on?"

I went through the rack. Most of the records there had been put back in the wrong sleeves. Dave Brubeck had landed inside Folk Songs from Israel, Miles Davis inside Dave Brubeck. No detective searching her apartment could have fingered Sally on this sort of evidence. She had contrived to keep herself to herself and all her options open.

Sally had embraced the adventitious as a sort of moral good, and it enabled us to improvise an instant common life. Within twenty-four hours, we fell into a routine that felt as set as if we'd been following it for years.

Each morning, the alarm went off at some dreadful time in the dark. Sally, trailing around the apartment in blouse and panty hose, would lose things—keys, bras, tape cassettes, skirts—and I would retrieve them for her. I burned the coffee and listened to the tinny squawking of the radio. At 6 A.M., the announcer sounded quite mad, his tidbits of news like the delusions of a fever victim.

"Scientists at New Mexico State University have recovered twenty-nine particles of antimatter from the upper atmosphere. Balloons were used for the ascent, and the particles were found at a height of 120,000 feet. This proves . . ."

"What the hell is a particle of antimatter?"

"I dunno. You seen my other shoe anyplace? I guess it's kind of like . . . Oh, God . . . my goddamn shoe."

At six thirty, we joined the slow shunt of suburban traffic down Route 40 in Sally's blue Volkswagen, our headlights slowly paling in the grubby half-light. On the final, looping stretch of elevated section, we'd see the Arch, an ellipse of tarnished silver framed between factory walls.

"You know," Sally said, "I *like* it. It gives me a kick to see it's still there every morning."

I was taken aback to realize that, as a resident of Clayton, looking in on the city from my fastness in the suburbs, I liked the Arch too.

Sally worked in a shiny black skyscraper. Outside it, we kissed decorously, I moved into the driver's seat, Sally was lost behind the uniformed doorman, and I joined all the other wives and homemakers who made up the convoy of cars returning to Clayton, Ladue, University City, Westwood, Richmond Heights and Frontenac.

I liked being a housewife. I didn't want my consciousness raised. I was sluttish over the morning's *Post-Dispatch*. I scribbled letters to friends on Sally's monogrammed notepaper. I dusted the Buddha, watered the potted plants and made a show of pushing the vacuum cleaner around the carpets. At ten, Sally would telephone from her office, and I'd hang on the details of her working day. She had an interview to do, a script to write, a tape to edit, a press conference to attend. I was appalled that anyone should have been able to buy Sally's electric busyness for $220 a week; I could hear her over the phone, being four people at once and trying to be a fifth to me.

I drove to our local supermarket, and came back with groceries in brown paper bags. I pored over Sally's only cookbook, a mint copy of *The Jewish Gourmet*. I worried a lot about how to make soufflés rise. In the cupboard under the sink I found a hoard of strange machinery. There were electric mixers, whisks, choppers, slicers, graters, mincers, dicers—all still in the plastic cases in which they'd been packed at the factory. I fitted a plug to one of these objects, and succeeded in turning half a dozen egg whites into snow.

"God," said Sally. "What's *that?*"

"White of egg. Where did you get all this stuff? Don't you ever use it?"

"Oh . . . they were gifts."

"They must have cost a fortune."

"I hate to cook. Like, I can boil eggs, you know—"

By afternoon, I would sometimes remember why I was supposed to be in St. Louis. I went to the Museum of Art, where there were three river paintings by George Caleb Bingham: *Jolly Flatboatmen in Port, Raftsmen Playing Cards* and *The Wood Boat*. I stood, rapt and critical, in front of the pictures. Once I had used Bingham as raw material for a dream of the Mississippi. Now I was able to match his river against mine on something close to equal terms. He had exactly caught the way the current twitched and folded over on itself, the leaden sheen of the water and the ruffled lights of the wind on it. I could steer a safe course through his paintings, watching where the river quickened over a submerged sandbar and made a swirling eddy in the crook of a bend. I had seen the faces of the men, too. They were still on the river, in a change of costume. The only picture that struck a really discordant note was *Jolly Flatboatmen in Port*. The surface of its paint was more chipped and cracked than that of the others, as if it had had to make more of a struggle to survive intact. In it, a barge was moored off-channel, by the warehouses of La Clede's Landing; and the

St. Louis waterfront was dense with steamboats, skiffs and rafts. I could redraw the whole thing, square inch for square inch. It would show fungoid green mud, broken cobbles and a convention of undertakers discussing (as I had found out) the problems of transportation involved after the mass suicide in Jonestown, Guyana.

When Sally finished work, I collected her from the lobby of her skyscraper looking drained and wan, the exhausted breadwinner. Our route home took us past the front of my old hotel. Who, I wondered, was up in the 1800s now? I guessed he had a copy of *Playboy* instead of *The New Yorker* . . . bourbon on the rocks from Room Service . . . Nooter Boilermakers and Crunden Martin out the window . . . six-o'clock panic with an empty evening ahead . . . my almost-double, the poor guy.

For me, Sally's office was a running soap opera in which I lived vicariously. For the ten miles along the darkening highway, I pestered her for the gossip of the day. I learned the names of her colleagues. Mildred and Bob and Harry and Jean became brilliant two-dimensional characters, with the exaggerated reality of people in *As the World Turns*. Life at the top of the black skyscraper was exciting stuff, with smoldering enmities, clandestine affairs, intrigues, conspiracies and sudden bolts from the blue. I lapped it up.

"So," Sally said, beginning the sad question that all working husbands have to ask all stay-at-home wives, "what did *you* do, hon?"

"I went to the art museum." I told her about the Binghams. As material for anecdote they were, if anything, a little flatter than my morning journey around the supermarket. In any case, Sally's interest in paintings was scant. Had she ever been made to confront the hoary question of grandmother versus Rembrandt in burning house, she wouldn't have hesitated for a second in putting her foot through the Rembrandt on the way to rescuing the grandmother. There was a framed print of Grant Wood's *American Gothic* propped against the wall by her dressing table, and a meaningless geometric abstract over her bed; and between them they made up as much art as Sally cared to handle in her life. She now lay stretched out in the passenger seat, blowing smoke rings at the sun visor.

"God, I ought to take you around to these friends of my family's. They got this art collection . . . Like, I mean to say, they've got sort of ten Picassos in every bathroom, you know?"

"What happens when the steam gets to them?"

"I dunno. What d'you reckon? Wilt. I guess."

At home, I mixed the drinks. I brought her little bowls of peanuts and raisins. Sally's face was scrunched in thought. Finally she said, "Plus: . . . oh, I dunno."

———

For days the fall wind, hot and wet, blew down our street like a monsoon. It came in gusts of fifty and sixty miles an hour, shredding the last leaves from the cherries, sycamores and maples. It croaked and chirruped in the metal fronds of the air conditioner. It made stoplights toss on their overhead wires; street signs shuddered on their poles; the knee-high swirl of leaves on every road gave Clayton the appearance of a lake city on stilts. One early morning, I made a detour around Wharf Street to inspect the river. It looked like an enormous fleece, with a single towboat struggling upstream in a caul of spray. If things went on like this, my own boat, locked away, off the river, wouldn't be launched again until the spring. Even without the wind, one could feel the press of coming winter. For the last week, the television ads for snowblowers had been falling thicker and faster between programs. On the day that I had collected my new set of charts for the Lower Mississippi from the Corps of Engineers, I had bought myself an Eskimo's quilted parka. I hid both it and the charts in my suitcase and said nothing of them to Sally.

———

Our weekends were snug and sociable. It occurred to me that my river charts might turn out to be like Ed's old railway timetable in Muscatine; out of date, good for nothing except grist for some fleeting annual fantasy.

Sally took me to the house where Picassos were rumored to be languishing on the bathroom walls. It was near Washington University, a pretty cottage in the St. Louis–Tudor style. From the outside, it looked like the sort of residence a woodcutter in Sussex in the 1540s might have been proud of; inside, it was more suggestive of the private quarters of a Medici prince. The owners were away in Europe, collecting more treasure, but Sally and I were let in by the light-skinned black maid.

A Monet, vast and blue, was hung over the chintz sofa in the sitting room; and the walls were checkerboarded with masterpieces. I couldn't take them in. Instead, I found myself looking at the leftover clutter of family life; the open books on tables, overshoes, half-emptied bottles, ashtrays, papers, coats and hats. Beside these ordinary things, the Picassos, Braques, Matisses, Courbets, Duchamps had the alienated splendor of exiled royalty in a seaside boardinghouse.

Embarrassed at finding my eye so numbed, I asked the maid which picture she liked best. She pointed at a big angular Picasso from the 1920s. "That's my favorite. I like all the straight lines. I ain't so keen on his figures." Like me, she found the paintings themselves difficult to come to terms with. Her face lit with real enthusiasm only when she explained how the house had been wired against burglars. "You know, you only have to touch a window, just light, like that, and the alarm goes off down in the police station? It's *wonderful!*"

In the study, I tried to concentrate on a lovely Courbet sketch.

Sally said: "What's all this worth? A million? Millions?"

"Tens of millions. Hundreds, probably. I don't know. Billions. Trillions. Squillions."

"God," said Sally, "I'm so innocent about that kind of thing," and suddenly hugged me. With my arms around her, I could feel her pulsing and sparking; it was like embracing a human-sized microchip with all its circuits on Overload. Next to us stood a skeletal Giacometti on a low side table. Its head was on a level with ours. Sally twisted her face around, stared at the sculpture, and looked back at me.

"Hey—do you think I'm too sort of, well, like, *skinny?*"

We went out into the garden. The swimming pool, drained for winter, was soddenly carpeted by dead leaves. Its marble rim was lined with reclining figures: fat ones by Henry Moore, thin ones by Giacometti and Arp. Together they suggested a group of badly out-of-condition old folks at some Californian hydrotherapy clinic. One expected nurses to come from out of the trees and ease them, one by one, into the pool.

That evening we met Sally's father at the St. Louis Club for dinner. Like just about everything else in the city, the club had moved west; it now occupied the fifteenth floor of an office building on a hill in Clayton, where its fumed oak, sporting prints and civic portraits were surreally suspended in their frame of concrete, glass and steel. From the club dining room, the hideous buildings of the central city looked innocuous and pretty. By night, at this height and distance, they looked like a fleet of lighted ships riding at anchor. We were a long, long way away from the St. Louis of gunmen, black magicians and wretched conventioneers.

Sally's father greeted his daughter with a look of deep mock melancholy. He raised his right hand and slowly clenched and unclenched it three times.

"The market's fallen?" Sally said.

"Fifteen points," her father said. "Tomorrow, know what I'm going to do? I'm going to buy some clothes." He encircled her with his arm. "There's a recession on: let's go shopping."

He was a big man with a frost of white hair over a pouchy, humorous face; a wise and wary ironist. I was frightened of his reputation. I'd heard of him before I met Sally, and he'd been described as "the one man in St. Louis who makes Wall Street listen when he talks." He was "sharp as a pistol." In the business aristocracy of the Midwest, Sally's father was a self-made duke. He handled the marriages and divorces of great companies. He was a conjuror with money. He could, so I was told, pull a handful of the stuff through a napkin ring and make it billow out into a fortune.

As he walked through the dining room, his importance was as manifest as the glow of light around a medieval saint. People stopped talking at their tables and nodded gravely to him as he passed. Waiters flew on wings ahead of him. When Sally announced that she was going to the ladies' room, I panicked at the prospect of being left alone with him.

"That one . . ." he said, half-lowering his large eyelids in the direction of Sally's back, "she's bright." It wasn't a father's fond indulgence so much as a neutral, financier's assessment of a stock.

"Yes," I said. "Isn't she. Very bright. Indeed."

I felt that my own rating on this particular question was already beginning to drop through the bottom of the market. I had only one idea I thought might arouse a glimmer of interest in him, and that was borrowed; from Edmund Wilson's *To the Finland Station*. Wilson had described Karl Marx as a man who had made a kind of poetry out of money and its movements. He had been able to apprehend currency as a sensuous object. He might have been a brilliant capitalist had he not felt revulsion for the financial system which, in his writing, he compulsively caressed, half in tenderness, half in hate.

I put the Wilson argument to Sally's father. Yes, he said; that sounded right. Money was something for which it was possible to have an artist's feeling for his medium. There was still for him as much creative excitement in the making of a deal now as he'd had in his twenties. He loved the sense of "swinging from the rafters." He stopped speaking. Something was nagging at him.

"Look," he said. "You take a book, like the one by this Wilson guy. How many copies would they have to print of that, to make a profit? Five thousand? Ten?"

I told him what little I knew of the commercial side of the book trade, fascinated by the way his eyes followed what I was saying. They were Trappist's eyes: serious, peaceful and contemplative.

"This must all seem terribly small beer to you."

"Small? A dollar interests me. Especially if it's a dollar profit."

Sally came back. Her father, swinging from the rafters between dour puritanism and gross excess, made niggardly sips at a glass of Coca-Cola while he lit each new cigarette from the butt of his last.

All through the meal he was courted by young men. They stood deferentially by the table in hound's-tooth jackets, striped ties and tortoiseshell glasses. Sometime . . . if he could spare a moment . . . perhaps . . . they'd appreciate it. One was thinking of buying a television station in Illinois; another had seen that a baseball team in Florida was up for sale.

"*His* family," said Sally of one of these young men, "they've got quite a bit of money, haven't they?" The question struck me as a shade redundant.

Her father sipped, smoked, smiled. "I haven't counted it," he said.

"Do you ever find yourself taking real pratfalls?" I asked.

"Unh-hunh. Something I learned right back at the beginning. You can make any mistake you like; it doesn't matter. Only never make the same mistake twice."

I talked of what seemed to me to be the cruel division between the deep woodiness of the western suburbs and the bald brick of the city ghettoes. I told Sally's father how my first view of St. Louis had been based on the newspaper story about the rapists who had been caught because their victim had seen a tree through a window. He considered the situation from all sides.

"Now, if they'd had the sense to cut that tree down, those guys'd be running free." He laughed. "Next time, I guess they'll pack an axe."

He left on the dot of ten o'clock. He was always in bed by ten thirty: a rule, he said, that he'd never allowed any boom or crash to interfere with.

"You stay on. Sign for all you want."

"Please," I said, "if I may, I'd like to—"

"No," said Sally. "Daddy *loves* to pay."

———

We went in for Sunday treats: bagels, fresh-squeezed orange juice, the multistoried edifice of the Sunday *New York Times,* its sections scattered around every room. We squabbled over who got to read the Book Review first. We annoyed each other by reading paragraphs of news out loud.

Former President Gerald Ford announced that he was definitely not available for the Republican nomination.

"That means he *must* be running," Sally said.

The Shah of Iran arrived in New York from Mexico for a cancer operation.

"Why can't they take his gallbladder out in Mexico, for godsake?"

"You know why the Mexican put his wife on the railroad tracks?"

"Why?"

"Tequila."

"Huh?"

"That's the funniest joke anyone's ever heard in Buffalo, Iowa."

"It doesn't sound funny to me. Is that some kind of hoosier place?"

We visited with Sally's friends, driving downtown to Lafayette Square. It was exactly as the broad Georgian squares of north London must have looked after the Blitz. There were bright little shops on the corners selling hand-sewn quilts and antique bric-a-brac, and London-like wine bars with gardens; but their gaiety was forced and defiant. For every smart "rehab" there was a blind ruin, its oxidized brickwork falling out, and weeds growing through the trash on its floors. In the sacked Victorian streets around the square one could sense the waiting shadows of Catullus Eugene Blackwater, 28, Hugh Saustell, 25, and all the other thugs who hadn't yet been honored by a mention in the *Whirl.*

Yet sprawled, talking, among colored scatter cushions on a floor of varnished pine, slopping wine from a flagon of Gallo into a tumbler, I felt uncannily at home. It wasn't just the bookish run of the conversation; it was St. Louis itself. The city was supposed to belong to the West. The full title of Saarinen's monumental loop was The Westward Expansion Memorial Arch, and the museum below it commemorated the great nineteenth-century drive west beyond the Mississippi; but St. Louis was the least obviously "Western" town I had been in since I'd started my journey. Its architecture had none of the happy eccentricity of places like Muscatine. It didn't go in for fake steamboats and boondocks-Greek. What St. Louis liked was solid Georgian, Queen Anne, Palladian and half-timbered Tudor. It wanted things to be in prim good taste. It would have got on very nicely over the teacups with my Wiltshire aunts.

Old, genteel St. Louis—T. S. Eliot's city—thought of itself as a slice of cultivated Europe. It seemed mystified as to how it had landed here, stranded on the wrong side of the big American river. Sally and I had spent an afternoon in the Forest Park section, drinking draft Bass in the Welsh pub off Kingshighway and rummaging in the bookstores along Euclid Avenue. *Kingshighway. Euclid Avenue.* Between them, the names defined the wistful snobbery of a city that was soft on royalty on the one hand and on the most severe of classical geometers on the other.

"Really . . ." I heard someone say; ". . . *really,*" and the voice had more of the throaty Anglophilia of Beacon Hill, Boston, than of the lolloping drawl of the Midwest. The woman next to me mentioned the word "Missour*a*." It was a pronunciation that had often puzzled me. Some people said "Missouri," others "Missoura." I had asked why before. I'd been told that the *a* was a south-of-state ending, that it was a west-of-state ending, that it was rural usage as against the urban *i.* No one really seemed to know. I said this to the woman.

"Oh, no," she said. "It's perfectly simple. New Money says 'Missouri'; Old Money says 'Missoura.' "

———

Somewhere in our garden there was a snake, but neither Sally nor I heard its giveaway rattle. The gales had died down; the temperature had settled. The carpet in the apartment was left unswept one morning while I laid out my river charts on the floor and plotted mileages. I didn't pack the charts away, and that evening Sally turned over their big pages until she reached a nowhere down in Arkansas. Not speaking, she put *Miles Davis in Concert* on the turntable and sat listening to it through stereo headphones.

"Martini?"

"Uh-uh." Her face made a quick, negative squirm.

In the Jewish country club in Westwood, where all the crockery was heraldically imprinted with a tennis racket crossed with a niblick or a mashie, we eked out a moody supper, overlit by crystal chandeliers. Passing friends of Sally's parents would save us from each other for five minutes at a time; we'd brighten for them, then fall back to listening to the noise of each other's knives and forks. Gloomily, I remembered that I'd been here before, and at the back of my mind I could see the oily gleam of the river opening out.

Next day the phone rang at ten. I picked it up. "Hi!" said a warm, kittenly voice.

"Sally!" I said. A new leaf. "I'm sorry—"

"This is a recorded message from several chiropractors in your neighborhood. . . ."

I slammed the phone back into its cradle. Sally didn't call.

For dinner we drove to the most expensive restaurant in Clayton, hoping that its showy glamour would restore a little of our own lost shine. We were met by a whole ship's crew of waiters in dress uniform: captains, lieutenants, quartermasters, stewards. It took half a dozen senior officers to escort us to a table for two, but when a pop singer came in, the entire company marched and piped him to his seat. Sally took in his black hat with a Mexican brim, his permed, shoulder-length hair, his beads, boots and caftan.

"That's what I *hate* to see—" But I knew that the singer, in his arrogant duds, was just a convenient stand-in for the man at Sally's own table.

We made a solemn, engrossed play of snapping the shells open around the rubbery bodies of our langoustes. *Rubber,* I thought . . . *bumper;* and tried to talk in our old, light way about the bumper stickers that had kept me half alarmed, half entertained on my rides around the freeways of St. Louis. GOD, GUNS & GUTS MADE AMERICA GREAT. DON'T GIVE GOD A VA-CATION: TAKE HIM WITH YOU WHEN YOU GO.

"I think the best one I ever saw was around Boston in 1973, just after Nixon had dumped Cox as Watergate Special Prosecutor. Practically every car in Cambridge had one. It said, 'Sack the Cox-Sacker.' "

"That's . . . obscene," Sally said, pronging a soggy tomato.

"You're being stupid and prudish."

"Plus, it's not even funny."

"I saw the weather forecast. It's okay. I'll get moving again tomorrow."

"You know? Something I didn't kind of see you as? You're a coward."

Dinner was our Reno. Before the check came, we'd had our divorce.

# Ned Rorem

## *Knowing When to Stop: A Memoir*

The swarthy American with the intelligent eyes walked by, spotted me, and sat down on the bench. This was Maurice R., about thirty, an instructor of romance languages in California. Within an hour we had decided to visit Acapulco together, if I could persuade my father to let me go. Which I did, but without saying that I was taking the trip with another person.

———

I have never gone back to Taxco. But early in 1968 I did see Acapulco again and found it unrecognizable. The town had become a city with stucco hotels, terraced lawns, menacing somehow, with its brothels and discos and money. La Playa Caleta is a country club today. In 1941 it was a wild near-empty beach of incandescent splendor miles from the center. It was here that Maurice and I settled after a five-hour bus ride, dangerous and affectionate, in a French pension on the south end, fifty yards up the hill. On another hill at the north end a mile away was a similar pension, and in between on the expanse of snowy sand that sloped into the emerald Pacific was a large *cabaña* with several tables and a jukebox that continually played the two sultry hits of that summer, "Esta noche" and "Amor," plus the standard frisky airs named for local cities, "Guadalajara" and "Tampico."

By day we swam and drank *cerveza* and made love in a hammock on the private deck, and by night we made love and swam and drank *cerveza* against a sonic blend of wind and chirping insects and the jukebox far down on the beach. The "making love" was not complex. I may have been promiscuous but was certainly no callous roué nor even very adventurous; it was almost sufficient to know I was desired, the knowledge replaced the act. Then, too, Maurice may have not wanted to damage the goods, knowing they would eventually be delivered back to Father. He would speak about Ravel's String Quartet, about his teaching curriculum, and then about my body "gleaming with a golden adolescent fuzz like the marble dust on a just-finished statue" (does one forget such words?), which gave me a feeling of power, as did my Gentile versus his Jewish aura. Once he said, "You know, in Taxco nobody believes your father is your father." I was surprised and offended.

When I told Father, he was not amused. He meanwhile had remained in Taxco, befriending Bu and a dozen others sitting around at Paco's, including Magda and Gilberte. They said to him, on hearing he was from Chicago, "A young composer from Chicago recently came to tea, but he didn't want to bring his father, imagine!" During this fortnight separation I don't remember how, or if, we kept in touch. I do know that when Maurice and I left the Pacific we hired a third-rate automobile with two chauffeurs and went straight to Mexico City, stopping in Taxco only for a quick tequila while the drivers refueled. So it must have been somehow understood that Father and I would rejoin each other in the capital. When night fell and an icy breeze wheezed through the car windows, Maurice and I covered ourselves in the back seat and made love unbeknown to the drivers, or so we thought.

# CHARLES NICHOLL

*The Fruit Palace: An Odyssey Through*
*Colombia's Cocaine Underground*

It was at the end of a long afternoon session with them that a boy came with a message from Waldino to meet him that evening at the Rincón Francés. It took me a while, surfacing through tropical mists of dope, to realize that this could mean business.

Soon after dark, rather the worse for wear, I tacked along to the French Corner, a low, opensided beer and cheap food *chingana* at the other end of the waterfront. There were American sailors in town, big men in white, with cigarette packs tucked into the tight sleeves of their T-shirts. There was a group of them outside the Pan-American, joshing loudly. A blond boy, chewing gum, shouted to a *costeña*, "Hey, baby, let's you and me go get weird!" The night was hot, and the Yankee presence made the town uneasy.

Waldino was at a corner table, well-placed for keeping an eye on the comings and goings of the beach drag. He was with another man whom I recognized, with a start, to be the tall *bingero*, the one who had moved with such deadly grace that night of the fight at El Molino. One is always trying to make sense of these places that live by different laws, and unexpected interconnections like this are unsettling. Was the El Molino crowd—Silvio, the Lone Ranger, the *bingeros*—mixed up in this deal? Were they Waldino's *trasportistas*? No, that was unlikely. They could well be his suppliers, though. The possibility jarred me, but I had already been spotted by Waldino, and had no more time to think before joining them at the table.

Waldino introduced the *bingero* as Alfonso. We shook hands. I'd seen him at Bingo El Portal, I said, and I'd heard him all along the seafront. He laughed, deep and sonorous. His voice was as slow and deadpan as it was calling the numbers over the microphone. He had a long thin scar down his left cheek, showing pinkish on the teak-coloured skin. He wore a trilby-style straw hat, perched at a raffish angle, and the same maroon jacket I had seen him in before. Underneath it, no doubt, was the gun he had flashed at the troublesome *costeño* that night.

I looked to Waldino for some cue, some indication that Alfonso was here regarding our business, but none came. We chatted aimlessly for a while. Alfonso was a Vallenato—"valley born"—from the lowlands of Cesar, round Valledupar. He asked me about London, about the four seasons, about the prices: all the usual chit-chat. There were plenty of opportunities to slide into the subject of cocaine, but none were taken. After a couple of beers he rose to leave. He looked me in the eyes and said *"Buena suerte,"* good luck, and I wondered if this meant I would need it. Waldino walked out with him to the sidewalk. They conversed for a while, Alfonso slow and emphatic, stooping as he talked to Waldino, straightening up and looking out to sea as Waldino in turn talked to him. They seemed to be arguing about something. I had the feeling that Waldino was the inferior, the deferential one, but then deference is generally due to a big Vallenato with a gun under his coat.

Waldino rejoined me, a picture of false, shifty-eyed bonhomie. "So," I said. "What did you want to meet about?"

"Ah yes. Very good news, Charlie."

"What?"

"We go meet the *trasportistas,* very soon, maybe tomorrow."

"Maybe?"

He shrugged. "I told you, it is difficult to be sure." He fiddled with his beard. I heard the distant boom of Alfonso's voice, as another session started at Bingo El Portal.

"You wanted me to meet you just to tell me that, Waldino? Come on. You've been telling me that for a week now. Maybe tomorrow. *Mañana, mañana . . .*"

"Charlie, I'm trying. Have another beer."

"You sure it was just that? What about Alfonso—is he something to do with it? I think you got me here so he could look me over."

He assumed the exaggerated air of surprise which Colombians fondly imagine will allay suspicions, and usually only increases them. "Charlie!

Alfonso's no *contrabandista*. He's a *bingero*, Charlie." He gestured vaguely down the drag to where Alfonso was intoning, *"Ochenta y ocho, los dos culebras!"*

"I know a bit about Alfonso," I said. Waldino's eyes narrowed. "He's with Silvio, isn't he, the guy who owns—"

"Hey, Charlie, *amigo!* You want to be careful here." He leaned forward and laid his hand on my arm. "OK. Look. Alfonso and I have certain . . . mutual connections. No more."

"Are they who you get your *perica* from? Is that it?"

Waldino was suddenly angry. *"Hijo de puta!* We said no questions, not a word about where it comes from. *I'm* your supplier, *amigo.* You remember that. Waldino can get it: that's all you need to know."

I was blundering, offending protocol. My damn fool inquisitiveness was going to blow everything. I sat back, ran my hand over my face. The beers were mixing badly with the *ron coco,* and I was coming down off the afternoon's cocaine into that dangerous, jagged hinterland. I felt sluggish and uneasy. I didn't like this intrusion of guns. I thought again of Alfonso dispatching the *costeño,* the sleek, sneering face of Silvio. My little game took another twist of seriousness.

Some of the American sailors, those sober enough to make it this far from the docks, drifted in, shouting, *"Cervezas pronto,* you honkies." After a few minutes the tarts began to muster, like gulls following a school of fish. The purlieu of the French Corner was one of their stamping grounds anyway, and the nights the US Navy was in town they came out in force. There was a group quite near us, lounging against the low wall that separated the tables from the sidewalk. The sailors called to them, motioned them over. A few peeled off from the group, and sauntered purposefully over to their table. Two girls remained. I eyed them with vague, theoretical lust. Waldino followed my gaze. "You like the *niñas?*" he said, in a jolly, let's-change-the-subject voice. I shrugged. "I can get them," he said automatically. "Of course you can," I sighed, and before I could stop him he was tipping his chair back to lean over the wall, and calling, *"Hola, chiquitas! Piropo! Vengan por acá!"* Over they came. The tall, blondish one swung her handbag like a Charleston flapper. She seemed to recognize Waldino. He looked up at her, said something I didn't catch. He put his arm right round her waist, and made to worm his pudgy hand down the front of her tight white jeans.

"This is Rosa," he said. He leaned forward to me and whispered loudly, "I hope she isn't as tight as her pants, you know what I mean?"

Rosa's hand snaked around Waldino's bushy head. She pressed it against her hip. Waldino winked at me. He puffed and pouted in a parody of lascivious pleasure. His hand began to delve below her waist-band. Then I saw Rosa's hand pressing tighter, the muscles in her arm tensing, and Waldino's face beginning to squash up against her tough flank. He broke away from her grip with a grunt of pain.

"Take it easy, monkey," she said, her brassy smile turned to a sneer. "Any lower and you have to pay."

A tall young negro, wafting *eau de cologne*, sat down at the next table. He pushed an empty chair out with a foot shod in alligator skin. "Sit down, Rosa," he said quietly. She turned her back on us and sat down. Waldino, crestfallen, rubbed his sore ear. The other girl was still standing beside the table. She was short and dark, chewing gum. Her breasts jutted impressively under her T-shirt: *tout le monde sur le balcon*.

Waldino rallied his battle-weary machismo. "And what's your name, little girl?" he asked silkily.

"Mabella."

"Take a seat, Mabella." She had to squeeze behind me to get to the vacant chair. I felt first one thigh, then the other, and something soft and ephemeral in between.

"You want a drink?" he asked. She gave a quick, nervy shrug that made her breasts judder, and chewed even harder on her gum. She had a young girl's face on a woman's body. Waldino called for three beers. The waiter spilt some on Mabella's trousers, tight, bright green and shiny. She swore and scowled as he roughly dabbed it dry with a cloth.

"I've brought you a nice juicy gringo," said Waldino, with that high-pitched titter of his.

"*Carajo!*" she said, without much obvious enthusiasm.

I heard my slurred voice saying "Hang on a minute." I had a headful of catarrh from too much *perica*. The best part of me wanted to wish them good night, head back to the hotel, and tuck up with a good book. Renaldo had lent me a leather-bound edition of Charles Waterton's *Wanderings in South America*, a trove of lore on preparing *curare* poison, removing ticks and chiggers, recognizing sloth's droppings, and much else. For bodily health in these "remote and dreary wilds" he recommends quinine bark, laudanum, calomel and jalap. For the soul, a small volume of the Odes of Horace. He says nothing about cocaine and black-eyed corner-girls.

So why am I still sitting here? As the poet says, *Video meliora proboque, deteriora sequor.* I see and approve the good, I follow the bad. Twenty minutes later the three of us were walking back up the beach-drag, past the sailors, past El Molino and the bingo stall, my arm around Mabella's shoulders, hers around my waist, our hips jostling.

At the Corona, leering like a pantomime pimp, Waldino patted us on the bottoms and ushered us in. Omar winked as he handed me the room key. They stood together, smiling encouragingly, thoroughly approving this time-honoured transaction. We walked hand in hand up the wide stone steps to my balcony room.

Inside, the dull air of the closed room made me feel ill. She locked the door behind her, leant against it, hands behind her back. Her breasts pointed accusingly at me.

"What do you want?" she asked.

I felt a headache plant itself above my right eye. "Well . . . How much is it?"

"Two thousand five hundred."

I echoed her, aghast. "You must be joking. I don't have that much."

"Two thousand five hundred to stay all night," she said.

I sat down on the bed. "I don't want you to stay all night," I said wearily. "Anyway, I can sleep all night for free."

She shrugged, then recited the rest of the tariff like a sulky waitress. Fifteen hundred pesos for a "fucky-fucky," two thousand for a *chupuda.*

"*Chupuda?*"

She looked at me pityingly. "Blo-joe," she said, "*el modo francés.*" She sucked once or twice at an imaginary lollipop to make it quite clear.

I was sweating heavily. I wanted to lie down and go to sleep. I went to turn on the ceiling fan. She thought I was coming at her, and dodged away. "No, you must pay first." Down in the courtyard I heard Waldino and Omar laughing together. I felt trapped. I couldn't just send her away. The absurd codes of machismo must be honoured. I thought of tom-cats sitting round on a wall, while one of their number services a hot mog.

After a bit of joyless haggling we settled on 1,000 pesos for a "fucky-fucky." She pocketed the note and immediately peeled off her T-shirt. Her breasts were brown and pendulous, with big, dark coffee-coloured aureoles. They made her look top-heavy. I suddenly thought how childish she looked.

"How old are you?" I asked. Unzipping her green trousers, she looked up in surprise. The breath of the ceiling fan caught her fine hair.

"Fifteen," she said sulkily. Whatever catch-all desire I had felt for her ebbed away in an instant, and in washed a tired, desperate and useless pity.

"Fifteen? No more? So young, *jovencita!*"

"I don't think so," she said, and pulled down her knickers. The stocky shoulders, the ripe breasts, the neat black triangle between her legs—these belonged to the *puta,* but the rest of her was just another under-nourished young girl, with her starch-fed belly and bum rounding out in different directions. She lay on the bed, idly tweaking a nipple. "Hurry up," she said. "A thousand pesos, twenty minutes, no more."

"Hang on!" I fished out a twist of cocaine from the drawer in the table. "Do you want . . . ?" She shook her head. "I think I'll just . . ." I heard again the laughter in the courtyard. My hands were clumsy with booze and sweat. A bit of crystal fluttered to the floor. I snorted the rest straight out of the paper, felt the slipstream surge, trying to push through the fogs of despair, failing. My headache was worse. I began to undress. I couldn't get the stud on my jeans through the buttonhole. Finally I was naked, tacking irresolutely towards the bed, where my pot-bellied Lolita, *mi muñeca de carne,* lay eyeing me with mild curiosity.

It was not a success, not a *nuit de passion* to linger in the memory. She lay inert and passive. I lay dutifully active. I pressed and fondled. I made one or two requests, in the hope of gingering things up a bit, but these apparently were not on the schedule. A "fucky-fucky" was the basic economy model. She was anatomically available, and that was it: a glove of warm flesh to slip into for a few minutes. Perhaps this is what turns on the average Colombian Joe. It didn't turn me on. I felt limper and guiltier with each minute that passed. It didn't even occur to me to kiss her.

In the end we lay side by side, in a sheepish parody of post-coital glow. I made excuses—too much of this, not enough of that, wait a few minutes and I'll be raring. She looked at her watch. Time was almost up. We talked a bit. She was from Bucaramanga, down in the Eastern Cordillera. She had been on the game for a year, ever since her father had died. She had worked the bus stations in Bucaramanga. It was all in the family: her uncle pimped for her. One day she took the train to Santa Marta, to get away from him. She had been here six months, sleeping by day in a little *residencias* near the Gobernacion, working the Rodadero bars and the dockside by night. She didn't like drugs because her uncle had made her take them. Basuko, pills, and a funny black power which you mixed with cobwebs, and which made you stupid, and you lay on the bed like you were para ... para ... yes, *paralizada,* while the johns came in and did their business on top of you.

I watched her get dressed. In that absurd way of things, I felt the twinges of desire return when she stood, wearing just her brief lacy knickers, and for the first time since I had met her, she smiled at me.

"It's OK, gringo. It happens."

"Come back to bed," I said.

She shook her head: she had to go back to the beach. Tomorrow night, maybe. I heard her sandals slapping down the staircase, then a burble of raucous comments from the pair down at the desk. They talked for a bit, then the street door was bolted, and all was silent.

She must have felt I was owed something for my 1,000 pesos, though. Next morning, with a sore, disgruntled head, I was greeted downstairs by Omar wearing an even wider grin than usual. Here we go, I thought. The gringo who can't even get it up with a *puta* ...

"So you had a good time last night?" he crowed. I shrugged non-committally. "That's what the *niña* says," he continued. "She says he may be a gringo, but he sure is one hot lover."

# Hugo Williams

## *No Particular Place to Go*

### Do You Faint or Anything?

Maggie came to the door in her nightie with a prove-it-to-me expression on her crumpled face. I got out the duty-free Scotch, which seemed to appeal to her, and tried hard to make five o'clock in the morning arrivals seem groovy. Quite soon we were both drunk in different ways. Maggie slyly amorous, me triumphantly slurred. Dawn broke and we were just about to cuddle up in bed when we were suddenly treated to a demonstration of ecstatic gasping from the woman next door. The walls were paper thin and you could hear every creak of spring, every suck of breath from this apparently lone enthusiast. We stopped talking the way you do when a clock strikes. The gasps became moans. The moans became cries—then this invisible love-goddess came in a great bellow of what sounded like disgust at something she had just discovered in the fridge.

Maggie smiled secretly to herself and said softly "She's great," as of some much-loved entertainer. I felt rather sober. We had another whisky then climbed gingerly into the narrow bed we had been sitting on. My eye was watering profusely by now, mostly with alcohol.

"Where did I meet you really?" asked Maggie eventually.

"At the party for Twiggy, wasn't it?" I guessed.

"Was it? I remember your brother doing a trick, but I think I met you somewhere else. Do you know Warren Beatty at all?"

"No."

"Didn't I help someone when you fainted or something? Do you faint or anything?"

"Look," I said, "I only fainted because someone was telling me about how he trepanned himself with a dentist's drill. Would you like to hear about it? He gave himself a local anaesthetic in the skull. I was just trying to get to the window . . ."

"A friend of mine went to a Christmas party where they had real snow."

"I think I'm beginning to fall asleep."

"I've got my period, you know."

The sex-machine next door was recommencing foreplay.

"Is it all right?" asked Maggie after a moment.

Oh it's great, I thought. I love blood everywhere. A Tampax thrown down like a gauntlet and something nasty in your shoe next morning. What more could one ask? I switched out the light. I had one of those tiredness erections which don't care what becomes of them so long as they aren't asked to get out of bed to pee. This seemed to be Maggie's condition also. She put her foot in the stirrup and swung a hungry leg over me. A forty yard dash followed by three hiccups and it was all over between us. I felt something warm trickling between my legs and wished I was back at the party.

Then came Maggie's verdict—a succinct phrase which I shall always remember in connection with my first sex-lag night in New York.

"I didn't like that," she said.

*　*　*

## LIFE AFTER MIDNIGHT

What shall I do now? It isn't even tomorrow yet.

The Curzon isn't a singles bar as such, but it is very cruisy: massive mahogany bar, gilt frames, darkened mirrors, burgundy or was it green drapes? It's the lobby of some old apartment block fashioned into a cock-tail lounge for the rhinestone cowboy set. And it closes at two on purpose so that these husky cow-hands don't start doing kinky things in the toilets.

I'm fascinated by the size and effect of dry martinis and three have opened my eyes. Did she wink at me, or did I wink at her? And why didn't her boyfriend mind? Here she comes now round the bar, presents herself for speech. This young lady is completely drunk. She has very short hair, big drunk eyes and a piece of glitter round her neck which has left a mark. She has silk pyjama bottoms on with no knickers. She drops her gloves, then her bag, then her whisky. Already she is buttoning and unbuttoning my jacket.

Oh God, here comes her escort. He greets me with a friendly self-introduction and invites us both to a party. That's very decent of him, but I can see this young thing isn't going to make it. Mister nice-guy has seen a convenient loophole in the evening and he's playing his cards correctly. I buy everything he has.

Denise works in Vidal Sassoon, she tells me. That's about all she can remember about herself, except that she is a girl. She tries to get me to acknowledge this fact on the floor of the taxi back to Howard's place.

The next problem is the dormer bed which seems to function with the aid of various springs and levers which make my head spin manipulating them. Done properly, a secret, spare bed springs up next to its parent bed, forming a double one. I get it to work and Denise sits down heavily, looking dazed.

When I come back from the bathroom Denise is sitting on the guest half of this dormer bed, but it has collapsed under her, apparently without her realising, and is in the process of withdrawing once more to its position under the other one, probably from embarrassment. Wearing only a short mauve blouse Denise looks like a road accident victim, suffering from shock. I want to put a blanket round her shoulders. The bleak spotlights and quiet of my bare room have wreaked a sobering effect on our rush to climax. There is a ringing in my ears from another world.

"Where are we?" asks Denise.

"In my apartment."

"Where's your apartment?"

"At 95 and Lex."

This address is definitely counter-romantic.

"My Gard! I taught you lived near the bar!"

"I'm sorry . . ."

"You're not American . . . ?" She looks suspicious now. This is beyond her reckoning for a night on the tiles. She leans over to switch on the reassuring tv. I have to tell her it doesn't work. She asks if she can use the phone and I tell her that doesn't work either. Then I fix the bed by putting a chair under it, put out the light and climb over her into bed.

## WHY HER BOYFRIEND DIDN'T MIND

The rest of the night is cloudy in my memory, but I do remember that it had at least one more surprise in store for me. This girl had breasts like cannonballs. Not big, but inflated to bursting-point. As I ran my fascinated hands over these curiosities I realised they must be the much-talked-about silicone substitutes. There they were, stuck there on her chest, hard as a rock, with their poor little nipples marooned on top of them like little rubber lighthouses. This idea Denise had of herself as an inflatable darling was going to wreck my impromptu characterisation. Suddenly she seemed all too human: just someone's little girl with a built-in sense of inadequacy. I was going to have to think fast to overcome these plastic passion-killers sweating coldly under my palm.

I cast around for the right erotic "peg" to hang the occasion on and remembered Apollinaire's necrophiliac nurse in "The Debauched Hospodar," grinding on the final erections of young soldiers fatally wounded in the Crimean war. This seemed to redress the balance.

In the morning I unplugged D's left nipple, rolled all the drink-laden breath from her imperfect carcass and returned her latex remains to the envelope marked ON APPROVAL.

"Just exactly where do you think you are?" shrilled Howard, putting a tousled head round the door. "This isn't a brothel you know. You walk out on a good friend of mine. I do my best for you. You make a complete fool of me. Now this. It's disgusting. I'm not standing for it. You can get out."

He called to the cat, who was curled up with us, but it wouldn't move.

"It's all my fault," said Denise, crying. Howard was looking at her in unrestrained horror. So was I.

"Can I use the phone?" I asked.

"No you can't. Get out!"

"I'm allowed one call by law."

"Just one then. You make me sick to my stomach."

My one call drew a blank. I checked my case at Penn Station, had a wash, and took out my address book. Under "Ambulance" it had "Omar, florist, room to let."

\*    \*    \*

## WHAT SHE SHOWED ME AT HOME

Vicky's bed was on a shelf up near the ceiling of a smart open-plan studio. I took one look at that high plateau, shrouded in mist, and could see straight away that once you got up there it would be difficult to turn back.

"You're not my ideal," Vicky said, "but you'll do for intersession." Intersession being half-term. She was doing American Literature, she said, showing me a letter from Ernest Hemingway to her husband. I read the letter, which was some boring point about sport. Then I asked about her husband. The man was an absolute charmer apparently, a handsome and witty stud with an ever-burning desire for her body, a heroin-addict and bisexual thief.

"Yeah, we had an amphetamine honeymoon Zak and I. One horny old beatnik and his child bride. He was erect for a month."

"What happened to him?"

"He wilted! He drifted west I think, then he went to prison of course."

Before long Vicky and I were sprawling on an uncomfortable couch, boasting and necking alternately. Every now and then she would disengage herself and run around looking for a signed copy of some book or other. She seemed to have slept with every author on her course. One exotic lover after the previous world famous admirer was paraded for my amazement, adding feather after feather to Vicky's imaginary plumage.

She would lean towards me with her sharp teeth showing and interrupt everything I thought of myself, her huge bright eyes alight with some fatal fever for celebrity. Every time I tried to get on top of her, William Styron or someone would come between us. Even death seemed to pose no barrier to her intimate knowledge of a man. Was it a test? Or had she got me round here just to have a nice row?

The excitement of being horizontally entwined with Vicky slowly ebbed, due to constant interruptions from the great. I stifled my disbelief and tried to stay awake. As dawn came up I must have dozed because I woke to find bits of Vicky's clothes coming away in my hands as if they had rotted with the great time we had lain there. But by then it was too late.

She was still talking, naturally, but now Marvin was there too, her flatmate, and she was addressing her discourse to him. He was trying to get to work, but she made him listen to a story about herself and Otto Preminger, shouting through to him in the kitchen while he made us coffee.

"I'm not a good lay," she told me later. "I only look like one."

The large print giveth, the small print taketh away.


ZAK PHONES

We woke that evening to find ourselves still on the day bed, exhausted, dirty and cross.

"When are we going?" asked Vicky.

"Going where?"

"New Orleans."

"New Orleans? Did I say that? I thought you had to go to school."

"Yes you did. So what if I do? I thought we were going for intersession. You said . . ."

"No, that was your idea. I meant next month, if I could get a car. I have these readings to do first."

"Well isn't that great? That's wonderful news. So we're not going, right?"

"Right."

"Zak phoned while you were asleep you know. All the way from the coast."

"Which coast?"

"There's only one coast, baby. The Coast coast. The Barbary Coast. The West Coast. He said he'd come over for intersession if I liked. I said, no, I was going to New Orleans. I'd met this guy who wanted to take me. Zak said that was cool, he wouldn't come this time. Now I'll miss him."

"Call him back."

"You wanna pay for the call?"

"Sure."

She scales the perilous fire-escape to her sulky sleeping area in the clouds. I'm just getting ready to go when Marvin enters.

"Hi Marvin honey child. Got any bread for me today?"

"No. Sorry." Marvin nods to himself like mad.

"Oh Marv, like you to meet, uh, like you to . . ." (peals of laughter) "What did you say your name was again?"

"Hugo, what's yours?"

"Marvin, that used to be Hugo."

# GEOFF DYER

## Out of Sheer Rage: Wrestling with D. H. Lawrence

What sticks in my mind about Oaxaca is how little I remember of it. We were on the Lawrence trail, of course, but already, even by that stage, the borders of the Lawrence trail were so vaguely defined that it was difficult to imagine an activity *not* undertaken with Lawrence in mind, that could not be justified by appeal to his name. I thought back to the Blue Line Trail in Eastwood, that narrow strip of paint taking the visitor on an efficient, carefully chosen stroll from one Lawrence-related place to another. *My* so-called Lawrence trail, on the other hand, was fast becoming unrecognisable, identified, if at all, by its lack of direction, by its overwhelming purposelessness, its capacity to encompass any and every detour. And yet I felt a determination to stick with it, to stick with the peculiarities of a path determined less by Lawrence than by an unswerving fidelity to the vagaries of my nature. By *straying,* I liked to think, I was following Lawrence's directions to the letter.

In retrospect it seems now that we went to Oaxaca simply to find a doctor for Laura who had fallen ill. We had quarrelled over some tuna steaks in Puerto Angel. The waiter assured us that the fish on the menu was not tuna. We ordered it and it *was* tuna, needless to say, a fish I detest more than all the other kinds of fish which I also detest but which, unlike tuna, I *will* eat if pushed. Tuna, though, I *cannot* eat and so I refused to taste even a mouthful since not only was this fish clearly tuna it was also a particularly revolting-looking tuna which Laura, in protest against my indignation, insisted on eating with relish. I stormed off to eat something marginally less revolting, and that was—or should have been—that.

It was a sad end to what had been an interesting day, to say the least, the culmination of what might be termed our *oceanic* experiences. We had spent the day in Zipolite, getting wasted. The name, Zipolite, means something to do with Death. It's a strip of beach a mile long. There are no hotels, just a few *palapas* offering beer, shade, and, if you are staying the night, a place to hang your hammock. It is possible to buy grass there and we had done so the day before, missing the last bus to Puerto Angel and walking back along the dirt road in the moonlit darkness. As far as I could make out it was never not a full moon in this part of the world. The grass was terribly strong and everyone in Zipolite was high the whole time. Naked too. To call it a nudist beach, however, is to dress it up in too many words. People say they feel naked without a favourite item of clothing. Here, so to speak, they felt naked without nothing on. The effect of this, as far as I could make out, was the opposite of what allegedly occurs in nudist camps: the de-eroticisation of nakedness. In Zipolite we were horny as rabbits all day. We had sex on the brain. Primitive, hair-pulling sex. Clothesless sex, naked sex. Also, like all women, Laura is completely at ease without her clothes, and felt quite at home naked on the beach at Zipolite. I couldn't get used to it. I am not really comfortable in shorts, let alone swimming trunks, let alone naked. And despite all the sun worship in his writing it is difficult to imagine Lawrence being happy without his clothes on. Easier to think of him trussed up in his tweed jacket, not wanting anyone to see his scrawny chest, clothing his embarrassment by sneering about the philosopher in *his* swimming costume: "Poor Bertie Russell! He's all disembodied mind!" Or—as in a photograph of Lawrence and Huxley—drawing his knees up to his chest, wrapping his hands around his knees so that his sleeves become a blanket, hiding the thin trunk the arms are joined to.

We are skinny, narrow-shouldered men, Lawrence and I. As a teenager I was so ashamed of my skinny legs that I played squash in jeans. Even before that, when I was a boy, I avoided wearing shinpads while playing football because, I felt, the bulk added to my shins and made my thighs seem even scrawnier. My father kept saying I would thicken out but I never did, never will. By the time I am fifty I will be one of those men with narrow shoulders and a droopy, kangaroo paunch. There was a time though, I found myself thinking as I sat naked, smoking dope on the beach at Zipolite, when, in my early thirties, I'd had strong shoulders, when I'd believed that you could not know what it meant to be a man unless you had strong shoulders and arms. Then, after a few years of pumping iron, my shoulders gradually reverted to their Cluedo-piece norm—but I have never quite shaken off the conviction that I was more of a man in that brief period than I was before or have been since. It was a good feeling, I reflected on the beach at Zipolite. Women like men with broad shoulders, men like my friend Trevor, for example, whose girlfriend I have often wanted to sleep with but whom I would never dream of sleeping with—whom I dream of sleeping with all the time but only dare *dream* of sleeping with—because I am always embarrassed at the thought of her seeing and feeling my bony shoulders and wishing they were more like Trevor's. Lawrence may have claimed that there was more to being a man than manliness, more to being a man, in other words, than having broad shoulders, but, equally, there is more to being broad-shouldered than having broad shoulders. The metaphorical connotations of having a broad back—of being able to endure things, of being resilient—are qualities by which Lawrence set considerable store. For my part, I thought to myself on the beach at Zipolite, even more than broad shoulders, I would like to have had the qualities of broad-shoulderedness but, metaphorically too, I am, as they say, a narrow-shouldered, long-necked kind of guy: incapable of enduring anything, lacking in resilience, weak, prone to sudden eruptions of temper over petty hindrances. "To be brave, to keep one's word, to be generous": this, for Lawrence, was what it meant to be a man. The narrator of Berger's story "Once in Europa" says something similar. According to her the men who deserve women's respect are "men who give themselves to hard labour so that those close to them can eat. Men who are generous with everything they own. And men who spend their lives looking for God. The rest are pigshit." I loved that even more than I loved Lawrence's version, even though it meant I was not a man who deserved respect, was pigshit, in fact. I do no work, I am mean with everything I own and . . . and the more I thought about it the worse I felt.

"I am so wound up in myself I am not even a man," I said to Laura, suddenly on the brink of tears.

"Yes you are, *hombre*," said Laura.

It would have been okay, I thought, if I had been here six or seven years ago when I was pumping iron, but now my nudity seemed to reveal the narrow shoulders which my swimming trunks contrived somehow to conceal. My swimming trunks padded out my shoulders. If I felt uncomfortable with no clothes on, however, I felt even more uncomfortable in my swimming trunks because they chafed somewhat so that I was actually more comfortable with no clothes on. Lying down was okay but when I stood up on my Bambi legs, naked, the idea of wearing chafing swimming trunks, even swimming trunks that chafed my skinny legs terribly, seemed preferable to standing there naked, skinny shoulders revealed for all the world to see. It was like this, being stoned at Zipolite: it was very good grass but you could easily find yourself drawn into a whirlpool of anxiety. To avoid being sucked under, engulfed by anxiety, I moved around in front of Laura who was dozing, one knee raised up, legs slightly apart so that I could see her cunt. After a few moments I became lost in the pleasure of looking at her breasts, her legs, her stomach, her cunt. My prick stirred into life. I thought of lying between her legs and licking her clitoris while she pissed, her piss running over my chin and immediately sizzling into the sand and disappearing. My prick became hard. I spat in my hand and rubbed saliva over the head of my prick—stopping abruptly when I realised that I was sitting on the beach at Zipolite with a semi-hard-on, right on the brink of masturbating, an activity which, to put it mildly, emphasised my nakedness and, therefore, my narrow-shoulderedness which was exactly what I had hoped to take my mind off by gazing at Laura's cunt. Besides, grains of sand were stuck in the palm of my hand and, even allowing for the lubricating effects of saliva, what I would have been doing would have been subjecting my prick to a form of highly animated chafing: mastur-chafing, as it were. I turned around, away from Laura, and stared at the ocean, letting my prick soften.

The ocean. Now that I was facing it I became conscious again of the motorway roar and crash of tide. Big thoughts were in order. The waves were huge: blue-white walls rearing up and pounding the beach. A couple of perfect Germans walked along the damp sand at the water's edge, a man and woman, naked, both with the same broad-shoulder-length hair, holding hands, taking it in turns to pull on a joint. It was paradise in a way, Zipolite: Anarcho-Eden-on-sea. You could probably fuck here, on the beach, in blazing daylight, and no one would bat an eyelid. The only thing you couldn't do, if you came across people doing that, was what you most wanted to do: watch.

# Richard Rayner

## *Los Angeles Without a Map*

We were stranded. I didn't mind. The situation had potential. Barbara said we should walk back to the main road and hitch a lift. That wasn't what I had in mind. I suggested we could perhaps take off our clothes and screw right there in the desert. Jesus could watch. She said, "If the snakes didn't get us, the scorpions would. Besides, I hate to fuck out of doors. It does something totally gross to the pores of my skin."

She picked up a blue-and-gold bag with "Los Angeles Rams" on the side and headed off down the rock-strewn track, telling me Michael had done something like this before, leaving her stranded outside Las Vegas. She'd had to hotwire a car. "It was easy," she said. "Mom made my sister and me take a lesson."

*In hotwiring a car?*

"She's a very far-sighted woman," she said.

"Did she remarry? After your father died?"

"Yeah."

"What's your stepfather like?"

"Mom's husband? He's a professional weight-lifter."

We climbed a dusty path to the highway. The heat left me breathless. A stretched Lincoln limousine with smoked windows went past on the boiling tarmac, then four teenagers in a pick-up, shouting and hurling beer cans. A truck lunged and swayed through a mirage, and stopped. The driver was fat and wore greasy blue overalls. "Strange place to be hitching a ride," he said, and Barbara informed him I was from England. That seemed to explain it: "Never met no one from there didn't need a saliva test," he said. We were passing through a town called Riverside when we passed the Mercedes which moved slowly on the inside lane. Michael stared in front of him, grasping the steering wheel so hard, his knuckles were white. A black swimsuit was wrapped samurai-style round his head and he had a hunting knife clutched between his teeth. Barbara and I looked at each other, and laughed. I asked her to come back with me to the hotel.

She said, "Why not?"

———

Gregory the desk clerk was in the hotel lobby with a group of Japanese tourists. There were about forty of them and they brandished cameras. "This," said Gregory as he stood beneath an iron chandelier, "is the precise spot where Paul Newman met Joanne Woodward in 1957." Barbara and I made for the lift.

In the room she looked out of the window. She said she had seen *Mad Max The Road Warrior* five times and she thought Mel Gibson was just the best. I placed my hands on her waist and kissed the back of her neck. She turned, pressing her lips against mine, running slender fingers down my arm. We undressed and lay on the bed. Her nipples were like peach-stones. My tongue explored a route down her body, past breasts, across belly and thigh to salty cunt. We fucked. I was lost to her reaction, lost to the honking traffic sounds that drifted up from Sunset, lost to everything. I couldn't believe this was happening. A fantasy had sprung to life. I was, actually, *in a movie*. Afterwards Barbara said (as I remember it) "That was so nice" and I lay unable to sleep, with her beside me, breathing regularly, head resting on the crook of her arm. I watched the rhythmic rise and fall of her shoulder. It had happened. I had made it happen.

I couldn't keep still. I got up to go to the bathroom. Barbara's bag was on the chair. I picked it up. The bathroom light shone bright off the tile floor, straining my eyes. I opened the bag. Here was: comb, lipstick, eyeliner, underwear (it was clean), California driver's licence, a crinkled black-and-white of a couple in their late twenties on a lake in a small boat (parents?), a paperback titled *Rich Is Better* and a plastic bag from Neiman-Marcus. Inside this bag was Barbara's Bunny costume. I looked in the mirror, thinking about Jane back in London, about Michael in the desert, about Barbara asleep in the bed a few feet away. My face was tired and drawn.

I had to stretch the band to make the velvet ears fit. I pulled on the tights, which were elastic, and then the corset, which was snug across the chest. The green stilettos pinched less than I would have expected. I hadn't realized Barbara had such big feet.

I went back into the bedroom and stood at the foot of the bed, watching as she stirred slightly in her sleep. Outside a police siren went *whoo-whoo-whoo*. I fingered the pom-pom on my arse. I was in Los Angeles, I was transformed, I had finally arrived: Bunny Richard.

by Methuen Publishing Limited. Reprinted by permission of Casarotto Ramsay & Associates Limited and Methuen Publishing Limited.

DAVID HIGHAM ASSOCIATES: Excerpt from *The Fruit Palace* (originally published by Random House) by Charles Nicholl; excerpt from *Ways of Escape* (originally published by Random House) by Graham Greene; excerpt from *Africa Dances* (originally published by Penguin) by Geoffrey Gorer. Reprinted by permission of David Higham Associates.

DOUBLEDAY, A DIVISION OF RANDOM HOUSE, INC. AND THE TRUSTEES OF THE SEVEN PILLARS OF WISDOM TRUST: Excerpt from *The Seven Pillars of Wisdom* by T. E. Lawrence. Copyright © 1926, 1935 by Doubleday, a division of Bantam Doubleday Dell Publishing Group. Rights outside of the United States are controlled by the Seven Pillars of Wisdom Trust c/o Tweedie & Prideaux, London. Reprinted by permission of Doubleday, a division of Random House, Inc. and the Trustees of the Seven Pillars of Wisdom Trust.

EDITIONS GALLIMARD: "So Be It" and "If It Die" by André Gide. © Editions Gallimard. Reprinted by permission of Editions Gallimard.

ELAND BOOKS: Excerpt from *An Indian Attachment* by Sarah Lloyd. Reprinted by permission of Eland Books.

ERIC GLASS LTD.: Excerpt from *Escape from the Shadows* by Robin Maugham. Reprinted by permission of Eric Glass Ltd. on behalf of the Estate of Robin Maugham.

FABER AND FABER LTD.: Excerpt from *The Letters of Rupert Brooke*. Reprinted by permission of the publishers, Faber and Faber Ltd.

FARRAR, STRAUS & GIROUX, LLC: Excerpt from *Christopher and His Kind* by Christopher Isherwood. Copyright © 1976 by Christopher Isherwood. Reprinted by permission of Farrar, Straus & Giroux, LLC.

GEORGES BORCHARDT, INC.: Excerpt from *Knowing When to Stop* by Ned Rorem (New York: Simon and Schuster, Inc., 1994). Copyright © 1994 by Ned Rorem. Reprinted by permission of Georges Borchardt, Inc.

GERALD DUCKWORTH & CO. LTD.: Excerpt from *Cleopatra's Wedding Present* by Robert Tewdwr Moss. Reprinted by permission of Gerald Duckworth & Co. Ltd.

GILLON AITKEN ASSOCIATES: Excerpt from *One Hot Summer in St. Petersburg* by Duncan Fallowell. Copyright © 1994 by Duncan Fallowell. Excerpt from *Old Glory* by Jonathan Raban. Copyright © 1981 by Jonathan Raban. Reprinted with the permission of Gillon Aitken Associates Ltd.

GROVE/ATLANTIC, INC.: Excerpt from *Quiet Days in Clichy* by Henry Miller. Copyright © 1935 by Henry Miller. Excerpt from *Keep the River on Your Right* by Tobias Schneebaum. Copyright © 1969 by Tobias Schneebaum. Excerpt from *My Life and Loves* by Frank Harris. Copyright © 1925 by Frank Harris. Reprinted by permission of Grove/Atlantic, Inc.

GROVE/ATLANTIC, INC. AND THE RANDOM HOUSE ARCHIVE & LIBRARY, A DIVISION OF THE RANDOM HOUSE GROUP LTD.: Excerpt from *Our Grandmothers' Drums* by Mark Hudson. Copyright © 1989 by Mark Hudson. Rights throughout Canada are controlled by The Random House Archive & Library, a division of the Random House Group Ltd. Reprinted by permission of Grove/Atlantic, Inc. and The Random House Archive & Library, a division of the Random House Group Ltd.

HARCOURT, INC.: Excerpt from *History of My Life*, Volumes 1 and 2, by Giacomo Casanova, English translation by Willard R. Trask. Copyright © 1966 and renewed 1994 by Harcourt, Inc. Reprinted by permission of the publisher.

HAROLD OBER ASSOCIATES INCORPORATED: Excerpt from *Hindoo Holiday* by J. R. Ackerley, published by New York Review Books. Copyright © 1932 and copyright renewed 1960 by J. R. Ackerley. Excerpts from *The Letters of J. R. Ackerley*, edited by Francis King. Copyright © 1975 by Francis King. Reprinted by permission of Harold Ober Associates Incorporated.

HARPERCOLLINS*PUBLISHERS*: Excerpt from *Walking in the Shade: 1949–1962* by Doris Lessing. Copyright © 1997 by Doris Lessing. Reprinted by permission of HarperCollins*Publishers*, Inc.

# ABOUT THE EDITOR

LUCRETIA STEWART was born in Singapore and now lives in London. She is the author of two travel books, *Tiger Balm: Travels in Laos, Vietnam and Cambodia,* and *The Weather Prophet: A Caribbean Journey.* Her novel, *Making Love,* was published in 1999.

A NOTE ON THE TYPE

The principal text of this Modern Library edition
was set in a digitized version of Janson,
a typeface that dates from about 1690 and was cut by Nicholas Kis,
a Hungarian working in Amsterdam. The original matrices have
survived and are held by the Stempel foundry in Germany.
Hermann Zapf redesigned some of the weights and sizes for Stempel,
basing his revisions on the original design.